Thomas North

A Chronicle of the Church of St. Martin in Leicester

During the Reigns of Henry VIII, Edward VI, Mary, and Elizabeth

Thomas North

A Chronicle of the Church of St. Martin in Leicester
During the Reigns of Henry VIII, Edward VI, Mary, and Elizabeth

ISBN/EAN: 9783337002558

Printed in Europe, USA, Canada, Australia, Japan

Cover: Foto ©Lupo / pixelio.de

More available books at **www.hansebooks.com**

A CHRONICLE

OF THE

IN LEICESTER

DURING THE REIGNS OF HENRY VIII. EDWARD VI.
MARY, AND ELIZABETH

WITH

SOME ACCOUNT OF ITS MINOR ALTARS AND ANCIENT GUILDS

Compiled from Original and Contemporaneous Documents

BY THOMAS NORTH

HONORARY SECRETARY OF THE LEICESTERSHIRE ARCHITECTURAL AND ARCHÆOLOGICAL SOCIETY

WITH ILLUSTRATIONS

LONDON: BELL AND DALDY, 186 FLEET STREET
LEICESTER: CROSSLEY AND CLARKE
1866

S. MARTIN.

(From Painted Glass, Christ Church Cathedral, Oxford.)

SUBSCRIBERS.

His Grace the DUKE OF RUTLAND, Lord-Lieutenant of the County.

The Right Reverend the LORD BISHOP of the DIOCESE.

The Worshipful the MAYOR OF LEICESTER. (Thomas William Hodges, Esq.)

The Countess of Harborough, Stapleford Park.
The Right Honourable the Earl Beauchamp, 19 Grosvenor Place, London.
The Right Honourable the Earl of Lanesborough, Swithland Hall.
The Right Honourable the Lord Berners, Keythorpe Hall.
The Right Honourable Lord John Manners, M.P., Belvoir Castle.
Sir George Howland Beaumont, Bart., Coleorton Hall.
Sir William de Capel Brooke, Bart., M.A., The Elms, Market-Harborough.
Sir Charles Wentworth Dilke, Bart, M.P., F.S.A., 76 Sloane Street, London, S.W.
Sir Henry Edward Leigh Dryden, Bart., M.A., Canon's Ashby.
Sir Henry Halford, Bart., Wistow Hall.
Sir Geoffrey Palmer, Bart., M.A., Carlton.
Lady Isham, Lamport Hall.

Adcock, Halford, Esq., Leicester.
Adcock, William, Esq., Melton-Mowbray.
Adcock, Mrs. Benjamin, Syston.
Akroyd, Edward, Esq., M.P., F.S.A., Bank Field, Halifax, Yorkshire.
Ashby, the Rev. Edward Quenby, M.A., Quenby Hall.
Ashton, John, Esq., Lubbenham.

Babington, the Rev. Professor Churchill, S. John's College, Cambridge.
Bacon, the Rev. John, M.A., Wymondham Rectory.
Baines, John, Esq., Leicester.
Baker, Charles, Esq., architect, Leicester.
Barfield, Mr. Samuel, Leicester.
Barker, Mrs. Fred. Raymond, Bisley, Stroud.
Barnard, C. W., Esq., Whitby.
Barrett, Mr. W. A., Pembroke Villas, Oxford.
Barrs, Mr. John, Leicester.
Beal, the Rev. William, LL.D, F.S.A., Brooke Vicarage, Norwich.

Beaufort, the Rev. D. A., M.A., Warburton, Warrington.

Bedfordshire Architectural and Archæological Society.

Bellairs, the Rev. S. G., M.A., Goadby Marwood Rectory.

Bellairs, George C., Esq., Leicester.

Benfield, Thomas W., Esq., Leicester.

Bingham, Henry Corles, Esq., Wartnaby Hall.

Billings, John, Esq., Thurcaston.

Billson, William, Esq., Leicester.

Bland, Mr. Thomas, Leicester.

Bonser, the Rev. James Armitage, S. Martin's, Leicester.

Bonser, Thomas Owen, Esq., Clare College, Cambridge.

Boulton, Mr. William, Leicester.

Bowmar, John, Esq., Leicester.

Bowmar, William, Esq., Leicester.

Bracebridge, Charles Holte, Esq., Atherstone Hall.

Bramley, Mr. T., Leicester.

Brand, J. S., Esq., Leicester.

Brandon, Raphael, Esq., architect, 65 Regent Street, London.

Brent, John, jun., Esq., F.S.A., Canterbury.

Brown, the Rev. Abner William, M.A., Honorary Canon of Peterborough, Gretton Vicarage, Uppingham.

Buckley, the Rev. William Edward, M.A., R.D., Middleton Cheney Rectory, Northampton.

Bunney, Mr. T., jun., Leicester.

Burdett, Charles, Esq., Lutterworth.

Burford, Mr., Leicester.

Burnaby, Miss C. C., Leicester.

Burnaby, the Misses, Evington House.

Burnaby, the Rev. F. G., M.A., Nursling Mount, Southampton.

CARLYON, the Rev. T. S., M.A., Glenfield Rectory.

Cartwright, the Rev. F. W., M.A., Aynhoe.

Chapman, Mr. George, Leicester.

Charlesworth, Mr. Thomas, Leicester.

Charters, Mr. Edward, Leicester.

Charters, Mr. Robert, jun., Leicester.

Checkland, George, Esq., Leicester.

Clagett, Major, Stapleford Park.

Clarke, Edward H. M., Esq., Melton-Mowbray.

Claughton, the Rev. T. L., M.A., Honorary Canon of Worcester, Kidderminster.

Clephan, Edwin, Esq., Leicester.

Coleman, George W., Esq., Glen Magna.

Collier, the Rev. Charles, M.A., F.S.A., Training College, Winchester.

Collins, Mr. J. Beaumont, Leicester.

Coltman, Mrs. Thomas, jun., Leicester.

Constable, Rev. J. P. Goulton, Cotesbach.

Cooper, C. H., Esq., F.S.A., town-clerk of Cambridge.

Cooper, Alfred, Esq., Leicester.

Copley, Mr., Melton-Mowbray.

Crick, Thomas, Esq., Rupert's Rest, Glen Magna.

Crick, Mr. Samuel, Leicester.

Crick, Mr. John, Leicester.

Crow, Mr. John, Leicester.

DALLEY, William Charles, Esq., Syston Villa (2 copies).

Davies, Robert, Esq., F.S.A., the Mount, York.

Deakins, Mr. Superintendent, Lutterworth.

De Lisle, Ambrose Lisle March Phillipps, Esq., Garendon Park.

Dent, the Rev. John Henry, M.A., Hallaton.

De Teissier, the Rev. G. F., B.D., R.D., Church Brampton.

Dickson, William, Esq., F.S.A., Alnwick, Northumberland.

Donisthorpe, A. R., Esq., Leicester.

Drake, the Rev. T., M.A., Mountsorrell.

Eames, Mr. R. F., Leicester.

Ellacombe, the Rev. Henry Thomas, M.A., F.S.A., Rectory, Clyst S. George, Topsham.

Elliott, Miss Ann (the late), Leicester (2 copies).

Ellis, Alfred, Esq., Belgrave.

Evans, John, Esq., F.R.S., F.S.A., Nash Mills, Hemel Hempsted.

Farmer, Rev. J., Croft.

Fenwicke, the Rev. G. C., B.A., Blaston, S. Giles.

Fisher, Edward, Esq., Over-seale, Ashby-de-la-Zouch.

Fisher, John, Esq., Kendal.

Fisher, the Rev. John, M.A., Leicester.

Fowler, the Rev. E. T. Straton, Cotmanhay Parsonage, Ilkeston.

Foster, Mr. S. H., Leicester.

Freer, Charles T., Esq., the Coplow, Billesdon.

Freer, William, Esq., Stoneygate, Leicester.

Freestone, Mr. Henry, Market-Harborough.

Fytche, John Lewis, Esq., F.S.A., High Sheriff of Lincolnshire, Thorpe Hall, Elkington, Louth.

Gantillon, the Rev. P. G. F., M.A., Cheltenham.

Garner, H., Esq., Market-Harborough.

Gillett, the Rev. G. E., M.A., R.D., Waltham-le-Wolds Rectory.

Gill, Miss Eliza, Leicester.

Goddard, Joseph, Esq., architect, Leicester.

Godwin, Edward W., Esq., F.S.A., 7 Apsley Place, Clifton, Bristol.

Goodacre, R. J., Esq., architect, Leicester.

Goodyer, Frederick, Esq., Leicester.

Greatorex, Mr. Samuel, Leicester.

Gregory, William, Esq., Leicester.

Gresley, the Rev. J. Morwood, M.A., Etwall Hospital, Derby.

Groocock, Mr. John, Leicester.

Grundy, Charles, Esq., 21 Abchurch Lane, London.

Hancock, Mr. J. H., Leicester.

Hancock, Mr. W., Leicester.

Harris, George Shirley, Esq., Leicester.

Harris, Joseph, Esq., Westcotes, Leicester.

Harris, Samuel, Esq., Westcotes Cottage.

Harris, the Rev. Joseph, Westcotes, Leicester.

Havergal, the Rev. Francis, M.A., Minor Canon of Hereford Cathedral.

Haxby, Joseph Barber, Esq., Leicester.

Hearn, John Henry, Esq., Ryde.

Herrick, W. Perry, Esq., Beaumanor Park, Loughborough.

Hill, the Rev. John Harwood, F.G.H.S., Cranoe Rectory.

Hickson, Charles, Esq., Apsley Place, Ardwick, Manchester.

Hickson, Thomas, Esq., Melton-Mowbray.

Hickson, Mr. Josiah, Melton-Mowbray.

Hughes, Thomas, Esq., Correspondiug Secretary, Chester Archæological Society.

Humfrey, R. Blake, Esq., Wroxham House, Norwich.

Hunt, Miss, Huncote, Hinckley.

Hunt, William, Esq., Stoneygate, Leicester.

Hunt, John, Esq., Thurnby.

Ingram, the Rev. Robert, M.A., Chatburn, Clitheroe.

Jackson, Mr. Benjamin Henry, Leicester.

Jackson, Mr. James, Leicester.

Jackson, W. H., Esq., Leicester.

Jacques, James, Esq. (the late), Birstall.

Jarratt, Miss, Leicester.

Jessop, Mr. Joseph, Leicester.

Johnson, Mr. Walter F., Leicester.

Johnson, R. W. Esq., architect, Melton-Mowbray.

Johnson, the Rev. R. H., M.A., Claybrooke,

Jones, the Venerable Archdeacon, Waterloo, Liverpool.

Jones, Mr. H. S., Leicester.

Kemp, Mr. Henry, Leicester.

Kempson, William, Esq., Leicester.

Kenrick, the Rev. John, M.A., F.S.A., Monkgate, York.

Kerrick, the Rev. Richard Edward, M.A., F.S.A., Cambridge.

King, the Rev. P. Meade, M.A., Norton Rectory, Atherstone.

Lane, Mr. Francis, Leicester.

Langley, the Rev. William, M.A., Wymondham House.

Lankester, H., Esq., Leicester.

Latham, William, Esq., Melton-Mowbray (2 copies).

Lea, Mr. C. J., Lutterworth.

Lee, the Rev. Fred. George, D.C.L., F.S.A., 19 Coleshill Street, Eaton Square, S.W.

Lefranc, Mon., Leicester.

Leicestershire Architectural and Archæological Society.

Leicester Literary and Philosophical Society.

Leicester Permanent Library.

Levien, Edward, Esq., M.A., F.S.A., British Museum.

Lloyd, James, Esq., Leicester.

Longstaffe, W. H. D., Esq., 4 Catherine Terrace, Gateshead.

Loseby, Mr. E., Leicester.

Luck, Richard, Esq., Plâs Llanfair, Llanfairfechan, North Wales.

Lysons, the Rev. Samuel, M.A., R.D., F.S.A., Hempsted Court, Gloucester.

Marriott, Mr. George, Melton-Mowbray.

Marris, Mr. W. H., Leicester.

Marshall, Mr., Governor, Borough Gaol, Leicester.

Martin, the Rev. Robert, M.A., Ansty Pastures.

Miles, the Rev. Lomas, M.A., Coreley Rectory, Tenbury, Salop.

Miles, William, Esq., Leicester.

Moor, Mr. William, Leicester.

Moore, Mrs., Museum Square, Leicester.

Moore, the Rev. W. B., Evington Vicarage.

Morley, Mr. Frederick Richard, Leicester.

Murdin, Mr., Leicester.

Neale, G. C., Esq., Skeffington.

Nevinson, G. H., Esq., Leicester.

Nevinson, Thomas, Esq., Leicester.

Nichols, John Gough, Esq., F.S.A., Corr. F.S.A. Scot. and Newc., 25 Parliament Street.

Nichols, Rev. W. L., M.A., F.S.A., Keynsham House, near Bath.

Norris, the Rev. Thomas, Tugby Vicarage.

Northcote, Rev. Dr., S. Mary's College, Oscott.

Ord, Mrs. J. E., Langton Hall.

Orton, Mr. John, Leicester.

Overton, Robert, jun., Esq., Leicester.

Packer, the Rev. George, Birstall.

Paget, Edward H., Esq., Leicester.

Paget, Mrs., Humberstone.

Paget, Mrs. T. T., Humberstone.

Paget, Thomas, Esq., the Coppice, Queniborough.

Paget, Thomas Tertius, Esq., Humberstone.

Palmer, the Rev. C. S., M.A., Owston Parsonage.

Paradise, Mr. Thomas, *Mercury* Office, Stamford.

Payne, Mr. W. G., Leicester.

Peacock, Edward, Esq., F.S.A., Bottesford Manor.

Pegg, Mr. W. H., Leicester.

Price, Mr. J., Leicester.

Reeve, Miss Isabella W., Leicester.

Rick, Mr. John, Leicester.

Richards, Mr. W., Belgrave.

Richardson, the Rev. W. K., M.A., R.D., Leire Rectory.

Robinson, Captain T. W. U., Houghton-le-Spring, Fence Houses, Durham.

Robinson, the Rev. W. K., the Rookery, Wymondham.

Russell, Jesse Watts, Esq., D.C.L., F.R.S., F.S.A., F.L.S., F.G.S., F.R.G.S., Ilam Hall, Staffordshire.

Sarson, Mr. Thomas F., Leicester.

Shaw, George, Esq., M.D., Leicester.

Shenton, Henry, Esq., architect, Leicester.

Simpkinson, the Rev. J. N., M.A., Brington Rectory, Northampton.

Small, the Rev. N. P., M.A., Market-Bosworth Rectory.

Snow, the Rev. Benjamin, M.A., Burton Rectory, Sleaford.

Spencer, Mr. James, Leicester.

Spurrett, Miss, Leicester.

Stafford, Mr. Robert, Leicester

Staples, Mrs., Leicester.

Staynes, Mr. George, Leicester.

Staynes, Mr. John, Leicester.

Stephens, the Rev. Richard, B.D., Belgrave.

Stokes, Thomas, Esq., New Parks.

Stretton, Clement, Esq., Fosse Road House.

Stretton, Miss Ann, Leicester.

Swain, Mr. Joseph, Leicester.

Thompson, J., Esq., Belgrave.

Thring, the Rev. Edward, M.A. Uppingham.

Tindal, Mrs., Melton-Mowbray.

Tower, the Rev. Ernest, Earl's Shilton.

Towne, Mr. John, Melton-Mowbray.

Trollope, the Rev. Prebendary, M.A., F.S.A., Leasingham, Sleaford.

Turner, Archibald, Esq., Leicester.

Tyssen, John R. Daniel, Esq., F.S.A., 9 Lower Rock Gardens, Brighton.

Tyssen, Amherst Daniel, Esq., Merton College, Oxford.

Vaughan, the Rev. D. J., M.A., Leicester (2 copies).

Vaughan, the Rev. E. T., M.A., Harpenden, S. Albans.

Vaughan, Mrs., Leicester.

Vaughan, Miss, Leicester.

Wale, Mr. Henry, Leicester.

Wale, Mr. William, Leicester.

Walpole, Reginald, Esq., Hanslope Park, Stony Stratford.

Ward, Thomas, Esq., Melton-Mowbray.

Warner, Mr., Leicester Abbey.

Warner, Miss, Leicester.

Webster, Thomas, Esq., Raven Holt, Scalford.

West, Mr. W., Leicester.

Whitby, Captain, Glenfield Frith.

Whitmore, John, Esq., Leicester.

Wilkinson, Mrs. E., Entwistle, Leicester.

Wilkinson, Mr. Isaac, Leicester.

Williams, J. H., Esq., Leicester.

Wilson, the Rev. Plumpton, M.A., Mowsley Rectory.

Wing, Vincent, Esq., Melton-Mowbray.

Wing, Vincent, Jun., Esq., Leicester.

Winterton, Mr. William, Leicester.

Wix, the Rev. Edward, M.A., Trinity College, Oxford.

Wollaston, Major, Shenton Hall, Nuneaton.

Woodd, Mrs. Charles, Roslyn House, Hampstead.

Wykes, Mr. Samuel, Leicester.

PREFACE.

THE following pages were commenced with the intention of preparing a Paper to read before the members of the Leicestershire Architectural and Archæological Society.

The work soon outstripped the length usually allotted to such efforts.

The writer is therefore induced to offer it to his friends and the public in its present form, with the hope that its publication may keep alive an interest in the Fabric of which it treats, and so further its Restoration, which has been gradually progressing for many years.

Any profit arising from the sale of this work will be devoted to that object.

For the copying and translating of Documents in the Tower and elsewhere in London, quoted in the following pages, the writer has availed himself of the professional services of Mr. Clarence Hopper, Palæographer to the British Archæological Association.

During the passing of this work through the press considerable alterations have been made in the portion of the church assigned to S. Dunstan's Chapel (p. 45). The remains of the ancient Chapel, and its many additions, have been entirely removed, and the present Chapel built, at the sole cost of a parishioner.

LEICESTER, *Easter* 1866.

CONTENTS.

SECTION I.

SECTION II.

SECTION VI.

SECTION VII.

ILLUSTRATIONS.

A CHRONICLE

OF THE

CHURCH OF S. MARTIN, LEICESTER.

SECTION I.

IN the vestry of most of our Parish Churches, or in some out-of-the-way place in the edifice, stands a large oaken chest of antique shape and fashion, its sturdy timbers firmly held together by iron binders, its lid ornamented with the same metal wrought into divers fantastic shapes, and its contents securely preserved from the gaze of the curious and the hands of the ruthless by locks, which, stout and strong, bid defiance to all unauthorised scrutiny. Not that the chest excites much curiosity—it is simply "the Church Chest," and the observer remarking, perhaps, upon its age or peculiar appearance, passes on without considering that its contents might possibly "many a tale unfold," at once original, curious, and instructive. It is much to be regretted that, notwithstanding the oaken chest, the iron binders, and the strong locks, our Parish Records are in so very many instances extremely few in number. The absence of ordinary care has sacrificed many to the effects of damp; and the natural decay arising from the want of proper arrangement, and from a too rough contact with each other, has not been sufficiently guarded against. Would that this were all. Ignorance of their value has doubtless in many—too many;—cases been the cause of their destruction: culpable carelessness also has frequently led to their being removed from their proper depository, whilst something very like the opposite of strict honesty has led to their not being restored.

When it is stated that the Parish Chests belonging to our Churches in Leicester now contain few or no documents of the Pre-Reformation period—that when Throsby* and when Nichols wrote their Histories, masses of such documents belonging to different churches in Leicester were in existence—the truth of the foregoing remarks will be evident. When these documents were removed, where they were taken, and what eventually became of them, are now—with respect to almost all—inquiries both useless and hopeless.† Such being

* Throsby, speaking of the Churchwardens' Accounts of S. Martin's parish, says, "which to the honour of the parish are by far the best kept I have ever seen." He makes many extracts from them, which, however, are frequently incorrect.

† Writing of the accounts of S. Mary de Castro, Leicester, Mr. Kelly says—"It is not known at what period these accounts were removed from the Parish Chest, but it was doubtless soon after the publication of Nichols' and Throsby's Histories of the Town. They were sold by auction in London many years afterwards, as appears by the following paragraph cut from the *Leicester Journal*, without date, but probably about the year 1830:—'Parish Records.—A curious collection of ancient writings was sold, last week, by auction, in Pall Mall, being deeds relating to Brokesbye, Great Bowden, Kirby, Coton, Bosworth, Barton,

the case, it was with feelings of extreme satisfaction and pleasure that the writer was enabled some time since to secure by purchase a large volume of Churchwardens' Accounts relating to the parish of S. Martin in this town,* with a view to its ultimate deposit in some public place of safety. The person from whom it was purchased stated that it had been in his possession for about fifty years, and that he bought it at a second-hand bookstall, and preserved it on account of its local character.

That this volume is of considerable local interest will be evident, when it is known that it commences with a statement of accounts for the year 1544, narrates by its simple entries the changes in the ritual of the Church under Edward VI., traces by its lists of expenditure the restoration of the pomp and magnificence of the Romish System in the reign of Queen Mary, and helps to elucidate the glorious revival and consolidation of religious truth under Elizabeth. Down to the year 1646, which is the date of the last account in the volume, there are notices of events having reference to the Parish Church and to the Borough in general, which must be both interesting and useful to the local antiquary or historian.†

In attempting, by the aid of this volume, and with such

Lubbenham, Huncote, and *St. Mary's Church, Leicester.* The collection was considerable, being deposited in five boxes.'"—*Ancient Records of Leicester*, p. 10.

* The same volume as that referred to by Throsby in his History.

† The volume contains 773 pages, bound in rough calf, and with strong brass clasps. It was purchased in London on the 14th day of February 1544, and cost four shillings and eightpence, as appears by the following entry (p. 5):—

Paid for this chirche boke Bought at London the xiiii. Day of Februarye Anno Dni 1544 . . . . iiij.s viij.d

assistance as was procurable from our Local and National Records, to place before the reader a chronicle of the Church of S. Martin, Leicester, during the time indicated in the title, the narrative will naturally, to a great extent, tend to show the progress of the Reformation in that Parish, as exemplified in the changes made in the furniture of its church and the accessories of its worship, and by the abrogation of local customs and peculiarities. In doing this we must not, even were we able, loiter in endeavouring to trace the early history of the Fabric, or of the introduction into this neighbourhood of those truths of Christianity which led to its erection. The truth of the tradition of a heathen temple having stood on the site of the present church is, it is presumed, now clearly demonstrated by the relics found during the late excavations. Considerable portions of walls and of columns, fragments of vessels, and several coins, attest the presence of the Romans on the spot, and the bones of animals and of birds, found in great profusion, point to the sacrifices there offered by their priests. There is little doubt but that a Christian Saxon Church would succeed the heathen temple at a very early period.* Near the close of the seventh century, according to the chronicler, Florence of Worcester,† a Christian bishop was established in Leicester; and here, as elsewhere, the site of the old temple would be chosen as a fit spot for the new church, partly on account of the old associations of worship connected with it, and of the consequent reverence of a half-

* Speed is most probably incorrect in saying that two martyrs suffered in Leicester during the persecution under Diocletian. Bede states that they were citizens of Chester.

† Bohn's Ed., p. 426.

converted population for the locality; and partly on account of the eligibility of the site, and the ample building materials at hand. However this may have been, we have undoubted evidence that when the Norman planted his standard of supremacy in ancient Leicester, and his power had become established, he swept away every vestige of the Saxon Church (supposing one to have here existed), and erected a new edifice in that style of architecture which bears his name. A portion of a Norman string, showing the billet—and, of course, the wall upon which it rests—at the eastern end of the north arcade of the nave on the northern side, is the only remaining portion of the ancient church of S. Martin erected shortly after the Norman Conquest.*

In the early part of the Fourth century the Roman army in Gaul numbered in its ranks a youth noted among his comrades for his humility, his mildness of temper, his sobriety, and, above all, for his boundless charity. He was the son of heathen parents, but had been early impressed by the truths of Christianity. He had, however, been enrolled by force in the Roman cavalry, and sent into Gaul, before he could be baptized. The severe winter of 332 found him quartered with his fellow-legionaries at Amiens, where, one day going out of the gate of the city, he was met by a poor naked beggar shivering with cold: the Roman soldier having nothing but his cloak and his arms, with his sword divided his cloak in twain, and gave one-half to the beggar, covering himself as well as he might with the other. He was shortly after this

* The lower portion of the Tower, with the stairs, both taken down in 1861, were portions of the ancient Norman Church.

baptized, still remaining for a considerable time in the army. At length, obtaining his discharge, he placed himself under the care and instruction of S. Hilary, bishop of Poitiers, who—almost against his will—conferred upon him minor orders, and sent him into his own country, Pannonia (Hungary), to convert his mother. He then led a retired and religious life for several years, after which he was raised in 371 to the Bishopric of Tours. As bishop, he showed himself the exterminator of Druidism and Roman Paganism, the powerful antagonist of Arianism, the enlightened and Christian opponent of punishment in ecclesiastical causes by the secular arm, judging that the excommunication of heretics by episcopal sentence was a sufficient punishment for their offence. He was also much opposed to the luxury of the clergy in Gaul, which, even at that early period, showed itself in their equipages, costume, and dwellings. In this exalted position his charity still burned brightly, for one day when preparing to perform one of the offices of the Church in the Cathedral, he beheld a wretched naked beggar, and desired his deacon to clothe the man. The deacon showing no haste to comply, the bishop took off his sacerdotal habit and threw it himself around the beggar. Many other acts of charity are related of this good bishop, who governed his diocese in great honour for nearly thirty years, and when he died, at the age of eighty years, two thousand monks formed his funeral train, and many heard the songs of the angels as they bore his soul to paradise.*

Such is a short sketch of the life (according to the page

* Count De Montalembert's *Monks of the West*, vol. i. p. 453; Mrs. Jameson's *Legendary Art*, vol. ii. p. 350.

of history and the voice of legend) of S. Martin, the titular saint of our church, one of the most famous saints of the West, and certainly one of the first to whose honour churches were dedicated in this country; for when Augustine, with his staff of missionaries, arrived in England at the close of the sixth century, he found a church—the one then used by Bertha, the Christian Queen of Ethelbert, King of Kent—dedicated to S. Martin.*

The Fourteenth century was, as is well known, characterised in England by a great Religious movement—a movement in which Leicestershire certainly took a prominent part, and in which Wicliffe, a Leicestershire priest, was a chief actor.

The causes which led to this movement, then commenced, are such prominent features in the history of the period as to render a recapitulation of them both unnecessary and undesirable, especially as we are now dealing rather with the external facts relating to a particular locality, than with the principles of a great National Religious Revolution. It may, however, be well to remember that the rapacity of the monks was securing, or had at that time secured, for themselves, the larger proportion of the livings of this country. Hence the majority of the parishes were handed over to the spiritual care of *Vicars*, with the small tithes as a miserable stipend, men—very many of them—with little or no learning, "mass-priests who could read their breviaries and no more"—"men of the lowest of the people, with all the gross habits of the class from

* According to *The Calendar of the Anglican Church Illustrated* (p. 135), we have now in England the large number of 160 Churches named after him.

which they sprang."* The Prayers of the Church, too, were in Latin, so that the ignorant worshippers (to use the words of the Preface to our Common Prayer) "heard with their ears only, and their heart, spirit, and mind were not edified thereby;" and even to the learned the services were so perplexing and varied, "that to turn the book only was so hard and intricate a matter, that many times there was more business to find out what should be read, than to read it when it was found out."† The services also were intermixed with observances and practices unknown in primitive times, the veneration of Saints and Relics engrossing the honour and worship due only to God. Preaching was neglected, the religious training of the young forgotten. Copies of the Scriptures were rare and costly, so that the common people had little or no knowledge of the contents of the Bible beyond what they gathered from the paintings upon the walls of their churches (which, however, more frequently depicted the leading events—fabulous or true—in the lives of the Saints), and from the Miracle Plays, as they are called, then frequently performed within the walls of their churches for their edification and amusement. These plays, however laudable the original intention of their compilers, became in time fearful, if not blasphemous, caricatures of scenes and incidents related in Holy Writ. The "Passion of Christ" was a favourite subject with these dramatisers. In the year 1478 a miracle play with that title was performed in Leicester,‡ and somewhat later (*i.e.*, in 1499) there was the sum of two shillings paid by the Churchwardens of S. Mary

* Blunt's *Reformation*, p. 66. † Preface, *Common Prayer*.

‡ Mr. Kelly's *Town Records*, p. 11.

de Castro "for a play in the church,"* and in our own church we shall have to note their presence.

The ignorance and superstition of priest and people, of which these glances at the state of religious teaching and knowledge are cursory reminiscences, were certainly among the many causes at work to produce that great revolution in religious thought and action in the fourteenth century which, gradually gaining strength and power, at length so leavened the mind of the nation as to prepare it for, and cause it to demand, those mighty changes in the Teaching and Ritual of the National Church, the purport and significance of which are tersely conveyed to us in the one word marking that memorable epoch, "The Reformation."

Not that even in the midst of all this ignorance and superstition there were no redeeming points. God has never left Himself without witness in the National Church of England. From its foundation in very early—if not in Apostolic times—to the present day, the Lamp of Truth has been always burning, however its rays may have been dimmed and its brightness obscured, by the weakness or sinfulness of many of those whose duty it was not to hide its bright beams, but to raise it on high, that all might walk in its light. There were always men holy, pure, and good, whose meek spirits sought, perhaps, the retirement of the cloister rather than encounter the roughness of the world, and mix themselves in the ambitious schemes, the covetous practices, of the so-called "religious" around them. There were those also raised up from time to time, as parish priests, or to fill high

* *Churchwardens' Accounts*, quoted by Nichols.

offices in the church, who showed by their lives of self-denial and high aspiration that, according to the light vouchsafed unto them, they were anxious to follow the right way, and lead the people under them in the old paths. Then, again, in the much-abused Monastery, it was not the lazy drones only who found a refuge from work, an excuse for their idleness, a cloak for their sins, but the wayfaring man found a shelter, the student a retreat, the disappointed, the weary, the conscience-stricken, a place of rest: there the young, with strong, loving heart, could give himself up to prayer and holy meditation; and there the old could find that calm repose and solitude so congenial to his nature. There, too, the diligent scribe could spend his life in the laborious, monotonous, yet not inglorious work of copying the Holy Scriptures, the Offices of the Church, the Works of the Fathers, the Lives of the Saints, or in multiplying copies of such works upon the Arts and Sciences as were then known in England; counting his life well spent in producing a few volumes, rich in illumination, radiant in colour, which, whilst they added honour to the House under whose roof he was sheltered, constituted it—what the Monasteries certainly were in the Middle Ages—one of the cradles of learning, and a preserver and perpetuator of the text of Holy Scripture.* Neither were bright and noble traits of self-denial and large-hearted liberality, in both clergy and laity, wanting in Leicestershire at this period.

* Count de Montalembert, in his able defence of Monastic Institutions, says the monasteries were "for ten centuries and more the schools, the archives, the libraries, the hostelries, the studios, the penitentiaries, and the hospitals of Christian society."—*Monks of the West*, vol. i. p. 107.

The fourteenth century was pre-eminently (especially in South Leicestershire) a church-building age. Very many of our beautiful parish churches were erected, rebuilt, or considerably enlarged during this period. These are bright gleams of light —flowers in the wilderness—signs of life and love, which, to the scanner of the times immediately preceding the Reformation, are indeed cheering, and should be eagerly grasped and recognised as tokens of God's mercy in never entirely leaving His Church, however grievously she had neglected her great mission, abused her power, and used her high prerogatives as stepping-stones in her career of self-aggrandisement.

It was in this district of South Leicestershire, too, that Wicliffe now appeared. He was presented to the Rectory of Lutterworth by the Crown* in 1375, but does not appear to have taken up his permanent residence in our neighbourhood until the year 1382. In that year he was banished from Oxford, in consequence of his religious opinions being condemned by the Convocation before which he was summoned to appear. Although now in comparative obscurity, Wicliffe helped forward by his pen, in as great a degree as he had formerly done by his more public preaching and discussion, the strong religious inquiry which was now so vigorously aroused in the heart of the people. Wicliffe had already done immortal service to his church and country by presenting to the people a translation—the first complete one—of the Holy Scriptures in their own tongue;† and he now—not

* In consequence of the minority of the then patron, Lord Henry de Ferrars.

† The general opinion of the supporters of the Romish system, with reference to this work of Wicliffe's, was not inaptly expressed by Knighton, a

disdaining to follow the example of the Mendicant Orders in the Romish Church—sent forth a large body of travelling itinerant preachers, called by him "Poor Priests," who, traversing nearly the whole kingdom, disseminated his opinions wherever they went. It is but natural to expect that in Leicestershire his doctrines would find many disciples, and his preachers be both numerous and energetic in their labours. That the former was the case, we learn from Henry of Knighton (a Canon of Leicester Abbey, contemporary with Wicliffe), who states that the Reformer's sect "was held in the highest honour in those days, and was become so numerous that you would scarcely see two persons in the highway but one of them was a disciple of Wicliffe."* Of the preachers, too, Knighton has left one or two portraits which may be worth our glancing at, as showing, to some extent, the state of

contemporary Canon of Leicester Abbey, who in his *Chronicle* thus alludes to it: "This Master John Wycliffe translated from the Latin into the *Anglican* (not *Angelic*) tongue the Gospel which Christ delivered to the clergy and doctors of the Church, that they should minister to laics and weaker persons, according to the exigency of the time and poverty of persons, agreeably with their mental hunger." . . . . "Whence through him (Wicliffe) it became common and more open for laics, and even women, to read that which was wont to be understood hitherto by literate and thoroughly intelligent clerks; and so the evangelic pearl is strewed and trodden by swine, even so that that which was wont to be precious to clerks and laics, now is rendered a mere common bauble to either, and the jewel of the clergy is turned into the mockery of the laics, and so that became for ever common to the laity which before was the talent from above [alone] to clerks and doctors of the church."—Twysden's *Decem Scriptores*, fo. 2644.

* Twysden's *Decem Scriptores*; Knighton's *Chron.*, fo. 2665. Speaking of Wicliffe, Knighton thus describes him:—"A.D. 1382.—At that time flourished Master John Wycliffe, Rector of the Church of Lutterworth, in the county of Leicester, a very eminent Teacher in Theology in those days. In philosophy he was reckoned second to none, in

things in Leicester at that period with reference to the religious movement under notice. Only we must remember that our Canon was a firm adherent of "Holy Church," and shows these "poor priests" and their followers in as bad a light, drawn with the most dingy colours, and with as ungainly shapes, as his monastic conscience would permit.

The first of these portraits represents a man "despicable and deformed in person," named from his trade—that of a chief metal-founder—William Smith. The deformity of his person, however it militated against his advancement in the good graces of the fair damsels of Leicester, certainly did not prevent the tender passion from gaining an ascendency over him, for Knighton tells us that, "wishing to marry a certain young maid, but being spurned by her, he rushed into such an ostentatious display of sanctity that he despised all the allurements of the world. . . . He renounced the use of linen, flesh and fleshly things, admitted in no wise fish and fishy things, refused wine and beer as if poison, going about with naked feet for many years. In the interim" (adds the Chronicler by way of severely showing the ignorance of the poor fellow) "he learned his A B C, and acquired the art of handwriting."* These might have passed as the vagaries of a disappointed man, but there was clearly something more than unrequited love at work in the bosom of the metal-founder, for when we next find him it is in the company of

scholastic learning incomparable. He especially endeavoured to surpass the ingenuity of others by the subtilty of his learning and profoundness of his genius, and to differ from them in their opinions."—Fo. 2644.

* Fo. 2661.

"Master Richard Waytestath," a chaplain. They by turns resided in the chapel of S. John the Baptist, near the Leper House, which was then used as an hospice and inn, and which stood at the lower end of the Belgrave Gate, Leicester.* There the followers of Wicliffe frequently met, and there these two—Smith and the priest—promulgated their novel opinions. One subject upon which they particularly commented was the practice of Image Worship. "They abhorred images" (says Knighton) "invidiously attacked them, called them idols, and despised them as [mere] figures," speaking of S. Mary of Lincoln and S. Mary of Walsingham as the witch of Lincoln and the witch of Walsingham.† They soon gave a practical proof of the sincerity of their teaching, for, to quote the Chronicler of our Abbey,—

"These two, Richard the Chaplain, and William Smith, by some chance conceived an ardent longing for vegetables; and when they had procured the cabbages, but had no fuel for cooking them, one of them, casting his eye into a corner of the chapel and seeing a certain ancient image standing there, carved and painted in honour of S. Catharine, "Look there, my dear fellow," quoth he, "God has forthwith provided for fuel to cook our cabbage, that we may satisfy our hunger. Marry now, this holy image shall be to us holy fuel, and so by axe and fire it shall undergo a new martyrdom, if peradventure by the cruelty of new tortures it may somehow be enabled to reach the kingdom of heaven." So one of them seized hold of an axe, while the other grasped the image,

* The present "Pack-horse" Inn and "Spittal House Brewery" mark the spot.

† Fo. 2662.

which they soon reduced to firewood, and therewith cooked their vegetables."* As a punishment for this horrible offence, as it would then be considered, they were quickly ejected from the hospice.

William de Swynderby, a priest, was another of these followers of Wicliffe, or "poor priests." He was called by the common people of Leicester "William the Hermit." He is described as having been a man "fickle and wavering in his life and habits. . . . . Whence he came, or where he originated, is not known." When he first appeared in Leicester, he signalised himself by descanting with considerable freedom and great pertinacity upon "the failings and pride of womankind. For he despised exceedingly," says Knighton, "the adornment of women, and contemned their vanity and gestures, and expressed his detestation of their foibles. And although they acted well, and notwithstanding they carried themselves correctly, he treated with too much importunity on this subject, because he never knew how to make an end. For to such a pitch did he provoke the anger of the women of the town, both the good and grave, as well as others, by the scurrility of his preaching and reprehension, that they proposed to hurl stones at him, and to stone him out of the town." He then attacked the merchants and rich men, nearly driving some "into the error of despair," by asserting "that no one could have the riches of this world and the affluence of temporal things, and possibly gain the kingdom of Heaven." Wishing to lead a life of seclusion, he retired into the woods of the Duke of Lancaster, which at that time came

* Fo. 2662.

nearly up to the walls of the town, and there resided for a short period, subsisting upon the bounty of the Duke, and frequently visiting the town. Growing weary of this kind of existence, he was received into the Abbey, provided with rations and a pension. He now visited many churches in the country, but wishing again to preach in Leicester, he left his retreat within the abbey walls, and we next find him in company with William Smith, the reformed metal-founder, with whom we are already acquainted. They, with other of Wicliffe's followers, met together in the chapel of S. John the Baptist—where Smith and Waytestath had often before preached. He now spoke against the corrupt lives of the clergy, their non-residence, their ignorance, and other abuses and enormities in the teaching and practice of the Church, frequently addressing the people upon these then exciting topics in the Churches of S. Martin and S. Margaret. That he obtained a ready hearing from the people of Leicester is evident from Knighton's remark, that "his preaching caught the court of the common herd, and gave them such a liking for him that they said they never saw or heard any one who could so expound the truth to them." Rumour of this preaching reaching the ears of the Bishop of Lincoln, he suspended Swynderby henceforward from all preaching in the chapel of S. John the Baptist, or any other church or churchyard within his diocese, and threatened all who should presume to listen to him with the greater excommunication. This did not deter the Reformer, for, being driven out of the chapel, he made himself a pulpit between two millstones which were placed for sale near its walls, and from thence addressed the people who flocked in crowds to hear him. He was at length, in 1389, cited to appear in the Cathedral Church of Lincoln. He was accompanied thither by many of the inhabitants of Leicester, who, when he was convicted, pleaded hard on his behalf. Their cries would not have saved him from the stake had not the Duke of Lancaster—who was then in Lincoln—interposed on his behalf. The end was, that Swynderby publicly recanted his opinions in the Cathedral Church of Lincoln, the Churches of S. Martin and S. Margaret, Leicester, and several Churches in the county. He afterwards went to Coventry, where, according to Knighton, he resumed the old style of his preaching, and was, in consequence, expelled from that diocese.*

Such is a sketch given by the Canon of our Abbey of some of the forerunners of the Reformation in Leicester—a sketch doubtless drawn by a most partial hand, the figures being distorted to throw ridicule and contempt upon a movement the strength of which he is at the same time compelled to admit, but nevertheless a sketch clearly showing the weakness of some of the instruments then used in preparing the minds of the people for the great change of which they were permitted to give but the warning sound.

The successful preaching of the followers of Wicliffe now fully aroused the fears of the ecclesiastical authorities, and immediate and energetic steps were taken in Leicester to counteract its influence. Richard II. issued a commission against the inhabitants, directed to the Dean of the College in the Newarke and others. Towards the close of the year

* Knighton, fo. 2665. See also Fox for an account of Swynderby.

1389 William Courtney, the Archbishop of Canterbury, made a visitation to the town, and took up his residence in the Abbey. He summoned several of the townspeople before him,* who, however, not appearing, were solemnly excommunicated by him from the High Altar of the Abbey Church. These, and other causes, seem to have brought about the desired effect, for early in the fifteenth century the inhabitants of Leicester appear to have forgotten the teaching of their favourite preachers, and to have returned to the observances and ritual of the Roman Catholic Church. This is evidenced, in some degree, by the fact that several Religious Guilds were formed about this period in Leicester. Early in the century (fifteenth) the Guild of S. George was formed.† The wealth of Corpus Christi Guild was much increased; and towards the close of the century the Guild of S. John the Baptist was established.‡ This apparent settlement of the disturbed elements was, however, merely that calm which usually precedes a tempest, that revival of the old decaying system which is so frequently a strong prognostic of approaching dissolution.

* The names of these are chronicled: Roger Dexter, Nicholas Taylor, Michael Scrivener, Richard Wagstaff, William Smith, Roger Goldsmith, and William Parchmener; and the proceedings against them, and the penances inflicted, are recorded at length in our Local Histories. It is worthy of remark, that the piece of ground opposite to the Great Meeting in Leicester was formerly known as "the Goldsmith's Grave," and it has been surmised that the above Roger Goldsmith, dying under excommunication, was there buried in unconsecrated ground, without the rites of the Church.

† Thompson's *Hist. Leicester*, p. 207.

‡ See Foundation Deed in *Midland Counties Hist. Col.* vol. ii. p. 344. William of Wigston founded the Hospital on the west of S. Martin's Church, formerly known as "The New Hospital," but now designated after him, "Wigston's Hospital," in 1512-13.

A mighty enemy to Despotism and Superstition now arose. About the year 1450 the first printed Bible appeared in Latin; and although, probably, neither that, nor the Greek Edition of the New Testament printed by the learned Erasmus seventy years afterwards—in 1518—found their way into Leicester, yet there is little doubt that Master John Tyndal's English translation of the New Testament, which appeared about the same time (in 1526) would, in spite of the vigilance exercised to prevent its circulation, be eagerly, though secretly, read by some of the ancient burgesses of this town. Henry VIII., too, was now on the throne of England. He ascended that throne a zealous champion of the Romish system, acquired the title of Defender of the Faith, and then, to replenish an exhausted exchequer, became the plunderer of the Church—to accomplish his own selfish wishes, became the opposer of the Papal Supremacy, and by his marriage of Anne Boleyn, in 1532, set the Pope at defiance. Such was, briefly, the state of things when Henry VIII., asserting his supremacy in matters ecclesiastical as well as civil, began his war with the Pope and the Papal system, by the suppression of the Religious Houses,* and by his allowing the English Bible to be set up in every Church.

In 1536 certain Articles of Religion were agreed upon and published, in which—though many old superstitions were upheld—Holy Scripture and the three ancient Creeds of the Church were made the standards of faith without any reference to tradition or decrees. Purgatory was declared uncertain, and the worship allowed to be offered before any

* The Commissioners visited and took possession of Leicester Abbey in 1537.

image was to be through it to God. In the same year Henry issued Injunctions to the clergy commanding them to publish to the people that the Bishop of Rome's usurped power had no authority in the law of God, and that the king's power was supreme over all persons in his dominion—to declare the articles lately published—not to extol Images or Relics for gain—to exhort the people to teach their children the Lord's Prayer, the Creed, and the Ten Commandments in English—to take care that the Sacraments were reverently administered—and lastly, those injunctions were to be observed under pain of suspension and sequestration.

In 1538 the English Bible was printed by Grafton, and all incumbents were enjoined to provide one and set it up publicly in the church, and not to hinder or discourage the reading of it. The people were to be taught by rote—sentence by sentence—the Paternoster and Creed in English—Sermons were to be preached at least once quarterly, and people were not to trust in pilgrimages, relics, or saying over beads what they did not understand.

In 1543 or 1544 the prayers for processions and litanies were ordered to be put into English, and publicly used; which was the case in S. Martin's Church, as appears by an entry in the Churchwarden's accounts for 1545-6.

Itm̄ to Wiłłm Mãby for ij. new englyche ꝓcessioñs bought ye last yere . . . . . vjd.

It must, however, be said that whilst Henry did much towards pulling down the Romish system, he did not do much towards the building up of Catholic truth. Towards the close of his life, after the passing of the Six Articles, the Reformation made little progress, and at his death, having (to use the words of Mr. Blunt*) "done all the work such an instrument was fit for," he left "a church which was little but a ruinous heap, its revenues dissipated, its ministers divided, its doctrines unsettled, its laws obsolete, impracticable, and unadapted to the great changes it had sustained."

Henry VIII. died in 1547, and the solemn sound then heard from the Bell Towers of England not only announced the fact of his decease, but also the downfall of the Romish system in this country. The death of that monarch is one of the early occurrences noticed in the manuscript volume of Churchwardens' accounts relating to S. Martin's Church, to the contents of which these remarks have now brought us :—

1546-47.—Itm̄ p^d. to the ryngers for kynge Henry the Eyght xij^d.
Itm̄ p^d. to the belman the same tyme . ij^d. †

* *Sketch of Reformation*, 194.

† That is, for summoning the people to the Church to hear mass for the repose of his soul.

SECTION II.

BEFORE, however, attempting to trace the changes in the ritual of the Church, and in the customs and observances peculiar to S. Martin's, which took place upon the death of Henry, it may be well to note a few of those customs, and to gain a view of that building as it appeared when he ascended the English throne.

The Church of S. Martin presented, at that time, a far different arrangement from the present, of the accessories of religious worship, to the gaze of the churchman, who, making due use of the Holy-water stoup at the door,* stepped

* According to the Roman Catholic liturgical writers, the Holy Water placed at the entrance of the Church, and into which it was customary to dip the fingers of the right hand, and make a cross upon the forehead, repeating an invocation to the Holy Trinity, signified that the worshipper must enter the sanctuary with a pure and clean heart, and must lift up pure hands to the throne of Him whose cross he had just figured upon his forehead. The Holy-water stoups erected at the doors of the Church of Melton-Mowbray, in this county, are thus noticed in the accompts of the wardens of that town (in manuscript) for the year 1556-7:—

Itm̃ pd. to Steven Andrew for iij. holy watr. stocks . vj.s viiij.d
Itm̃ pd. for iiij. stone of leed towards ye makyng of iij.
leed pannes to sett in ye Holy watr. stocks . . iiij.s

Sometimes these stoups at the church doors were provided with "strinkels" where with to sprinkle the water:—

1484: Item paide . . . for a chene of irren with an Holy water
stik at the south chirche door 0 0 4d

—*Churchwardens' Accts. of Wigtoft, Lincolnshire; vide* Nichols' *Illus.* p. 83.

over the threshold of the western entrance. Before him, spanning the easternmost Tower arch, was the Rood-loft,* bearing the Crucifix in the centre, and on either side the figures of the Blessed Virgin and S. John, whilst at the foot of the Crucifix gleamed the "Rood-light." Rich curtains or "clothes" hung in massive folds about the Loft; under its beam would be a screen of open-work tracery, through which the eye would catch a glimpse of the High Altar covered with an altar-cloth, decorated with its rich frontal, and enclosed at the sides by costly hangings of "damask and velvet," the colours of which were changed to mark the recurrence of the different holy seasons of the Church's year. Upon the Altar itself, or rather upon a low narrow shelf resting upon the inner edge of the Altar, where it touched the wall, stood a crucifix,† probably of silver, and a pair of candlesticks, bearing the two tapers or lights, afterwards enjoined to remain at the Reformation "for the signification that Christ is the very true Light of the world."‡ Upon the

* The entrance to the steps leading to the Rood-loft is still distinctly visible in the masonry on the right hand entering the north chapel from the north transept; and during the recent alterations the opening into the loft itself above was uncovered on removing a portion of the old wall. For a description of the Rood and the Rood-loft, see further on, under "The Rood-loft and Sepulchre."

† I do not think that the crucifix generally superseded the cross earlier than the fourteenth or fifteenth century. —Mr. Bloxam's *Gothic Arch.* 389 (10th Ed).

‡ The placing of more than two lights upon the Altar seems not to have been practised in the English Church; for a careful inspection of ancient illuminations, and the perusal of the numerous lists of church plate and ornaments made at the Reformation, shows that two candlesticks for the High and other Altars were all that were provided. They, in common with many other vessels and ornaments belonging to the Altar, were frequently made of "latten"

Altar, too, the rich plate required in the various Offices of the Church shone in profuse splendour—the Chalice and Paten*—the Pix, wherein the Host was kept reserved for

—a compound metal composed chiefly of copper—or of brass: thus, in an inventory of goods belonging to Merevale Abbey at its dissolution is:—

It' ij. candelstycks of latten.—*Mon. Ang.* v. 484.

And in the accounts of our own Church are several charges for scouring the candlesticks of brass.

In the richer Churches silver or more precious material was used:—

Peir of churche candellsticks of silver parcel gilte.

Pare of Candellsticks parcell gilte for an aulter.

Peir of Candilsticks of Burrall.—*Inventory of Plate received by Treasurer of Henry VIII.'s Jewels from divers surrendered Monasteries, Mon. Ang.* i. 66-7.

In our Cathedrals they were more generally of gold, very considerable in weight, and made as rich in their design, ornamentation, and workmanship, as the skill of the goldsmith could render them: take, for example, a description of those belonging to Lincoln Cathedral in 1536, as preserved in an Inventory then taken:—

Imprimis, two great and fair candlesticks of gold standing on great feet of one fashion, with twenty buttresses of gold in either of them, standing on one base pierced thorow like windows, with four void places for arms, with four great buttresses, and four less, in each one of them; and above every buttress one pinnacle, one of the greatest pinnacles wanting; and betwixt four of the greatest buttresses of every of them are four windows, graven hollow with a stile, having a great knop, with diverse buttresses like the making of a monastery, with eight pillars on every of them, and in the height of them is a bowl battled and buttressed like a castle, with one pike to put candles upon; of the gift of John, the son of Edward, King, and Duke of Lancaster, weighing four hundred and fifty ounces.

Edward VI., in his Injunctions issued in 1547, commands the two lights upon the altar to remain. In the year following, Cranmer in his Visitation Articles allows "two lights upon the High Altar" (Sparrow's *Col.* 326, Ed. 1684); but Ridley, in his Injunctions given in his Visitation 1550, forbids "the setting any Light upon the Lord's Board" in the time of Holy Communion (Burnet's *Ref.* ii. part ii. 287), thus showing a diversity of custom in the reign of Edward VI.

* From the earliest times the holy vessels of the Church used in the cele-

the immediate use of the sick,* with the Lamp before it†—a Ship for frankincense‡—a Sacring Bell§—a Chrisma-

bration of the Eucharist have been, when circumstances permitted, of the most costly description (see *Bingham's Antiq.* ii. 450), and in the English Church before the Reformation the Chalice was frequently encrusted with precious stones, or ornamented with the most precious enamels. A beautiful specimen of a Chalice, apparently of the sixteenth century, is in the possession of the Right Hon. the Earl Howe, and was exhibited by him at a meeting of the Leicestershire Architectural and Archæological Society held at Ashby-de-la-Zouch in 1857. This magnificent Chalice is richly embossed, chased, and set with six enamels, and no less than three hundred and fifty-four precious stones. The enamels represent the Annunciation and the Salutation of the Blessed Virgin, the Nativity, the Adoration of the Magi, the Presentation in the Temple, and our Lord disputing with the Jewish Doctors. The Paten—said in the catalogue of the exhibition to belong to this very ornate Chalice—is entirely devoid of ornament.

* See Note A, at the end of this Section.

† Money or land was frequently left for the maintenance of this, as of other lights in the Church, in Pre-Reformation times: thus the Churchwardens of S. Margaret's parish, Westminster, in 1509, say:—

Item received of certain land lying by Brentbrigge in the parish of Hendon given to the intent to find a lamp before the Sacrament in the said church by one Richard Wise for a hole year 0 15 0

—Nichols' *Illus.* p. 6.

‡ See Note B, at the end of this Section.

§ A Sacring (or holy) Bell was a small handbell rung at different parts of the Office of the Mass.

Belonging to the Priory of Kirby Bellers in this county, at its dissolution, were, in the choir—that is for use at the High Altar—"a sacryng bell;" in "Seynt Andrew's Chapell," and "our Lady Chappell" the same; and in "Seynt Thomas's Chapell" were found "Two sacryng bells."—Nichols' *Leicestersh.* i. cxxxviii.

Cranmer, in his Visitation Articles, 1549, condemns the use of "ringing or *sacrying* Bells" in the time of Communion. He classes it among the customs kept up by those ministers who "Counterfeited the Popish Mass;" and Ridley, soon after his appointment to the Bishoprick of London, issued Injunctions (1550) for that diocese in which he forbids the "ringing of the *Sacrying* Bell." Indeed its use—that of warning the people that certain portions of the office were about being performed—passed away when the Reformed Liturgy, or Order of the Holy Communion, was commanded to be used in English in 1547.

tory for oil* in the (so-called) Sacrament of Extreme Unction—the Pax for the kiss of peace†—Censers‡—Cruets from which the water and wine were poured into the Chalice at the Eucharist§—Offering Basons—a Holy-water Stoup

* See Note C, at the end of this Section.

† See Note D, at the end of this Section.

‡ Censers or Thuribles were frequently architectural in their design, with openings at the sides somewhat in the form of windows, for the emission of the fumes of the incense when swung to and fro by means of the chains attached to them.

A censer of the fourteenth century is in the possession of Mr. M. H. Bloxam, and is figured in his last edition of *Gothic Architecture*, p. 392. Among the Plate belonging to Lincoln Cathedral in 1536 appear—

> Item two pairs of censers of silver of bossed work with six pinnacles and six windows and every of them having four chains.—*Mon. Ang.* vi. 2280.

Incense, in addition to being used symbolically as the outward sign of the prayers of the assembled worshippers, was otherwise extensively used in the church before the Reformation. It was customary to incense pictures, sacred vessels, etc., which was probably one cause of its being disused in the Reformed liturgy.

Occasionally charges for Frankincense are met with—"for frankynegsens, vj[d.]"—*Churchwardens' Accts. of Minchinhampton*, 1556.

§ The mixture of a little water with the wine in the Chalice at the Holy Communion was a very ancient and general custom in the Church. In the rubric to the first order of the Holy Communion, issued by command of Edward VI. in 1547, the Priest, after receiving the Sacrament himself, is directed to "bless and consecrate the biggest Chalice or some fair and convenient cup or cups with wine with some water put into it" (Sparrow's *Col.* 20). Also in King Edward VI.'s first Prayer-book (1549), in which many alterations were made in the above-mentioned Office, the rubric still directed the priest to put to the wine in the Chalice "a little pure and clean water." And although, in the next review of the Liturgy, the order respecting the use of water was omitted, and the practice has fallen into general disuse, still it was never condemned—so far as I can learn—by the English Church; indeed it is specially ordered to be used in the Form of Consecration of a Church or Chapel and of the Place of Christian Burial drawn up by Bishop Andrewes (Sparrow's *Col.* 395-6), and Archbishop Laud and others are said to have used it.—*Origines Liturgicæ*, ii. 77.

and Sprinkle,* and other vessels then used, there all found their appointed place. At the back of the Altar, upon the

In the collection of W. Maskell, Esq. (and shown by him in the Loan Exhibition, South Kensington, 1862), is a pair of small silver altar cruets of the latter half of the seventeenth century, on the lids of which are respectively the letters A. (*Aqua*) and V. (*Vinum*). Amongst the goods belonging to the altar of S. Thomas in the Priory of Kirby Bellers in this county, at its dissolution, were "Two crewets" probably of latten, valued at twopence; and in an Inventory of plate belonging to the Cathedral Church of Ely, taken 30th November, 31 Henry VIII., a chalice and "two crewets" are mentioned.—Nichols' *Illus.* p. 136.

* It was the custom in the English Church, before the Reformation, to sprinkle the altar and the people, before commencing the celebration of High Mass, with Holy Water, or water which had been blessed by the priest. The Holy-water Stoup, or vessel containing the water so blessed, was frequently called a vat or "fatte;" thus in a list of ornaments, etc., belonging to the Nunnery of Kilburn, Middlesex, at its dissolution, is—

Item a holly water fatte of brass.

And then belonging to Fountains Abbey, Yorkshire:—

One holy water fatt with a strinkil of sylver ungilt weighing fifty-three ounces.

In an Inventory relating to the monastery S. Frideswide (now Christ Church), Oxford, taken 19th May, 37 Henry VIII., it is called a bucket:—

Itm̃ a halliwater bokett, and a sprinkell whitt sylver weing 33 ounces.—*Mon. Ang.* v. 290, ii. 167.

In certain Articles of Religion agreed to in 1536, the symbolism of the use of Holy Water is thus explained in the one intituled "of Rites and Ceremonies"—"Sprinkling of Holy-water to put us in remembrance of our Baptism, and the Blood of Christ sprinkled for our Redemption upon the Cross."

And in the Injunctions given to the Clergy and Laity within the Deanery of Doncaster towards the close of the reign of Henry VIII., already referred to, is found the following, which explains the custom, and the then mode of its application:—

Item you shall every Sunday, at the time of your going about the Church with Holy-water, into three or four places, where most audience and assembly of People is, for the declaration of the Ceremonies, say, distinctly and plainly, that your Parishioners may well hear and perceive the same, these words:—

Remember Christ's Bloodshedding, by the which most holy sprinkling, of all your Sins you have free pardon.

Cranmer, in his Visitation Articles, 1549, classes Holy Water among the "Abuses and Superstitions, contrary to the King's Majesty's Proceedings."

wall, would be placed a table or picture, or there would be hung a super-frontal, or reredos, probably richly embroidered with a subject from Scripture or the Lives of the Saints.* Near the Altar, too, on its northern side, at Easter-tyde, was a mimic sepulchre, before which the "Sepulchre Light" was kept burning, and where, at the same season, certain rites were performed commemorative of the death, burial, and resurrection of our Saviour;† and within the Chancel, or near its entrance, stood the brass Eagle which then adorned the Church, and from which the Epistle and Gospel were read.‡

Bringing the eye from the eastern end of the Church—which would naturally first claim attention—on the right hand as he entered, the visitor would see, divided from the nave by a parclose or carved screen-work, the Chapel of the Guild

* Occasionally in our large wealthy churches the wall at the back of the high altar was decorated with both a super-frontal of embroidery and a "table," or representation by painting or sculpture of some sacred subject. That was the case at Winchester, as we find from the Inventory given in by the Prior and Convent to Cromwell, Vicar-General to Henry VIII. Speaking of the high altar, the report says—

Imprimis. The nether part of the high altar being of plate of gold garnished with stones. The font above being of broidering work and pearls, and above that a table of images of silver and gilt garnished with stones.

† See further on, under Rood-loft and Sepulchre.

‡ Unfortunately I am not aware that there is any Inventory extant of the plate belonging to S. Martin's Church at this period; I find much was sold as per "pticuler byll thereof," in 1545-6.—Most of the ornaments and vessels I have mentioned above will be found among the articles enumerated hereafter as sold in the reign of Edward VI., thus showing their existence at the period now under review. Some are incidentally noticed in other parts of the churchwardens' accounts; of these latter I may quote:—

of Saint George. There, in addition to the Altar and all its fittings, stood a large figure of S. George upon horseback

1545-6.—Itm̃ for mēdynge of a box for ye pyx & for the sylṽ therto . . . . xij.d
Itm̃ to ye same Robt. (Sexton) for mēdynge ye Holly Wat' stock & for spryncles . . . . . iij.d

1544.—More oing to the chirche the same day by Henry Maybley for the sepulcre-lyght . . . . . . x.s
Pd. to Robard Goldsmyth for me'ding the pix . . iiij.d
Paid to ij. Pore wemen for scowring the Eygle of brasse the candilstix and aliwatr. stop . . . . xxj.d ob.

Also in Queen Mary's reign will be found—

1554-5.—Itm̃ pd. to Robt. Huseley for oyle & creme & mendyng of the crysmatorye . . . . xij.d

Among some ancient documents belonging to the churchwardens of Melton-Mowbray in this county, which I some time since partly arranged and transcribed, I find the following :—

Sylvyr Juells of the Churchys.

Ima. a crosse of Selvyr and parsell geltt. ij. crewetts of selver psell gelt.

Itm̃ ij. paxes of selver psell geltt and a shyp of clene selver.

Itm̃ a grett chalys gelt. a grett pyx & ij. sensyns of sellver.

Itm̃ remaynying in the church a Cresmatary of selvyr, & a Hooselyng coppe selver & gelt, a pexe on the high auter.

And as a further illustration of the richness of the church plate belonging even to small churches before the Reformation I may quote from the manuscript accounts of the same Churchwardens, under date of 1547, where I find the following receipts :—

Itm̃ recd ffor a pere silṽ sensers & a pax weyng xxxiij. oʒ & ð & ð a quarṽ. at iiij.s viij.d ye oune sma . vij.li xvj.s xj.d

Itm̃ recd ffor a pix Sylṽ. & Gilt sold att London v.li ix.s iiij.d . . . . . .
Itm̃ ffor a pere sensers Sylṽ. a ship ffor ffrankynsense of sylṽ. & ij. cruytts of sylṽ. psell gilt . . } xv.li xiiij.s ix.d

Itm̃ recd ffor the crosse of silṽ & gilt sold at london xix.li x.s vj.d . . . . . .
Itm̃ ffor ij. Images Mary & John a pix sylṽ. & Gilt lvj.s x.d Itm̃ ffor a cheyn silṽ. & psell gilt iiij.s } xxij.li xi.s iiij.d

trampling under foot, or transfixing with his spear, the fierce dragon—type of the evil one and all sin. Following the course of the beautiful series of columns dividing the two south aisles, the eye would reach the Chapel of Our Lady, which occupied the eastern end of the most southern one. This, with its sedilia (yet remaining) for priest, deacon, and sub-deacon, its Altar richly clothed, its richly-carved screens, its figure of the Virgin, the symbols and other decorations of the Guild of Corpus Christi, whose priests served at this Altar, and all the concomitants of the sensuous ritualism of Rome, would present a gorgeous and impressive appearance.

Rather more eastward, at the eastern end of the first south aisle, in close proximity to the present vestry, most probably, was the chapel and altar of Saint Dunstan, whilst nearly opposite to that, looking north, was the chapel and altar of Saint Catharine, which, as it will be shown, there are

The amazing wealth of our venerable Cathedrals and larger churches in plate and ornaments can only be estimated by a perusal of the inventories taken at different periods, and now happily in some instances preserved to us as memorials of the self-sacrifice of our forefathers in this land in their desire—actuated by whatever motive—to add to the honour of God's House, and to enhance the majesty and solemnity of His worship. As instances, see the wonderful lists of Plate and Vestments formerly belonging to the cathedral of S. Peter at York, now preserved in Dugdale's *Monasticon* (vol. vi. 1202), and the equally marvellous lists of those belonging to the cathedral church of Lincoln in 1536 to be found in the same valuable work (vol. vi. 1278). When Henry VIII. laid his sacrilegious hands upon those belonging to the latter church—then the cathedral church of Leicester—in the year 1540, he took out of that church at one swoop, in gold, two thousand six hundred and twenty ounces; in silver, four thousand two hundred and eighty five ounces, beside a great number of pearls and precious stones which were of great value, as diamonds, sapphires, rubies, carbuncles, etc. etc.—*Mon. Ang.* vi. 1286.

good reasons for believing occupied that portion of the church now known as Heyrick's chancel, against the eastern wall of which the altar of S. Catharine rested. And the Rood Chapel, too, with its large Rood or Cross, would not fail to attract attention. In addition to the effect produced by the presence of these chapels and altars—respecting each of which we must enquire more particularly presently—with their rich and gorgeous accessories, there was much to add to the rich effect of the whole building. The floor shone with many a stone inlaid with brass or incised with curious and elaborate ornamentation; the light poured through windows radiant with colour, where were depicted many a simple story, many a mystic symbol, many an escutcheon and heraldic device,* and sometimes, it must be added, many a bitter sarcasm.† The walls, too, as in other churches, would be covered with paintings illustrative of incidents mentioned in Holy Writ, or of real or supposed events in the lives of the saints;‡ whilst on brackets, by the altars in the chapels, and in other parts of the Church, were sculptured figures of Saint and Martyr, Bishop and Confessor,§ in richly-carved taber-

* In Burton's time (1622) there were several of these remaining.—*Description of Leicestershire*, 1st edition, 165.

† Nichols in his History says there was depicted "in the great window of the North Cross aile" in 1730, a Fox preaching to Geese, and under it a Latin perversion of the text, Phil. i. 8, thus—"God is my witness how I long after you in *my* bowels." This was no doubt a satire upon the monks, between whom and the parish priests there was constant and bitter warfare.

‡ See under S. Catharine's Chapel.

§ The figures of saints were sometimes covered during Lent as appears by the following curious entry in the Inventory of goods in the Infirmary Chapel of Peterborough Monastery, taken 30th November 1539:—

Item Old Cloaths to cover Saints in Lent.—Gunton's *Peterborough*.

nacles,* before which lights would continually be burning,† and at the feet of which were stools or hassocks for the use of the devotee.‡

Such is a faint sketch—not a fancy one, but one founded on facts, as we shall see when we come to speak of the changes effected under Edward VI.—of the state of S. Martin's church in the reign of Henry VIII., as it then presented itself to the eye of the visitor curious to view its furniture and fittings at a time when no religious service was being performed within its walls. And if even then, when his own footstep was the only one heard within the building, and his eyes were the only ones gazing upon the many curious and beautiful works of art before him, a feeling of awe crept over him, and his imagination became captivated by the outward semblance of holy things around him, how must that feeling have been increased, and the power of the gorgeous ritualism of Rome over the imagination have been strengthened, had he visited our ancient church when public worship was going

* Belonging to the Abbey of Owston, in this county, and standing in its choir at its Dissolution, were:—Two images, one of Seynt Andrew, the other of Seynt Peter, with feyre tabernacles of wood.—Nichols' *Leic.* i. cxxxviii.

† It was not unusual for persons to make provision for the maintenance of these lights in their wills. Thus Agnes Complyn of Wyke, near Winchester, by her will, dated 30th September 1503, bequeathed to the light burning before the image of our crucified Saviour in that church, twenty pence; to the light of the Blessed Mary, three ewe sheep; and to S. Christopher's light six ewe sheep.—*Journal Brit. Arch. Assn.* 1863, p. 200.

‡ In Evington Church, Leicestershire, projecting from the north wall of the south aisle, near the east window, is a stone bracket for an image, and from this bracket projects a smaller one in which is a small orifice into which a taper was inserted to burn before the image.

1548-9.—Itm̃ rec. for the fote stolls of the tabnacles, ij^s.—*S. Martin's Churchwardens' Accts.*

on. Then the priest officiated at the High Altar in rich vestments of "tissue," of "blue," "green," or "red" velvet or silk, curiously embroidered and enriched,* attended by his acolytes

* To form a proper estimate of the splendour and costliness of the Vestments of the Church before the Reformation, the reader should, as before recommended in the case of church plate and ornaments, consult the Lists of those then belonging to the Cathedrals and Monastic establishments, as preserved in many of the Inventories taken in the time of Henry VIII. One instance may be taken by way of illustration. On the 30th of November 1539, an Inventory of articles belonging to the then monastery of Peterborough was taken, in which the following list of vestments occurs :—

Albes.

Red Albes for Passion-week, 27.

Item, Eight Albes with Crowns and Moons.

Item, Fourteen red Albes.

Item, Forty blue Albes of divers sorts.

Item, Seven-and-twenty other Albes to be worn on single Feasts.

Item, Six Albes with Peter-keys.

Item, Six Albes called The Kydds.

Item, Seven Albes called Meltons.

Item, Six Albes called Doggs.

Item, One old Albe richly embroidered.

Item, Eight Albes with Apples of cloth of gold.

Item, Eight Albes with Apples of blue Tissew.

Item, Five old Albes with red Tissew.

Item, Eight Albes embroidered with Vines.

Item, Five old Albes embroidered.

Item, Fourteen Albes embroidered with divers sorts.

Item, Thirty Albes of old Cloth of Bawdkyn.

Item, Nine Albes embroidered with green.

Item, Thirteen Albes of divers sorts.

Item, Fourteen green Albes with counterfeit Cloth of Gold.

Item, Four Albes called Ferial White.

Item, Seven Albes called Ferial Black.

Vestments.

Item, One suit of Crimson Velvet upon Velvet with a Cope, and Albe suitable to the same.

Item, One Chesible with an Albe called The Burgon.

Item, One suit of blue Damask with a Cope, and thirteen Albes to the same.

Item, One suit of Purple Velvet embroidered with Flowers and Angels, with a Cope and five Albes.

Item, One suit of black Velvet with a Cope, and four Albes with Flowers.

Item, One suit of rich White Cloth of Bawdkyn with seven Albes.

Item, One suit of blue Velvet with five Albes.

or by his deacons, who now and again swung the censer to and fro, from which ascended a fragrant scent, typical of the

Item, One suit of red Velvet with ragged staves, with three Albes of green Bawdkyn.

Item, One suit of crimson Velvet with Flowers and one Cope, and three Albes.

Item, One suit of red Satin with three Albes.

Item, One suit of red Tissew with three Tunicles.

Item, One suit of blue Tissew with two Tunicles.

Item, One suit of cloth of gold with orphers of Tissew.

Item, One suit called The Crowns with two Copes.

Item, One suit called The *Londus* with four Copes.

Item, One suit of *Peter* Keys with two Copes.

Item, One suit of the Doggs with two Copes.

Item, One suit of the *Meltons* so-called with eight Copes.

Item, One suit called *Overtons* with three Copes.

Item, One white suit called *Godfreys* without a Cope.

Item, One suit of white silk called The *Georges* with eight Copes.

Item, One suit called the Kydds with four Copes.

Item, One suit called Red Needle-work with two Copes.

Item, One suit of green silk called Martyrs with four Copes.

Item, One suit called the Squirrels with two Copes.

Item, One suit of green silk called The Cocks with two Copes.

Item, One suit of green velvet with one Cope.

Item, One suit of yellow silk with two Copes.

Item, One suit of changeable silk with one Cope.

Item, One suit called The Daysies with one Cope.

Item, One suit called The Popinjays without a Cope.

Item, One suit of Purple Velvet without a Cope.

Item, One vestment of black Velvet with one Albe.

Item, Three Tunicles of black woorsted.

Item, One suit of course red without a Cope.

Item, Three Tunicles with *Peter* Keys.

Item, One vestment called The Vines.

Copes.

Imprimis, Eighteen of red Tissew.

Item, Two Copes called the Burgons.

Item, Three Copes called The Golds.

Item, Six Copes of red Velvet.

Item, Three Copes of red Bawdkin.

Item, One Cope of red Damask.

Item, Six Copes of blue Tissue.

Item, Two Copes of dun Tissue.

Item, Nine blue Copes called The Roots.

prayers of the faithful worshippers. Then the organs sounded, and the voice of song wafted heavenwards, now in strains

Item, Five Copes of blue Velvet.

Item, Thirteen Copes of blue silk called The *Georges*.

Item, Seven Copes of blue Bawdkin called The Hindes.

Item, Four copes of old Black Bawdkin.

Item, Seven Copes of Sattin of *Cyprus*.

Item, Three Copes of red silk.

Item, Three Copes of green silk.

Item, Four Copes of red Needlework.

Item, Four Copes of green velvet.

Item, Thirteen Copes of white silk.

Item, Two other Copes.—Gunton's *Peterborough*, 59-61 (1686).

In addition to this list there were many more vestments belonging to the Lady and the other numerous chapels. "Bawdkin" was a precious stuff composed of silk interwoven with threads of gold, and the peculiar names given to some of the vestments had reference to their ornamentation. Thus the vestment called "the Vines" was undoubtedly richly decorated with needlework in imitation of grapes and vine leaves; whilst others would appear to have been named after the donors of them to the Abbey. For instance, the suit called Godfrey's had been probably the gift of Godfrey of Croyland, who was elected Abbot in 1299, and who spent much money in vestments and ornaments for the Abbey Church. Henry de Overton, again, another Abbot, was perhaps the donor of the vestments bearing his name. The garments in the above list specially called "Vestments" were chasubles, the outer coverings of bishops and priests in the office of the mass.

This list, extravagant as it may appear to our poor, scanty, modern notions of what is due to the service of God, discloses to us comparatively nothing as to the extreme richness and splendour of the Church vestments in and before the the reign of Henry VIII.: nothing was too gorgeous, too costly, too precious to use in their manufacture and ornamentation. The most costly velvet, the richest silk, the most precious cloths of gold and silver, the most beautiful needlework and embroidery that English fingers—the most famous in the middle ages in those arts—could produce, were unsparingly used. The Eucharistic Chasuble was ornamented with its orphreys before and behind set with pearls, with plates of gold enamelled, with falcons, dragons, leopards, angels, or branches of gold, with images of needlework, its back being also sometimes gorgeously decorated with a symbol of the Trinity, images of the Virgin or of the Saints, texts of Scripture, or heraldic device. The Cope, too—the magnificent processional vestment,—was perhaps even more splendid and costly in its material and ornament, its hood and morse giving scope for the display

slow and plaintive, then with the full gushing flood of sound, speaking of thanksgiving, jubilation, and victory. Picture all

of much precious workmanship. Among the two hundred and fifty-four Copes belonging to Lincoln Cathedral in the time of Henry VIII., almost all of which were equally magnificent, the following, by way of example, may be quoted :—

"Item, a red Cope called The Root of Jesse, of red velvet broidered with images of gold, set with roses of pearls, with a precious orphrey, having a morse of cloth of gold.

Item, a red Cope broidered with images of gold and historics of apostles and martyrs.

Item, another Cope of cloth of gold having in the orphrey little images, birds and roses, set with pearls.

Item, a costly Cope of blew velvet, with costly orphreys of gold, with images set with pearl, and in the morse an image of Our Lady with her Son and four angels, in the hood the Trinity set with pearl and stone, and in the back a large image of the Assumption garnished with pearl and stone, with many angels and gold set with pearl."—Dugdale's *Mon. Ang.* vi. 1281-3.

The morse, or clasp holding the Cope together on the upper part of the chest, was made the vehicle of many a curious and sacred symbol or device, the name or arms of the donor.

Neither was it the venerable cathedral or the wealthy monastery only which possessed vestments rich in material, in colour, and in design; the parish churches too had their costly and gorgeous habiliments, though fewer in number, and less complete, perhaps, in their arrangement. Our Church of S. Martin, as we shall see in the course of our narrative, was not entirely destitute of them, notwithstanding its poverty, which was so great in 1535 that there was "no other priest than the vicar, whose living was so poor that he could not afford to pay a priest to assist him in the performance of his duties." And the parish of Melton-Mowbray, in this county, possessed, as I find from the manuscript records of the church, the following among other vestments, which are only incidentally mentioned, so that probably many more were there provided :—

1553-4
Sute of whit vestments.
1562
A Coope of red velvett.
A Vestment awbe wth amys & that w[ch] belongeth to y[t].
A Vestment of Stoole worck.
A Vestment wth awbe & amys.
A Vestment of satyn.
ij. Coopes of yallow sylke a Ratchyt & iiij serplycs."

Again, in the few extracts from the Records of the neighbouring church

this, and is it strange that, without the open Bible, without the faithful teaching of God's truth from the pulpit, men should have been so long held as it were spell-bound by a rich ritualism, backed as it was by the great spiritual power exercised by the priesthood?

of S. Mary de Castro, Leicester, preserved by Nichols in his History of the County, are the following references to vestments formerly belonging to that church:—

1505

Paid for mending 3 white copes	0	3	6
For the black cope . . .	0	2	6
For ribband for it . . .	0	0	8

1507

Paid for a day's work mending all the red copes of silk .	0	0	4

1525

Edward Lydurland and John Baynesford churchwardens, with the consent of the parish, bought 3 copes with a vestment and 2 . . . . . of which . . . . . damaske flowered with . . . . . flower de luces	£20	0	0

It was customary for the vestments and other things connected with the offices of the church to be hallowed or set apart for their special purpose. Thus, in the same list of extracts relating to S. Mary's Church, Leicester, Nichols gives:—

1499

Item, paid for hallowing Mr. Pryke's cloth 2 stolis and 2 corporasses &c.	0	1	2

1500

Paid for hallowing a vestment and three altar cloths at the abbey	0	1	8

But very few of these ancient English vestments are now in existence to authenticate the description given of them above, or to compare with the concise entries in many an Inventory made at the Dissolution of the Religious Houses by Henry VIII. The Loan Exhibition, South Kensington (1862), contained, however, some extremely valuable and precious examples which must have been viewed with much interest by the many thousands of visitors who were privileged to see that exquisite collection of antiquities and works of art.

THE CHAPELS.

Any description of the appearance and fittings of S. Martin's Church previous to the Reformation would of course be very incomplete without at least a passing allusion to its chapels and minor altars. Unfortunately so little is known respecting these, that anything approaching to a detailed account of them is rendered impossible. There are, however, a few notes which may not be without interest, or be altogether unworthy of preservation.

THE LADY CHAPEL.

When we reflect that for many hundred years the adoration of the Virgin Mary prevailed through all Christendom; that the most beautiful of the Works of Art—whether pictures, statuary, or architectural enrichments—which the Middle Ages produced had reference to her attributes, her person, or her history, surely we must look upon that portion of the fabric of our Church which was set aside to her honour, and for the special use of her votaries, with great interest. Judging from the architectural features of the great south aisle of S. Martin's Church, that noble addition to the edifice was made at the close of the thirteenth or very early in the fourteenth century, at a time when the worship of the Virgin had reached its meridian—when her votaries abounded—when chapels dedicated to her were added to our larger churches and cathedrals—when her altar appeared in almost every parish church—and when Guilds or Brotherhoods claiming the protection and patronage of "Our Lady the Virgin" were established in many of our towns and villages. Soon after the erection of this portion of the church the Guild of Corpus Christi was founded by license from King Edward III. Probably the chief contributors to the cost of the building were the first members of the Guild; and here, at the eastern end of this aisle, stood "our Lady's altar," at which the priests of Corpus Christi served, and where they performed those services for the ghostly welfare of its members, living and dead, which will be more particularly referred to when the ancient Guilds of S. Martin's Church are brought under notice. That this was the altar used by the Guild Priests is shown by an Account of the Receipts and Payments of the Stewards of the Guild of Corpus Christi for the year 1525–6, which is preserved among the Records belonging to the Corporation of Leicester. This interesting document the writer was, with the assistance of Mr. Kelly, fortunate enough to discover, and it will be found, with others, transcribed in its proper place. There are found charges for "washyng off the Awter clothes & oth^r. the ornyments abowt the Awter in our lade chappell," . . . "ffor waxe spent at o^r ladise Awter," . . and "ffor garneshyng off the Awter."

One consequence of this altar being served by the Guild Priests is, that we know little of the arrangement or fittings of this chapel previous to the Reformation; nearly all the furniture belonging to it, being the property of the Guild, had disappeared before the Injunctions of Edward VI. reached Leicester, and before the existing records of the Church begin. That it was richly decorated, and wanting in none of those accessories to its religious services which the Mediæval Church knew so well how to employ, we may well believe, when we remember the wealth of the Guild, and the purposes for which that Fraternity was formed. Even its present appearance attests as much. Its goodly proportions—fragments proving the existence of its former rich geometrical windows—its sedilia for priest, deacon, and sub-deacon, appearing here and at the high altar only—its almery (?)—its piscina (which, if I mistake not, a rap on the plaster will still discover)—the many recumbent gravestones from which the rich brasses have been ruthlessly torn,—all speak of a time when it would be wanting in none of those appurtenances which we have seen abounded at the High Altar and in the other portions of the church. Its altar, we may infer, was a massive one, as it took "Robert Sekerston and hys fellow" a week to remove it in 1550–1, as we shall notice under that date. By the altar was a "tablet," upon which were written the names of the founders, etc., of the Guild, and which was placed before the chaplain in order that he might name them every day in his mass. A "table in our lady chappell" also, or picture*—probably of the Blessed Virgin, similar to the

* A picture, and the piece of carving, sculpture, or metal work placed over the back of the altar, was called a "table" at the period now under notice.

In the Churchwardens' Accounts of Melton-Mowbray, under date of 1558, I find :—

"R$^{d.}$ off Mast^{r} Gyles ffor y^{e} Pynakell whyche was on y^{e} gryt table of y^{e} aulter . xij.^{d}"

And again, in a Memorandum at the end of the Accounts of the same Churchwardens for the year 1562 :—

"Item in the hands of Goodman Carver . . . . all ye ymagies in y^{e} table of the hye alter."

In an Inventory of goods, etc., belonging to the Monastery of Peterborough, taken 30th November 1539, are the following :—

one formerly in the church of S. Mary de Castro, which represented her Coronation—and a "crowne of wode Kyverd w[t.] sylv̾," which, it is not unlikely, was placed upon the head of a figure of the Virgin upon festive and great occasions,* were numbered among the treasures of the Church.

It may deserve remark, that formerly, as now, this chapel was used for business purposes connected with the church.

In 1546 the Accounts of the Churchwardens were passed "on Palme Sonday . . . . in o[r] lady's quere w[th]in the same churche;" which Accounts, by the way, were always passed under the supervision of the mayor, in conjunction with the principal inhabitants of the parish, in obedience to an order made at a Common Hall on the Feast of S. Matthew, 2 Henry VIII., which enacted "that the mayor for the time being shall every year take the accompts for the church of S. Martin within his time, under pain of forty shillings."

"In the Quire. Item at the upper end of the Church three altars, and upon every altar a Table of the Passion of Christ, Gilt, with three stained Fronts.

In the South Ile. Item in S. Oswald's Chappel . . . . one Table, Gilt, of S. Oswald. Item in S. Bennet's Chappel . . . . one Table, Gilt, with the story of S. Bennet."—Gunton's *Peterborough* (1686), 61, 62.

These "tables" were sometimes moveable. Belonging to Fountains Abbey, at its dissolution—

"One table for the high altar on principal days, with three images of silver, gilt, with beads and plate of silver, and some parts of gold set with stones.—*Mon. Ang.* v. 290.

* In "our Lady Chappell," in the Priory of Kirby-Bellars, Leicestershire, was standing, at its dissolution, "an Image of our Lady."—Nichols' *Leic.* i. cxxxviii.

S. Dunstan's Chapel.

S. Dunstan—whose chapel we now proceed to notice—claims our attention for a brief space, not only as an English Saint, but as a very prominent figure in the history of the English Church in the tenth century. According to Mrs. Jameson, he was born in the year 925, in the beginning of the reign of Athelstan, the grandson of Alfred. His early years were passed in the neighbourhood of Glastonbury, where he afterwards became a professed monk. The famous abbey of Glastonbury belonged to the Benedictines; which noble order was established in 529, and was introduced into England about fifty years after the death of its founder. The Benedictines soon became a most numerous, powerful, and, it must be added, eminently useful body of men. They were the early missionaries of Northern Europe—the sole depositories of learning and the arts through several centuries of ignorance —the collectors and transcribers of books—the fathers of Gothic Architecture (the Cathedrals of Canterbury, Westminster, Winchester, Durham, Ely, Peterborough, Bath, Gloucester, Chester, and Rochester were theirs)—the earliest illuminators and limners—the first instituters of regular schools of music; added to all which they were the first agriculturists who brought science to bear on the cultivation of the soil. Such was the Order to which Dunstan joined himself, and if history be true, he became a not unworthy member of a society of men who have been described as the thinkers and writers, the artists, the farmers, and the schoolmasters of mediæval Europe. He himself became not only learned in books, but an accomplished scribe, a painter (a drawing by him is now extant), a musician (he built an organ), and an excellent artificer in metal. It was when he was engaged in the latter pursuit that he had the famous encounter with the Devil, which is perhaps the best-known incident in the life of the saint. At a later period, be it remembered, Luther threw his inkstand, according to his own account, at the same unbidden visitor. Dunstan repaired early to court, where he was at first a great favourite with King Edmund, but his rare acquirements procuring him the reputation of being a sorcerer, he was driven from the royal presence. He was afterwards recalled and appointed Abbot of Glastonbury, and Treasurer to the king. Upon the accession of Edwin, Dunstan was again driven from Court—(whether the frequently repeated story of his treatment of the young king and Elgiva is true or not, in all its details, is an open question)—only, however, to be raised to higher honours when King Edgar was placed upon the throne. The Abbot of Glastonbury was then created successively Bishop of Worcester, of London, and at length Archbishop of Canterbury. In the year 960 he visited Rome, and received from the hands of the Pope—John XII.—the pallium as Primate of the Anglo-Saxon nation. Upon his return to England he founded many monasteries and schools, and aided much in the cultivation of knowledge and the civilising arts. Dunstan, "the chief of monks," as he is called by William of Malmesbury, died in 988, and his festival was ordered to be kept throughout England by a Synod held at Winchester in the year 1021. A solemn translation of his relics to a more honourable place in Canterbury Cathedral was effected by Archbishop Lanfranc after the rebuilding of the Cathedral, which had been burnt down in 1074. His monument was on the south side of the high Altar, where his relics were found in 1508 by Archbishop Warham in a leaden chest with the inscription "Here reposeth S. Dunstan, Archbishop." * The Calendar of the English Church still marks his anniversary on the 19th of May.†

* Mrs. Jameson's *Legends of the Monastic Orders. Notes and Queries,* 3d Series, ii. 77. William of Malmesbury's *Chronicle,* chaps. vii. and viii. Dr. Hook's *Archbishops of Canterbury,* i. 382-426.

† The accompanying engraving is an outline, facsimile, of a figure of S. Dunstan in an Anglo-Saxon Manuscript in the British Museum (Cotton. MSS. Claudius, A iii. fo. 7, drawn, probably, early in the eleventh century), and is here given not only as an illustration to the remarks upon the saint and his chapel in S. Martin's Church, but also to show the ecclesiastical dress of the period.

Dunstan is represented sitting on a Faldstool, which, from the ease with which it could be folded up, was usually carried about by the Bishop in his progresses through his diocese; over the Faldstool is spread a cloth or "hanging;" his right hand is held up as if he were in the act of speaking, his left holds an open book. He is vested in a Chasuble—the outer vestment of bishop and priest during the Sacrifice of the Mass. This vestment was anciently made of a piece of material semicircular in shape, which was folded in two, the straight sides being then sewn together within a few inches of the right angle, where an opening was left for the head of the wearer to pass through. It then fell—as will be seen in the annexed engraving—in graceful and easy folds about the person. This vestment was made of the most beautiful and precious stuffs, and was, in S. Dunstan's time, ornamented with a peculiar decoration called "the Flower," which consisted of a mass of rich needlework, in gold or silk, about the shoulders, the chest, and the upper part of the back, while round the opening through which the head passed ran a broad band, frequently of gold studded with jewels. The needlework of "the Flower," in our figure of S. Dunstan, is (in the original illumination) represented as wrought in red needlework, that being also the colour of the deep fringe which falls from it over the upper part of the chest.

S. DUNSTAN.

(From Anglo-Saxon Manuscript in British Museum—Catton, Claudius, A. iii. fo. 7.)

Much more can be told of the saint than of his altar in S. Martin's Church. The position even of the latter is uncertain. It probably stood, as before intimated, at the eastern termination of the small south aisle, in the neighbourhood of the present vestry, which is a comparatively modern addition to the church. The only reference to S. Dunstan or his altar

Over the chasuble, about mid-way between the shoulders and the elbows of the wearer, will be noticed the Pallium or Pall which, as remarked in the text, S. Dunstan received personally from Pope John XII. in 960. This mark of Metropolitan dignity had, in the time of S. Dunstan, assumed the form given in the illustration, and which form—with the exception of the pendants being now much shorter—it has ever since retained. The Pall was then, and still is in the Roman Catholic Church, a band of woollen material about three inches in width, encircling the person as before mentioned, where it is kept in its place by being attached by hooks or pins to the chasuble. From the band were two pendants, one hanging down the front of the wearer, the other hanging in a similar manner behind. Both the band and the pendants were ornamented with crosses. Under the chasuble S. Dunstan wears the Dalmatic, with its richly-ornamented hem or border, from under which the two ends of the stole are visible. The vestment under the Dalmatic, and reaching to the feet, is either the Alb or the Tunicle; probably the former. The head-dress is well worthy of careful notice, it being the precursor of the mitre which, as is well known, was for several centuries the episcopal covering for the head: it is simply a white kerchief fitting close to the head, and kept in its place by a long fillet or bandage tied behind, the ends of which are seen. Several exquisite specimens of ancient Ecclesiastical Vestments were exhibited in the Loan Exhibition (1862), South Kensington Museum; and the Very Rev. Dr. Rock, in the catalogue of that section, and in his published works, gives much information respecting them.

For the vestments and insignia of the Bishops of the English Church shortly before, and at the period of the Reformation, see the Monumental Brasses of Thomas Cranley, Archbishop of Dublin and Warden of New College, Oxford, A.D. 1417, in New College Chapel; and of Thomas Goodrich, Bishop of Ely A.D. 1554, in the south aisle of the Choir of Ely Cathedral; both engraved in Mr. Bontell's *Monumental Brasses of England.*

which is to be met with in the church records is one which, although out of place here as to date, is quoted :—

1549/50 Itm rec. for a sellyng oṽ sent dunstones alṗ sold to Mr. Cort . xvj.[d]

S. Catharine's Chapel.

Standing in S. Dunstan's chapel and looking through the parclose which then probably screened the opening from that chapel into the chancel, the eye would rest upon a fine mural painting which then adorned the opposite wall on the left hand of a corresponding opening on that—the north side—of the chancel, through which, again, the eye would reach the chapel at the east end of the north aisle. This painting was a figure of S. Catharine of Alexandria, to whose honour the altar in the adjoining or north chapel * was dedicated, and was probably painted in this conspicuous place outside the chapel in obedience to the Canons, which required that the name of the saint under whose invocation each altar had been erected to Almighty God should be written either upon a tablet affixed to the altar itself, or somewhere near upon the walls of the sacred edifice.†

Among the many beautiful allegorical legends with which the literature of the Middle Ages abounds, perhaps few can compare for poetic incident and charming grace with that of S. Catharine of Alexandria; and well this painting epitomised her story. She was represented crowned in right of her royal

* Now known as Heyricke's Chapel.

† Dr. Rock's *Church of our Fathers*, i. 227.

S. CATHARINE.

(From Mural Painting in S. Martin's Church, Leicester, now destroyed.)

birth and as a sovereign princess : in her right hand she held a book to signify her learning, for at the age of fifteen years she was incomparable in her knowledge of the learning and philosophy of the ancients ; at her feet was a wheel armed with teeth, her especial emblem, the intended instrument of her death, but from which she was miraculously delivered ; in her left hand she held a sword, the weapon of her final martyrdom ; whilst under her feet she trampled the pagan emperor Maximin, who, after in vain attempting to make her swerve from her profession of Christianity, and after failing, by offers the most splendid and threats the most fearful, to corrupt her virtue, caused her to be beheaded. When she was dead, angels—according to the legend—carried her dead body over the desert and the Red Sea, and deposited it on the summit of Mount Sinai, where it rested in a marble tomb, and where a monastery was afterwards erected over her remains.* Under the painting was a Latin inscription in honour of the saint.† Over the altar in the chapel itself was a "voyte"

* Mrs. Jameson's *Legendary Art*, ii. 78.

† The figure of S. Catharine referred to in the text was discovered on the wall in the position indicated during the restoration of the Chancel in 1847. A correct tracing was taken by Mr. Brandon's instructions, from which the illustration here given is engraved ; and Mr. Goddard of Leicester also took a tracing, which he has kindly permitted me to inspect. The height of the painting, including the inscription, was about five feet. The dress—a close-bodied gown, with a mantle and tippet faced with miniver—leads to the inference that it was painted about the time of Richard II.—the end of the fourteenth century. According to Nichols, the chancel was rebuilt in 1409 : it might have been painted then. The tracing of the inscription, which was partly obliterated —the commencement of each line being wanting—is not translatable. It has been shown to several scholars and antiquaries, and the one opinion is, that the tracing being made by a person unskilled in palæography, any attempt at

or canopy; and by the altar stood a "table" or picture. On its south side was the piscina,* which is still partially remaining.

So popular was S. Catharine in England that her name was retained in the calendar of the Reformed Church, where it will be found under the date of 25th November.

S. George's Chapel.

The Legend of S. George, the Patron Saint of England, the Great Martyr of the Greeks, is too well known to call for repetition here. That his person and attributes were purely ideal there is no doubt. The Legend represents the power and victory of truth and holiness over falsehood and iniquity, and so strongly had it obtained possession of the imagination of men even in the earliest ages of Christianity, that we find one of the first churches erected by Constantine, after his profession of the Christian religion, was in honour of S.

a certain and finished translation would be futile. Its general import, however, is as given in the text.

* The Piscina, which is still found in most of our ancient churches and side chapels, was a shallow stone bason, with a hole in the centre communicating with a drain, fixed at a convenient height from the floor, and placed within a niche on the—in England—south side of the altar. Its use was to receive the water in which it was customary for the priest to wash his fingers after the Gospel and in the office of the Mass, and also the water with which the chalice was rinsed. This custom was referred to and condemned by Cranmer and Ridley in their Visitation Articles. The former, in 1549, charging that "no minister do counterfeit the Popish Mass," mentions among the ceremonies used by those who did so, "washing his Fingers at every time in the Communion;" and the latter, in 1550, referring to the same thing, enjoins: "Item, That no minister do counterfeit the Popish Mass in . . . washing his Hands or Fingers after the Gospel or the receipt of the Holy Communion."

George. Richard I. in his Crusades invoked the aid of S. George for the protection of himself and his army. In 1222 his feast was ordered to be kept a holiday throughout England, and when, in 1330, the Order of the Garter was instituted, S. George was firmly established as our Patron Saint.* And long he held his own, for when Richmond addressed his followers on the Field of Bosworth, in 1485, preparatory to leading them in deadly fight against Richard III., he still bade them advance in the name of God and S. George; and later still, when Henry VIII., in 1536, issued his order for the abrogation of certain holidays, the "feests of the apostles, of our blessed lady *and of Saynt George*," were specially excepted from the regulations therein made;† and even now a reference to our Church Calendar will show that April 23 is marked "S. George. M."

The Guild of S. George in Leicester, as before remarked, had its altar in S. Martin's Church, and tradition has always pointed to the Western end of the great south aisle as the position formerly occupied by it. The Chapel itself would be separated from the other portions of the church by a parclose or carved screen-work. Upon the altar—over which was a "vowte" or canopy,‡ and at the back of which, or near

* Mrs. Jameson's *Legendary Art*, ii. 5.

† Sparrow's *Coll.* 168, ed. 1684.

‡ I say "vowte or canopy" ("vowte" is the word used in the Churchwardens' Accounts), because, if I mistake not, the "sellyng" over S. Dunstan's altar, the "voyte" over S. Catharine's, and the "vowte" over S. George's—which were probably of carved or otherwise enriched wood-work or metal, inasmuch as they were saleable—were the comparatively modern representatives of the ancient Ciborium or canopy, which we have seen was placed over the altars in the ancient church: the difference pro-

to which, hung a "painted cloth"—were a "chalis," a pix, and the other usual sacred vessels required by the officiating Guild Priest.* In this chapel was a series of stalls, probably for the use of the Master and Stewards of the Guild, curiously carved. One of them had a projecting bracket or "miserere" on the under side, which, when turned up for use, exhibited in bold carving a "dragon or flying serpent with long talons and expanded wings" of a black leaden colour, under which were two human skulls. Through the sitting-board of this stall was a hole large enough to admit a thick wand or similar badge of office during the performance of religious service.†

But by far the most conspicuous object in this chapel, if not in the whole church, was a figure of S. George on horseback, who, as the patron saint of the Guild, was—to use the words of old Throsby—"harnessed in the church splendour

bably being, that while the ciborium was supported on four pillars rising from the four corners of the altar, the "vowte" over S. George's altar was attached to the wall at its back, and overshadowed it above, somewhat like—to use a term applied in Domestic Architecture—a penthouse.

In the sixteenth century the term was, I think, synonymous with vault. In a letter to Lord Cromwell by John Portmari, describing the progress made in the destruction of Lewes Priory, he says: "I told yor. lordshyp of a *vaute* on the ryght syde of the hyghe altare, that was born up wt. fower greate pillars, having abowt it v. chappells, whych be compased in wt. the walls lxx. steks of lengthe, that is fete ccx. . . . now we are pluckyng down an hygher *vaute*." And in a Survey of Tykford Priory, Bucks, in the time of Henry VIII., is found:—"Itm̃, the chauncell there is *voted* with ston and tymber work oṽ the same . . ." —*Mon. Ang.* v. 10, 206.

* In the Churchwardens' Accounts for 1544 is—

"Paid to Robard Goldsmyth for mẽding the chalis belongyng to sent georgs chapell and a pix xvj.d"

† Nichols' *Leicestersh.* i. 592.

of the times," and elevated on a "florth" and vente—that is, on a floor or plinth of, perhaps, considerable height.*

Leaving the Chapel of S. George,

The Rood Chapel,

of the existence of which there is abundant evidence in the Records of the Church, would claim attention. It derived its name from a large Cross or Rood which stood therein, and which was of sufficient importance in mediæval times to give a designation to the edifice—S. Martin's being then not unfrequently called S. Cross. It is so referred to by Knighton in his Chronicle written in the reign of Richard II.,† and even in comparatively modern times the street on the north side of the church was called Holy Rood Lane, it being so designated in the Accounts of the Chamberlains of the Borough for the year 1594-5.

It is presumed that at the foot of this Cross in the Rood Chapel was an altar, and that there offerings were made by the people; for Charyte, a Canon of Leicester Abbey, who made a Rentale of the possessions and emoluments of that House about the year 1348, speaking of S. Martin's Church, says the High Cross—*Alta Crux*—produced yearly eleven pounds.‡ Indeed, we know that some of the fittings mentioned as belonging to other chapels where there were undoubtedly altars, were also here, for "ye table in ye rode

* The word "vente" is difficult of explanation in its use here.—Vide *Glossary of Architecture*—"Vent."

† Twysden's *Decem Scriptores*, fol. 2665.

‡ Nichols' *Leicestershire*, i. 113, app.

chappell" will be found among the articles sold in the year 1550-1. That this High Cross mentioned by Charyte was the one in the Rood Chapel, and not the large Cross or Rood, which here, as elsewhere, then stood upon the Rood Loft, is, it is thought, proved by the fact of his mentioning a further sum as derived from offerings made at "the foot of the Cross" —*Per Crucis*—and which will be noticed again when the sepulchre and its ceremonies are referred to.*

The position of the Rood Chapel is unknown. It is not even traditionally marked out, and although it is mentioned several times in the Churchwardens' Accounts, the only record we have there of the Cross itself is a reference to its destruction under the date 1568-9 where we shall find—

> Payd to Bodeley for Caryinge ye stones and Ramell away where ye Crosse stoode . . . . viij.[d]

The Rood Loft and the Sepulchre.

Reference has been made to the Rood Loft which, in S. Martin's, as in most other churches before the Reformation, was placed over the screen dividing the Chancel from the Nave. This was sometimes simply a beam, and was called

* It should also be mentioned, that in the Taxation made by Edward I. about the year 1291—known as Pope Nicholas' Taxation — the following entry occurs relative to S. Martin's Church :—

"Estimaco obvencionu' Sc̄e Crucis in eadem ecclesia . . 6 13 4."

Whether this refers to the High Cross in the Rood Chapel, or to the Crucifix on the Altar, or rather in the Sepulchre, is not clear.—*Taxatio Ecclesiastica, P. Nich.* iv. 65.

the Rood-beam, or, from the number of lights burning thereon, the Candle-beam. In the loft, or upon the beam, was a large rood * or crucifix, on either side of which were figures of the Blessed Virgin and Saint John looking west, which were said to symbolise the Christian and Jewish Churches, and which were so placed to meet the gaze of the worshippers in the nave, and also in accordance with the tradition that the aspect of our Saviour upon the cross was to the west. In addition to these figures were frequently those of angels and the Patron Saint of the church.† The passage to the Rood Loft was usually up a flight of stone stairs through the wall of the nave; sometimes on the north side, as in S. Martin's, traces of which are still visible; sometimes on the south side, as in the church of S. Mary de Castro, Leicester; and occasionally there were stairs at both ends of the loft, as at S. Saviour's, Dartmouth. The Rood in S. Martin's occupied a loft of sufficient size to admit of persons passing along it. It was, as before remarked,

* Fuller, alluding to the position of the Rood upon the loft, says:—"And wot you what spiritual mystery was couched in this position thereof? The church (forsooth) typified the church militant; the chancel represents the church triumphant; and all who will pass out of the former into the latter, must go under the Rood-loft, *i.e.* carry the cross, and be acquainted with affliction."

† The Churchwardens of S. Helen's, Abingdon, charge in 1555:—

Payde for peynting the roode
Marie and John and the patron
of the churche . . . 6s 8d

For the roode Mary and John
with the patron of the churche 18s 0d
—*Archæologia*, i. 14.

The Churchwardens of S. Mary Hill, London, charge in 1497:—

Item to Undirwood for peynting and gyldyng of the roode, the crosse, Mary and John, the iiij. evangelists, and the iij. dyadems . . . .—Nichols' *Illus.* 103.

The figure of S. Martin, which we shall see existed in the church, probably stood upon the Rood Loft.

decked with rich drapery, which "hengyd beffore" it. The "rode lyght" burned before the crucifix:—*

$\frac{1558}{9}$ pd for lyght to burne by the roode . ij.[d]

Whilst along its extent tapers were gleaming:—

$\frac{1555}{6}$ Itm̃ pd for ix. taper dysshes for the Rode loft . ix.[s]

The Rood-screen was frequently painted with the figures of saints, with sacred devices, and with texts of Scripture and other inscriptions.† From the loft announcements were made to the congregation, and there certain devotions were performed, and hymns and psalms were chanted. There, too, "the Passion," or a portion of the Gospel descriptive of the Passion and death of our Saviour, was read or sung on Good Friday by a priest standing by the Rood,‡ which is probably the custom referred to in the Churchwardens' Accounts for the year 1544, and in those for the two following years:—

Pd on Palme Sonday to the proffit (prophet) for ale at the reding the passhon § . . . . . ij.[d]

1545. Item p[d] to y[e] ꝑphete & for ale on Palme Sonday . ij.[d]

1546-7. Item p[d] to y[e] ꝑfet of Palme Sonday and that he dranke . . . . iiij.[d]

* Cromwell, in certain Injunctions to the clergy issued by him in the name of Henry VIII. in 1538, ordered that they should suffer from thenceforth no candles, tapers, or images of wax to be set before any Image or Picture, but only the Light that "commonly goeth across the church by the Rode-loft, the Light before the Sacrament of the Altar, and the Light about the Sepulchre, which, for the adorning of the church and Divine Service, they shall suffer to remain."

† The fine screen preserved in S. Saviour's Church, Dartmouth, may be quoted, among others, as an example.

‡ *Glossary of Architecture; Notes and Queries*, 3d Series, ii. 233 and 177.

§ In some churches the Passion was

Passing under the Rood Loft in Holy week, the churchman would—during the reign of Henry VIII., the date at which we are supposed to be inspecting the church of S. Martin—see on the north side of the High Altar an imitation in wood of the sepulchre in which the body of our Saviour was laid after his crucifixion.

1545-6. Itm̄ for thered for ye sepulcar ij. yere . . j.[d]

This was erected—where a stone one did not permanently exist*—according to the custom of the English Church, on Maunday Thursday. The altar was then, or on the following day—Good Friday—stript of its decorations, to denote the penitential season; and the crucifix and the Host (which was there reserved for the sick in a pix, or, as it is now termed, a ciborium) were deposited in the sepulchre and covered with a pall or veil.† This was of course to signify the entombment. A Light, called the Sepulchre light, was kept burning before it, which was frequently in a lamp or on a standard of a massive and elaborate character. Thus, at S. Martin's the "sepulcre light, waying iij. score and xv.[li]" is mentioned.

partly dramatised on this day by one person (perhaps the "Prophet" referred to in these extracts) reciting the words in the Gospel assigned to our Saviour, the choir singing the portions recording the outcries of the Jews, whilst the deacon read the "middle text," or the descriptive portion.—See Brand's *Popular Antiq.* i. 127 (Bohn's Ed.)

* Several fine specimens of sepulchres in stone still exist in our churches. See the *Glossary of Architecture*, 5th Ed. pp. 421–2, where a curious and full description of one formerly in the church of S. Mary Redcliffe will be found.

† The Cathedral Church of Ely possessed (according to an Inventory of Plate, etc., taken 20th November 31 Henry VIII.) "a red pall for the sepulture."—Nichols' *Illus.* 137.

The sepulchre was watched* from the time of its erection until Easter morning, when the crucifix and the Host were again placed upon the altar with much ceremony. The most peculiar custom, however, connected with the sepulchre was the one called "creeping to the cross," which from very early times was practised in the English Church. Dr. Rock† quotes the Canons of Ælfric, the Anglo-Saxon homilist, to show that the custom was prevalent in his time: "And let them (on Good Friday) pray to the holy rood so that they all greet the rood of God with a kiss." Offerings were made at the sepulchre,‡ which, from the circumstances attending their presentation—the people creeping on bended knees—were called "creeping silver."§ The offerings made at the foot of the cross in Holy week and on Easter morning in S. Martin's amounted to a considerable sum, and were part of the vicar's

* In remembrance of the soldiers watching the Holy Sepulchre:—

Item to Rych. Rysley for watchyng the sepulker . . . xij.[d]
to John Long for watchyng . vj.[d]
—*Accounts of Churchwardens of Minchinhampton, Gloucestershire*, 1551.

The Churchwardens of S. Helen's, Abingdon, expended in 1555:—

To the sextin for watching the sepulter two nyghtes . . 0 8[d]

And again in 1559:—

To the sexten for meat and drink, and watching the sepulture according to custom . . . 0 22[d]
To the bellman for meat, drink, and coales, watching the sepulture . . . . . . 0 19[d]
—*Archæologia*, i. 14, 16.

† *Church of our Fathers*, i. 308.

‡ Or perhaps at an altar in a side chapel, upon which the crucifix was temporarily placed at certain intervals during these days for that purpose.

§ The original offertory basin for the receipt of the "creeping silver," or offerings made at the Sepulchre at Easter, still exists, and forms a portion of the structure called the Holy Sepulchre on the north side of the chancel of East Kirkby Church, Lincolnshire.—*Transactions of Associated Arch. Societies*, 1850, 22.

endowment.* Charyte, in his *Rentale*, already referred to, drawn up about the year 1348, says they produced annually ten pounds, eleven pounds, or twelve pounds.† On Holy Saturday the Paschal Candle was blessed by the deacon, who stood upon an elevation or pulpit, and sang an Exultet. This hymn was frequently written upon a scroll of parchment of considerable length, gorgeously illuminated and enriched with miniatures.‡ This candle, which was several feet in height, and proportionably thick,§ was regarded as an emblem of Christ, and was placed upon what is called, in S. Martin's Churchwardens' Accounts, the "pastall stock," that is, a tall standard or candlestick.‖ Before the candle was blessed the

* Charyte's *Rentale*, quoted in Nichols' *Leic.* i. 113, app.

† "Per crucis reddebat x.[li] xi.[li] vel xii.[li]"

‡ See a facsimile of an Exultet of the eleventh century in Agincourt's *Hist. of Art*, Plate 53.

§ "Item for vij.[li] off wax to make the pascall taper, the faunt taper, and makyng . . . . . vij.[s] iij.[d]
—*Accounts of Churchwardens of Minchinhampton*, 1555.

In the large churches the Paschal Light must sometimes have been of colossal proportions: thus, in 1557, we are told "the Pascal taper for the abbey church of Westminster was 300 pounds weight."—Brand's *Pop. Antiq.* i. 158 (Bohn's Ed.)

The Churchwardens of S. Mary Hill, London, in their Accounts for the year 1489, charge:—To the wax chandlyr for the Pascall taper for 2 yeres each yere weighing 30 lb at 1[d] per lb . 0 5 0

Special gifts were sometimes made to a church for defraying the cost of the Paschal Light. The churchwardens of Heybridge, early in the reign of Henry VIII., say:—Item receyved of Wylliam Barrett for a yeres rente of Paschalles croft due at our Lady day in Lente 0 7 0
—Nichols' *Illus.* 94 and 152.

‖ Among the goods belonging to the Abbey of Owston in this county, at its dissolution, was "a paschall."—Nichols' *Leic.* i. cxxxvii.

Occasionally the Paschal light consisted of more than one taper or candle, and was many-branched. The centre or upright stem was then, Dr. Rock says, called the "Judas of the Paschal," the origin of which name, he adds, is un-

deacon inserted in it five grains of incense,* to signify the wrapping of our Saviour's sacred body in linen clothes with spices; the grains themselves were placed in the form of a cross, and, from their number, were said to have reference to the five wounds inflicted upon the body of Christ at his crucifixion. The Paschal candle, when unlighted, was supposed to be figurative of our Saviour's death and repose in the tomb; when lighted, it represented the splendour and glory of His resurrection.† On Easter even, too, the hallowed fire was lighted :—

1544. P[d] for charcole on East evin . . . ij.[d]
1545-6. Itm for a stryke of chercole on Easter even ij.[d]

known.—*Church of our Fathers*, iii. Part ii. 244.

In corroboration of this Brand quotes from the Accounts of S. Giles' parish, 1519:—"Paid for making a Judas for the pascall, iiij.[d]"—*Pop. Antiq.* i. 160 (Bohn's Ed.)

It would, however, appear that the "Judas Light" was sometimes quite distinct from the Paschal, for the churchwardens of Eltham, in Kent, charged in their Accounts for the year 1557—

"Itm paid for xvj.[li] of newe waxe for the pascall and for the tapers about the sepulchre, and the rood lofte with the 4 tapers and Judas lighte at xij.[d] amounteth . . . . xvj.[s]
—*Archæologia*, xxxiv. 52.

Mr. Corner, F.S.A., in his notes upon this extract, says, Judas Light was "a taper which represented Judas Iscariot, and which, at a certain part of the ceremony on Good Friday, was suddenly extinguished, and left to stink."—*Ibid.* p. 54.

Large Torches borne in Processions were also sometimes called "Judas Torches." The churchwardens of S. Mary Hill, London, in their Accounts for the year 1511, give the following explanation of the Judas :—Mem. that the Judas of the pastal—*i.e.* the tymbre that the wax of the pastel is driven upon—weigheth 7 lb.—Nichols' *Illus.* 107.

* "A taper great, the Paschall namde,
with musicke then they blesse,
And franckencense herein they
pricke, for greater holynesse."
—*Popish Kingdome* (Googe's Trans.): Brand's *Pop. Ant.* i. 158 (Bohn's Ed.)

† *Hierurgia*, 406.

And again, in 1558 :—

P[d] for a stryke of charcole for the hallowed fyer . v.[d]

The hallowed or holy fire was kindled in the Church Porch* on the morning of Holy Saturday (Easter eve), and was obtained from the sun by means of a crystal or burning-glass, if the morning was bright; if not, a flint and steel were used. This fire was blessed by the priest, and from it the Paschal Candle, the lamps in the church, and the candles on the altar were lighted—the latter at mass on Holy Saturday, which was anciently performed immediately after midnight—that is, early on Sunday morning—and which was in honour of our Lord's Resurrection. This service, however, was in process of time allowed to take place by anticipation on Saturday morning. The people, too, took home with them (according to Dr. Rock) a light from the sanctuary, and the hearth that had been allowed to become cold and brandless then became warm

* *Notes and Queries,* 3d Series, ii. 276, 318, 395, 439.

It should be remembered that the Church Porch was used much more before the Reformation than at present. Part of the Baptismal and Matrimonial Services were then performed there, and it was used upon other occasions. I may here mention that there was, until late in the last or early in the present century, a porch to the south as well as to the north door of S. Martin's Church. It is figured in Nichols' History of the county, and is referred to in the Churchwardens' Accounts for 1599-1600 :—

"Item paid to Henry Halpenny for slates lyme and sand, and for workmanshipp aboute the ij. porches . . . xvj.[s] iiij.[d]

There is also an entry, under the date of 1570-1, relating to the North Porch, which I cannot explain, inasmuch as I find no trace of the existence of the chamber over it therein mentioned :—

"Payd unto Mr. Herycke for plaster y[t] mended the northe churche porche and the chamber over it . . . . ij.[s] iiij.[d]

and bright once more, and the evening candle shone brightly again with a flame from the new-hallowed fire.

The practice of "creeping to the cross," and making offerings thereto, continued during the reign of Henry VIII. In certain "articles about Religion," subscribed by Cranmer and many other bishops and abbots, drawn up about the year 1536, mention is made in the one "of Rites and Ceremonies," of creeping to the Cross, and humbling of ourselves to Christ on Good Friday before the Cross, and offering there unto Christ before the same, and kissing of it in memory of our redemption by Christ made upon the Cross; setting up of the sepulchre of Christ, whose body after his death was buried. And these are stated to be "laudable customs, rites, and ceremonies, not to be condemned and cast away, but to be used and continued as things good and laudable to put us in remembrance of those spiritual things which they do signify, not suffering them to be forgotten, or to be put in oblivion, but renewing them in our memories from time to time; but none of these ceremonies hath power to remit sin, but only to stir and lift our minds unto God, by whom only our sins be forgiven."*

Before dismissing the notice of the many customs observed

* Burnett's *Refor.* i. Part ii. 470.

In Archbishop Cranmer's Articles of Visitation, 2 Edward VI., there is this condemnatory inquiry :—

"Item, whether they had upon Good Friday last past the Sepulchres with their lights, having the Sacrament therein?"

Bishop Ridley, too, in his Articles of Visitation, 1550, asks, "whether there was any Sepulchre on Good Friday?"

Similar means were taken to prevent the continuance of the use of the Paschal Candle, the Hallowing of Fire, etc etc.

in Holy week, and brought before us in the Accounts of the Churchwardens of S. Martin's, reference should be made to one incidentally brought to view by the following entry :—

1557-8.

P[d] to Wiłłm . . for steynnyng* the veyle . vij.'

This reminds us that it was customary in the Pre-Reformation Church to cover or screen the Rood, at this season, with a veil or cloth, which, during the Procession on Palm Sunday, was drawn up by a cord, the priest and people kneeling and repeating an invocation.†

Having thus, it is hoped, brought before our mind's eye a picture of the church, its chapels, and some of its more attractive garniture and fittings, as it appeared when Henry VIII. ascended the English throne, it will be well, as was suggested, to note—in addition to those already mentioned—one or two customs peculiar to S. Martin's, or to the teaching of the Romish Church, as brought before us by references to them in the existing Records of the parish.

* Steynnyng or painting.

† This custom is illustrated by the following extract :—

Makyng of iiij. polesis of bras and iron work and lede that served for the vayl	o	5	8
Thirty-eight yards of liste for the vayl . . .	o	1	1
For sewynge and trymming of the same vayl and rynges	o	1	o
For echyng of the same vayl 10 Elnes of lynnen cloth .	o	7	7

—*Churchwardens' Accounts of S. Mary Hill, London;* Nichols' *Illus.* p. 98.

The altar was also sometimes veiled in Lent :—

1518. Itm̃ a cloth called a vayle of Whyte Lynnen, to draw affor the awter in Lent tyme . . . .—*Churchwardens of S. Martin Outwich, London;* Nichols' *Illus.* p. 272.

NOTES TO SECTION II.

NOTE A, p. 25.

IN some of the early Christian Churches, soon after images and pictures began to creep into use—towards the close of the fourth century—the Holy Spirit was typified by a silver or golden dove suspended over the font, and by a like symbol over the altar. The latter was suspended under the *ciborium* or ornamental canopy, which was supported on four pillars rising from each corner of the altar, and about which rich curtains or hangings were placed. When it became customary to keep at the altar the Eucharist for the sick, which before had been reserved elsewhere, or had been in the private custody of the priests, this dove, suspended as just described, or an ark upon the altar, at the foot of the cross, was chosen as its receptacle (see Bingham's *Antiq.* ii. 445).

In process of time, in England, where the dove-shaped tabernacles were very uncommon, the form of the receptacle assumed, generally, that of a cup or chalice with a cover, still made of the most precious materials, and frequently suspended, called a pyxis or pix. Fine specimens of the ancient pix containing small patens for the Host are preserved among the plate belonging to Corpus Christi College, Oxford. Occasionally, however, in this country the Sacrament was reserved in an adjacent recess or "Almery." Thus, in the accounts of the Parish Church of Thame, Oxfordshire, an "Aumbreye for the Lordes Boddye" is mentioned, and in the "*Fardle of Facions*" (1555)—"Upon the right hande of the highe Aulter, that ther should be an Almorie either cutte into the walle or framed upon it: in the whiche thei would have the Sacrament of the Lordes Bodye; the holy oyle for the sicke, and Chrismatorie, alwaie to be locked."—See *Glossary Arch.*, "Almery."

The practice of placing a movable Tabernacle upon the altar as a place of deposit for the pix does not appear to have prevailed at all generally in the English Church until a few years preceding the Reformation, for although the pix is of course enumerated in almost all the numerous lists of church plate made by command of Henry VIII., the tabernacle or shrine, which has since become so general in the Romish Church, is seldom mentioned. Moreover, the old custom of suspension is noticed by William Bruges, Garter-king-of-Arms, who in his will, dated 26th February 1449, bequeaths to the church of S. George, Staunford, "one coupe of sylver in the whych is one litel box of yvory, to put in the blessed sacrament; and to hang over the high awter" (Nichols' *Illus.* p. 112). It is also, I think, not unfrequently referred to incidentally in the lists just mentioned. For instance the following pix, one among many then belonging to the Cathedral of Lincoln, would appear from the "ring" to have been capable of suspension :—

Itm̃ a pyx of ivory bound above and beneath with silver and gilt, having a squared steeple on the top, with a *ring* and a rose, and a scutcheon in the bottom, having within a case of cloth of gold with J. H. S. of every side set with pearls.

And there then belonged to St. Frideswide's monastery (now Christ Church) Oxford :—

In the Quere: Itm̃ a *canoby* with a pixe of coper.—*Mon. Ang.* vi. 1279, ii. 166.

Among the rich altar-plate sold by the churchwardens of Melton-Mowbray in this county in the year 1547 I find :—

A pix sylv[r] & Gilt lvj.[s] x.[d] Itm̃ ffor a *cheyn* silv[r] & p̄sell gilt iiij.[s]

The tabernacles for the reception of the pix which were finding their way into the English Church at the period of the Reformation, and which became —as just stated—so general in the Romish church afterwards, were usually diminutive temples made—where circumstances permitted—of costly materials; as for instance in the monastery at Peterborough there was upon the High altar "a little shrine of copper, enamelled, for the sacrament," but occasionally they formed elaborate pieces of sculpture, and covered with their accompanying decorations a considerable space behind the altar. There are two extremely interesting examples, though not in their original positions, of the latter kind of Tabernacle, now preserved in Aberdeenshire: one in the church—or rather without the church, for it is against its western wall—of Kintore, and the other in the ruined church of S. Michael and all Saints Kintell.—*Hierurgia,* 506; Gunton's *Peterborough; Gent. Mag.* vol. ccxiv. 311; see also p. 482 in same vol. for *Dissertation on Mediæval use of Tabernacle.*

The Eucharist was usually in the reign of Henry VIII. borne to the house of the dying in the Pix in which it was reserved on or over the altar; but, if I mistake not, in our more wealthy cathedrals and churches, a small box was kept for that special purpose: thus at Winchester Cathedral they possessed "Item one little box of gold with his cover to bear the holy Sacrament" (*Mon. Ang.* i. 202), and belonging to the Church of S. Martin Outwich, was "a box off selver ffor the Sakerment in vessitaciones" (Nichols' *Illus.* p. 271). The procession from the church to the house of the sick man was made as imposing as possible: a clerk going first bore a cross, then came another bearing a silver hand-bell, and others with torches in their hands walked either immediately before or about the priest. Among the jewels belonging to "oure Lady chirche" at Sandwich in 1483 was "a bell of sylver to be boryn with the Sacrament of ix. ounces j. quarter" (Boys' *Hist. Sandwich*, p. 374); and in 1374 Jeffery de Drayton of Great Yarmouth bequeathed to the support of the light of Corpus Christi to be carried to the town for visiting the sick vj.[s] viij.[d] — Swinden's *Hist. Gt. Yarmouth*, 807.

In poorer places one attendant at least accompanied the priest, bearing a lantern and ringing a bell, in order that all might know the holy Eucharist was being carried by, and, according to the then teaching of the Church, pay reverence to it.—Dr. Rock's *Church of our Fathers*, ii. 461-4, who quotes the last two extracts.

Belonging to Melton-Mowbray Church I find were a handbell and a lantern, probably used for this purpose :—

1546. Itm̃ payd for mēdyng of the lytyll bell . . . . . v.[d]

1548. Itm̃ to John . . . . for mendyng ye church lant'n vj.[d]

—*Churchwardens' Accounts.*

And the Churchwardens of S. Margaret, Westminster, charge—

1554. Also paid for a lantern to be borne before the Sacrament in visitacion 0 2 10

—Nichols' *Illus.* p. 14.

Cranmer, in his Visitation Articles, 1549, refers to this custom and condemns it :—

Item, That going to the sick with the sacrament, the Minister have not with him either Light or Bells.

In some churches a special pix was provided for Rogation days and other occasions, when the Host was borne under a canopy in procession through the streets, or round the churches, accompanied by the clergy singing solemn litanies. For example, we find among the church plate formerly belonging to Lincoln Cathedral—

Imprimis: one great feretrum, silver and gilt, with one cross isle, and one steeple in the middle, and one cross in the top, with twenty pinnacles, and an image of our Lady in one end, and an image of St. Hugh in the other end, having in length half a yard and one inch: and it is set in table of wood, and a thing in the middle *to put in the sacrament when it is borne*, weighing three hundred forty and one ounces, of the gift of John Welborne treasurer, wanting a pinnacle.

And again :—

Item a round pyx of chrystal having a foot of silver and gilt, with one image of our Lady in the top, having a place for the Sacrament *for the Rogation days*: weighing twenty-one ounces one quarter and half.—*Mon. Ang.* vi. 1278-9.

These processions were strongly reprehended by Edward VI. in his Injunctions issued in 1547, and commanded to be discontinued; the Litany in English only was ordered to be used, in these words :—

To avoid all contention and strife, which heretofore hath risen among the king's majesties subjects in sundry places of his realms and dominions, by reason of fond courtesie, and challenging of places in procession, and also that they may the more quietly hear that which is said or sung to their edifying, they shall not from henceforth, in any Parish Church at any time, use any procession about the church or churchyard or other place, but immediately before High Mass, the Priests with other of the Quire shall kneel in the midst of the church, and sing or say plainly and distinctly the Litany which is set forth in English, with all the suffrages following, and none other Procession or Litany to be had or used but the said Litany in English, adding nothing thereto, but as the King's Grace shall hereafter appoint. —Sparrow's *Col.* 8.

In addition to the receptacles for the Host already mentioned, there was yet another in which to place it for exhibition to the people in order to receive their adoration, and for use during what was called the Benediction with the Blessed Sacrament. That was the Monstrance or Remonstrance—now called an Ostensorium in the Romish Church—which was usually a receptacle made of crystal or some other transparent material, through which the wafer could be seen, and which was mounted on a stand or ornamental pedestal. In a List of Plate accruing to Henry VIII. by the surrender and visitation of certain Religious Houses and Cathedrals is the following description of a Monstrance:—

Item delivered unto his saide maiestie the same daie a mounstraunce of silver and gilte, garnished with counterfett stones, with twoo greate glasses of Birrall in the myddes lackinge dyverse pinnacles and garnishinge, weinge altogeither with the birrall three score and thirteyn unces.

At that time there belonged to S. Augustine's monastery, Canterbury—

One monstrance silver gilt with four glasses.

Occasionally, too, a special monstrance was provided for a particular feast—as for Easter, the feast of feasts—for I find among the plate belonging to Lincoln Cathedral—*temp.* Henry VIII.—

Imprimis, an image of our Saviour, silver and gilt, standing upon six lions, void in the breast for the Sacrament for Easter day, having a beral before, and a diadem behind, with a cross in hand, weighing thirty-seven ounces.—*Mon. Ang.* i. 66, 125; vi. 1279.

The Adoration of the Host was one of the first things condemned by the Church of England in the reign of Edward VI.; and as tending thereto, or as fostering a superstitious reverence for the outward signs in the Sacrament of the Holy Communion, the Elevation of the Consecrated Elements in the consecration thereof, the carrying the same in processions, and finally, the reservation of them for the sick, were all in succession ordered to be discontinued. This is shown by reference to the concluding rubric of the first Order of the Communion put forth in 1547, which directs the consecration of the wine to be done "without any *levation or lifting up*"—to the concluding paragraph of the Article "of the Lord's Supper," in the Articles agreed upon in Convocation, 1552, which states, "The Sacrament of the Lord's Supper was not commanded by Christ's ordinance to *be kept, carried about, lifted up*, nor worshipped"—to the rubrics of the Office for the Communion of the Sick in the First and Second Prayer Books of Edward VI., in the first of which (1549) the Priest was directed as follows:—"And if the same day there be a celebration of the holy Communion in the Church, then shall the priest reserve (at the open Communion) so much of the sacrament of the body and blood, as shall serve the sick person, and so many as shall communicate with him (if there be any); and so soon as he conveniently may, after the open Communion ended in the church, shall go and minister the same, first to those that are appointed to communicate with the sick (if there be any), and last of all to the sick person himself." In case of there being no open Communion in the church, the priest was directed to reverently celebrate the same in a convenient place in the sick man's house. The reservation here was restricted to a few hours, and for a special purpose, but in the rubric of the Second Book (1552) no mention whatever is made of reservation, the priest being directed to celebrate reverently in the sick man's house and to communicate himself with him and such as were appointed to join with him.

NOTE B, p. 25.

THE Ship was a vessel so called, used for holding the frankincense required for the censers or thuribles in different portions of the divine offices; it was usually provided with a spoon, with which to take out the incense when required. In the then Cathedral Church of this Diocese (Lincoln) was, at the time now under notice, one which is thus described in an Inventory taken in 1536:—

Item, a ship silver and gilt with two coverings, having two heads, wanting six pinacles, and one flower: having a spoon with a cross in the end, weighing with the spoon thirty-three ounces and a quarter.—*Mon. Ang.* vol. vi. 1278.

At its dissolution, Fountains Abbey numbered among its vessels for the altar:—

One schipe for incense of silver and gilt with a spoon gilt weighing twenty-five ounces @ 4/4 . . £4 11 0
—*Ibid.* v. 290.

And in 1547 the Churchwardens of Melton Mowbray sold "a ship ffor ffrankynsense."

In form these ships resembled the vessels of the period, were frequently richly enamelled, and for convenience in use were generally on four wheels. Indeed, there is no reason for thinking that they differed in form from the Nef or Ship introduced on the tables of the wealthy in England in the Middle ages, as a receptacle for the alms of the guests. It was there called an "Elemosinaria," or alms-dish. That belonging to Henry VI. is described as a "grete almes disshe of silver, overgilte, made in the maner of a shippe, ful of men at armes feyghtyng upon the shippe syde."

NOTE C, p. 26.

A CHRISMATORY was a small phial or receptacle containing the holy oil called Chrism, used in Baptism. It was, however, usual to fit up a case containing three of these phials; one containing the *Chrism*, another the *Oleum Catechumenorum*—both, apparently, at the period of the Reformation used in the Sacrament of Baptism, though in earlier times used, the one at that Sacrament, the other at Confirmation—and the third the *Oleum Infirmorum*, used in the administration of the (so-called) Sacrament of Extreme Unction.

This description of the Chrismatory is well illustrated by the following extracts from an Inventory of the Jewels, etc., belonging to the Cathedral Church of Lincoln, made by Master Henry Lytherland, Treasurer of the same Church, in the year 1536:—

Chrismatoria.

Imprimis, a crismatory, silver and gilt, within and without, having sixteen images enammelled with ten buttresses without pinacles, battelled about in the covering with two crosses and one crest, having within three pots with coverings for oyl and cream, without slyces, having three letters above the covering, S. C. J., standing in a case, of the gift of William Skelton, sometime treasurer of the Church of Lincoln, weighing twenty-seven ounces."—Dugdale's *Mon. Ang.* vol. vi. 1281.

The "slyces" were probably instruments for taking out small quantities of the different oils when required. We now use the word—as fish-slice, butter-slice, etc. The letters S. C. J. would guide the priest to the particular oil he required, in the same way as the letters A. V. on the cruets, mentioned in the note page 27, guided him to the water or the wine.

The different oils, however, for the sake of convenience in use, and in carrying about, were prepared and kept in separate receptacles, each of which was provided with a spoon, which answered the purpose of the "slyce" in the larger chrismatory, as we find from the same Inventory:—

Ampullæ pro Oleo.

Imprimis, an ampull plain, with a foot silver and gilt, and a cover chased, parcel gilt, with broken gemmels, and a spoon with an acorn, ordained for cream.

Item, one other ampull silver, with a

cover chased, with a spoon within, with an acorn, ordained for oleum sanctum.

Item, another ampull silver, with broken gimmels with a cover chased, and a spoon, having an acorn on the end, ordained for oleum infirmorum.—*Ibid.*

Belonging to the Cathedral of S. Peter, at York, were formerly three large phials of silver—two for the holy oil and oil for the sick, and the third, gilt, for the chrism.—*Ibid.* p. 1203.

The Cathedral Church of Ely, too, possessed, according to a list of its plate made 20th November, 31 Henry VIII., "a crysmatory of lether with 3 boxes of silver."—Nichols' *Illus.* p. 136.

The use of oil in the Sacraments or Offices of the Church of England was, with one exception, gradually discontinued at the Reformation. In the Administration of Public Baptism in Edward VI.'s First Prayer Book (1549), after the child had been "discreetly and warily" dipped in the font thrice, and been clothed by the priest in a white vesture called a Chrism—which Chrism, it may be remarked, was provided by the Church, and returned, or a new one in its stead, by the woman, with "other accustomed offerings," at her Purification—the priest was directed to anoint the infant upon the head, saying an appropriate prayer. In the Second Prayer Book (1552) the office of Public Baptism was much altered, and this rubric omitted.

Again, in the Office for the Visitation of the Sick in the First Prayer Book of Edward VI. (1549) the rubric says, "If the sick person desire to be anointed, then shall the Priest anoint him upon the forehead and breast only, making the sign of the cross, saying thus," etc. It will be observed the anointing was not then enjoined, but only permitted when requested by the sick person, and that instead of all the organs of sense being anointed, as previously, the forehead and breast only were to be touched. In the Second Prayer Book even this was omitted.

The only exception to the discontinuance of the use of oil in the Offices of the English Church, is in that used for the Benediction and Coronation of Kings, in which, at the place appointed, the "Dean of Westminster, taking the *ampulla* and spoon from off the altar, holdeth them ready, pouring some of the holy oil into the spoon, and with it the archbishop anointeth the king in the form of a cross, on the crown of the head, and on the palms of the hands, saying," etc.

The Hallowing of the oils, which took place on Maunday Thursday, was an imposing ceremony in the Pre-Reformation Church.

NOTE D, p. 26.

IT was the universal custom in the Primitive Church to give, as a mark of Christian love and unity, the kiss of peace in the church before receiving the

Holy Communion. That custom is referred to in the *Apostolical Constitutions*, and some particulars are there given as to the performance of the ceremony: "Let the Bishop" (it is there said) "salute the church and say, *The peace of God be with you all;* and let the people answer, *And with thy spirit.* Then let the Deacon say to all, *Salute one another with a holy kiss;* and let the clergy kiss the Bishop, and the laymen the laymen, and the women the women" (quoted in *Archæologia*, xx. 534).

In the churches of the West when the simplicity of earlier times was departing, and when, probably, the sexes were not so rigidly separated during divine service as formerly, it was found desirable to give up this apostolic custom, and its place and its significance were sought to be supplied by the introduction of the *Osculatorium*, or as it was usually called in later times in England, the *Tabula-Pacis*, or Pax.

The Pax appears to have been first used in the English Church in the twelfth or thirteenth century. It was first kissed by the priest, then by the laity. The ordinary Pax was usually of silver gilt, flat, about three inches long by two wide, with a scriptural subject engraved on the face, and at the back was a handle by which to hold it. Among the "sylvyr juells" formerly belonging to Melton-Mowbray Church were "ij. paxes of selver psell geltt." Some, however, were extremely costly, being most beautiful and elaborate in design and execution. Several specimens were shown in the Loan Exhibition, South Kensington, 1862 (see the *Catalogue*, pp. 54, 60, 684); and in *Archæologia*, vol. xx. p. 536, will be found an engraving of an ancient one preserved in the neighbourhood of Wolverhampton.

The Pax was used in the English Church down to the close of Henry VIII., as is shown by certain Injunctions issued to the clergy and laity within the Deanery of Doncaster at that time—the exact date is uncertain—in which the following direction occurs:—

"And the Clarke . . . shall bring down the Paxe, and standing without the church door, shall say loudly to the People these words:—*This is a Token of joyful Peace, which is betwixt God and Men's Conscience: Christ alone is the Peacemaker, which straitly commands Peace between Brother and Brother.*"—See Burnet's *Refor.* ii. book i. 109.

The use of the Pax leading to abuses from the fact of an undue reverence being paid to the sacred subjects depicted upon it, was omitted in the Reformed Liturgy, its place being well filled by the call to charity contained in the exhortation preceding the Confession. Chaucer refers to the use of the Pax in his Parson's Tale:—and yet there is a privy species of pride that waiteth to . . . kiss the pax . . . before his neighbour.

SECTION III.

AMONG the religious processions or pageants—irrespective of those of the Guilds—during the middle ages in Leicester, those formed from the Churches of S. Martin and S. Mary—and probably also from the other churches in the town—to S. Margaret's at Whitsuntide, were the most conspicuous, and tended most to show the splendour and gorgeousness of those attractive observances of the Mediæval Church. The priests and inferior clergy in their richly-embroidered processional vestments — their attendants, some carrying crosses of silver, some banners of varied hue and strange device, others bearing aloft figures of the titular saints of their churches richly apparelled — the twelve apostles, represented by twelve men, each with the name of the apostle he personified attached to his bonnet*—music, and the solemn chant of the priests, as they wended their way down the north, and along the sancta via (the present Sanveygate, said to have obtained its name from these processions); the whole adorned by the presence of the virgins of each parish, probably in dresses of white, who formed a not unimportant part of the procession—produced a picture with which Rome delighted to amuse and lead captive the imagination of her votaries.

There is little to add to the account given by Nichols in

* Nichols' *Leicestershire*, i. 159.

his History of the Town respecting this procession from S. Martin's, and although there were similar ones from the other churches on the same day, still their origin is wrapt in obscurity. It may, however, be surmised that Whitsuntide was celebrated by the people as a holiday season, and that the Mediæval Church, in providing these processions to, and services in, the churches, simply took that prominent part in the every-day life of the people which was one of her most pleasing traits, and at the same time one of her great sources of strength.* There are a few entries in the accounts of the Churchwardens of S. Martin's which may tend to throw a little light upon, and to illustrate the custom.

Thus in the year 1544 are found the following charges :—

Paid to the viker, prests, and clarks for the presesshon at
Sent mgetts on Whissun moday . . . . . xiij.[d]
Pd to Danyell for mēding the vestmets . . . ij.[s] viij.[d]
Pd for the chargs of the presseshon on Whissun monday
as Doth apeyre in a bill . . . . . . x.[s] ij.[d]
(Which "bill" unfortunately is not forthcoming.)
P[d.] for a yard of grene silke and x. skeynes thred . . viij.[d]

* There were processions at Melton-Mowbray at Whitsuntide, and oblations were there made at the altar in the church, both apparently in a similar manner to those at S. Margaret's, Leicester. In the Churchwardens' Accounts of that town I find—

1557-8.—Item recd in y[e] overplusse of y[e] offerings of the processions at
Wissondey . . . . xiij.[d]
1558.—Rec. off y[e] offrynge ffor Meltō att Whytsontyde . viij.[s] iij.[d]
Rc clerc off y[e] offrynge off the cuntye (*i.e.* the country
—the hamlets) . . . . vij.[d]
1549.—Item reseved of Whitson mundey in oblacons as ap-
parith bye the ꝑticuler reseyte . . . vj.[s]

Paid for brayd and ale on Whissun mōday . . . xij.d
Paid for mēding ẜtyn things belonging to the Preshcsšhon wiche was nedefull to be done . . . . . xij.d
Paid to the Sm̄nars at Sent Margarets for the offring viij.d

And again, in 1545, the Churchwardens place among their "Receytes:"—

Itm̄ at Sent m̄grets churche at Whitsontide . ij.s ij.d

And among their payments:—

Whitsontyde.—Itm̄ pd fyrste for paper pȳnes & poynts at Whitsontyde . . . . iii.d
Itm̄ for bred & ale, kakes in the churche . xiiij.d
Itm̄ for the costs & charges of all the reste & prešsion . . . . . xj.s j.d
Itm̄ to ye somners on Whytsonmonday . viij.d
Itm̄ to ye prests of or chirche of the offerynge vj.d

The bread and ale "in the churche" may refer to the "church ales," or "Whitsun ales," then given away or sold at the door of almost every church at that season, but more probably the charges are for refreshments for the banner-bearers and others, because we find a similar charge, with the addition of "gloves," in the following year:—

Itm̄ pd for bred, alle, glouys & all such thyngs as belongyd to the prossessyon, wth money & all things clerye . xvij.s

We also find that those who took part in the procession from S. Mary's Church were thus rewarded, usually in lieu of money payment. Thus, under date of Whitsuntide 1494, as quoted by Nichols, the Churchwardens of that parish paid 3s. 4d. "for bread, ale, flesh, &c., for the apostles and others." The payment to the virgins in 1518 was threepence. The "Sm̃nars" were probably the summoners or apparitors—conductors of the procession—who made an offering at the altar on behalf of the company.

The "paper, pins, and points," were for the use of the apostles and others, the "points" being tagged laces used in their dresses.

The figure of S. Martin was, as before stated, borne aloft in the procession, his coat—"sente Martens cowt" as also "ij sherts yt was for syente Nicoles" will be found mentioned in the list of articles sold in the years 1552-3. In 1546-7 the Copes—the processional garment of the priests—were repaired.

Itm̃ pd to Roger . . . . for mendynge of the cops x.[d]
Itm̃ pd for thred to mend the coppys . . . . iiij.[d]

S. Martin being a saint of a less degree than S. Mary was not carried under a canopy in this procession, neither was music played before him as was the case before the figure of "our lady" carried in the procession from S. Mary's Church.*

Apart from these Processions to S. Margaret's Church there was another Whitsuntide custom not peculiar to this church or the churches of Leicester, but practised very commonly throughout the country both before, and in many parishes for some time after, the Reformation, which we can hardly expect was unobserved in S. Martin's parish. It was usual to have in the parish a house belonging to the church called "the Church House." In this house a quantity of ale

* Four that bore up the canopy received one penny each, and two pence was paid for playing the harp before "the Mary" by S. Mary's Churchwardens in 1523.—*Nichols*, vol. i. 569, and vol. i. 591.

was brewed from malt contributed by the parishioners or purchased from the church stock, and at Whitsuntide—in some places quarterly—a "church ale" was held in the house (or where a church-house did not exist the ale was sold in the church porch), where the parishioners contributing the provisions or money for them, and buying the ale, met and made merry together. After the expenses were paid the balance went to defray the repair and expenses of the church. In S. Martin's parish there was a house called the church-house, sometimes alluded to as the treasure-house and store-house, which was probably used for this purpose. In 1544 is

> Pd to Robart Croft for a day work at ye store hows . v.^d^

In 1547-8

> Itm̃ pd for a Kay for the Tressure howse dore ij.^s^ iij.^d^

In 1552-3

> Payd to roberte croftes and rycharde symson for ij days wourke of thc chyrche house . . . . vj.^s^

The Churchwardens credit, in their earliest preserved accounts, quarterly offerings for "church work," but whether they were derived from this source is uncertain.

Consequent upon the Romish doctrine of Purgatory was the belief in the efficacy of prayers for the dead. Provision was frequently made by will or otherwise by which persons not belonging to the Guilds secured the celebration, after their death, of certain religious services for the repose of their souls, or for their more speedy deliverance from the pains of purgatorial fire. These services, which in ordinary cases were celebrated upon the anniversary of the death of the person on whose behalf they were performed, were from that circumstance called "Obits." There were several such celebrated in S. Martin's Church, and the Churchwardens credit their accounts with the amounts received apparently for the use of the bells upon those occasions.

Under the head of "other obbytts"—that is, not obits of the Guild—in 1544 we have

Rychard Fynnes obbyt iiij bels .		xx.[d]
Itm̃ Thoms Draks obbyt iiij bels		xx.[d]
Itm̃ Mr. Jhōn Wigstons obbit v bels	iiij.[s]	
Itm̃ Mr. Wymeswolds obbyt iiij bels		xx.[d]

During these services, to which the parishioners were summoned, masses were sung and the mass-penny collected; doles of bread, money, or fuel, were frequently afterwards given to the poor. By Mass-penny must not be understood always an actual penny, but the gift or offering was so called.* These remarks are illustrated by an example connected with S. Martin's parish. George, third Lord Hastings, and first Earl of Huntingdon, dying on the 24th March 1543-4, ordained in his will "that his executors should cause a thousand masses to be said or sung in as short a time as might be after his decease, by secular priests and others, in the county of

* For instance we are told that at the funeral of King Edward IV. "on the morn' aft' the comendacions, beganne the masse of our Lady songen by the byshop of Duresm, at which masse Sir Thomas Bourgchier offered the *masse peny*. . . . After that masse done, beganne the masse of the Trynyte songen by the bisshop of Lincoln, at which masse th'erle of Huntingdon offred the *masse peny*." . . .—*Archæologia*, i. 380.

Leicester, and other places adjoining.* Besides this provision in his will he gave a garden to the town of Leicester, apparently upon the condition that his obit should be celebrated in S. Martin's Church, for in 1544 the Churchwardens say:—

> Rd. for my lord of Huntingdons obbit of a gardin geven to the Towne of Edmond Cowper . . ij.s iiij.d

and they carried out his wishes thus:—

> Itm̃ paid for ryngenge for ye masse peny & to ye belmā at my lord a Hūtingdons obbet . . vj.d
> Pd. for my lord of Huntingtons obyt . . . xj.d

Henry Lord Grey, Marquis of Dorset, father of the unfortunate Lady Jane Grey, possessed at this time, and occasionally occupied, the family mansion at Bradgate. The nearness of his residence to Leicester gave the Mayor and his brethren many opportunities of recognising the claims which his high position had upon their polite attentions and marks of respect. He was a frequent visitor to the town, and at the abbey and the various inns where he took up his temporary abode, he not unfrequently received from the Corporation presents of wines and confectionary. This was the case in 1547 when he was staying at the White Hart, and in the following year similar presents to him and "my lady m'ques" are recorded in the Chamberlains' accounts. It was probably upon one of these occasions that the Marquis was accompanied by his chaplain, who preached in S. Martin's Church, and who received his full share of wine through the liberality of the

* Nichols' *Leicestershire*, iii. 576.

Churchwardens, as they show in their accounts for the year 1546-7 :—

> Itm̃ pd for iij quarts of claryt wyne that was gyven to my lord m̃ques chapplyn the sonday after xx[l.] day ix.[d]
> Itm̃ pd to Thõm Hallam for a quart of malmysey for the same mã at the same tyme . . iiij.[d]

In 1549 Lady Jane Grey herself received a present of wine and confectionary from the Corporation.

That due regard and affection for the memory and for the relics of those who by the purity and holiness of their lives shed a lustre and a glory around the Christian faith which they professed, or who by their martyrdom sealed the truth of their convictions by their blood, which had always been felt and acknowledged by the Catholic Church, did, as is well known, assume in mediæval times a character and a prominence against which the English branch of the Church—finding no warrant in Holy Scripture for the superstitious reverence then awarded to them—most energetically protested at the Reformation. The real or supposed relics of a real or supposed saint were eagerly sought after as a means—it must generally be confessed—of obtaining honour to the particular fraternity, monastery, or church possessing them, or as a means of exciting the superstitious feelings of the people, and so adding to the wealth of the church by means of the offerings made at the shrine or at the altar where the supposed relics were deposited. That these relics were of an extremely heterogeneous character may be gathered from a notice of some of those said formerly to have been in existence in Leicester. In addition to the thorn from the crown with which our Saviour was degraded at his crucifixion, which was placed upon a socket of pure gold near the altar of the once existing Collegiate Church in the Newarke, Leicester,* there were many relics belonging to the other religious houses or Churches in the town; for according to Mr. Staveley,† "in the time of King Henry VIII., upon the dissolution of the Monasteries in Leicester, a multitude of false miracles and superstitious relicks were detected: and amongst the rest our Lady's girdle shewn in eleven different places, and her milk in eight: the penknife and boots of S. Thomas of Canterbury and a piece of his shirt . . . the coals that roasted S. Laurence . . . Malchus' ear, the parings of S. Edmund's nails; the bell of S. Guthlac, and the felt hat of S. Thomas of Lancaster, both remedies for the headache, etc. etc."

That the memory of Thomas of Lancaster should be cherished in this town is not singular when it is remembered that he was Earl of Leicester as well as of Lancaster and Derby, and that he was considered by many to have died a shameful death in a good cause; neither is it surprising that in addition to the article of apparel mentioned above we should find another relic of him, and that in our Church of S. Martin—the central church of the town. Charyte—from whose Rentale of the Abbey we have before quoted—says that the foot of Thomas of Lancaster in S. Martin's Church answered, or paid, in 1348, six pounds ten shillings per annum.

Pes Thome Lancastrie respondebat . vj.[li] x.[s]

* Throsby, 227.

† His MSS. quoted by Nichols, i. 225.

This is the only reference to this or any other relic formerly existing in this church, and even this entry in the monk's account of the emoluments of S. Martin's may refer to the oblations offered at the foot of a figure of Thomas of Lancaster, though that is hardly probable, more especially when we find his hat among the list of those articles esteemed worthy of the respect, and capable in some way of alleviating the pain, of his fellow-mortals.*

Before entirely dismissing the consideration of matters connected with our church of S. Martin in the reign of Henry VIII., it may not be without interest to show from what sources the churchwardens at that time derived the income from which they kept the fabric in repair, paid the fees or wages of the officials, and provided for what are now called

* Very many of our parochial churches possessed, before the Reformation, one or more supposed relics of departed saints—some of them sounding to our ears extremely ludicrous, and sometimes grossly irreverent; whilst our larger churches, cathedrals, and monasteries had on or about their altars very many in number and various in kind and degree. Our then Cathedral Church of Lincoln possessed many what would be thought precious relics, including a finger of S. Katharine, teeth of S. Paul, S. Hugh, S. Christopher, S. Cecile; joints of S. Margaret and of S. Sebastian; bones of S. Stephen the first martyr, of S. Lawrence, and of the head of S. John Baptist; the chest bone of S. Thomas Cantilupe sometime Bishop of Hereford, the chain with which S. Katharine bound the devil, and many others. And Dr. London, one of the visitors appointed by Henry VIII. to inspect the monastery of Reading, sending to Lord Cromwell an inventory of the relics then belonging to that house, concluded a long list by saying:—

"Ther be a multitude of small bonys &c. wich wolde occupie iiij. schets of papyr to make particularly an inventorye of euy part therof. They be all at yo[r] lordshyps commaundment."
—*Mon. Ang.* vi. 1202, iv. 48.

The feeling against the superstitious use of Relics showed itself strongly in the reign of Henry VIII., as is shown by the injunction issued by several of the Bishops at that time.

the incidental expenses of public worship. Perhaps a transcript of the Churchwardens' accounts for the year 1545-6 will best show this, and at the same time exhibit the way in which the accounts were then kept. The statement for that year is thus headed :—

J. H. C.

An^{o} Dni 1.5.4.6.

Thacom̄pte of Richarde Reynsforde and Henry Mabley churche Wardens of sent m̄tyns in leic^{r} made on palme sonday the xviij^{te} of Ap^{r}ell In the yere of o^{r} lorde god Mccccxlvj^{ti} before Mr Cotton then maire of the towne of leic^{r}. M^{r} gyllot Mr Renolds Mr Wood Mr May Mr Vicare wth dyv̄s other in o^{r} ladys quere w^{t}in the same churche.

Receytes.

Imp'imis	Recevyd of Wiłłm Manby my ꝑdicessor of the foote of his Ac̄ompte in money of the churche stocke at my firste entre vz: on Palme sonday the xxix^{ti} of marche an^{o} dni Mccccxlv^{ti} sm̄ .	x.^{s} vj.^{d} ob.
Offeryng Days	And Rd on schere thursday* & at ester of the ꝑyschyonē at godds borde sm̄ xv.^{s} iij.^{d} ob. Itm̄ at sent m̄grets churche at whitsontide ij.^{s} ij.^{d} Itm̄ at mydsom̄ quart^{r} . v.^{s} ix.^{d} Itm̄ at Michalmes v.^{s} vj.^{d} and at c̄stemas vj.^{s} ij.^{d} . .	xxxiiij.^{s} x.^{d} ob.

* "Sheer Thursday," the Thursday in Holy Week, usually called Maunday Thursday. The meaning of this old English term is quaintly explained in

Plate solde	And Rd. of Mr. tallance then maire of covētre the xj.th day of auguste for ₰ten plate sold to hym as apperith by hys ꝑticuler byll therof sm̄	xxiiij.li v.s x.d
obyttes	And Rd. at thobbet of Mr. Wymeshold for iiij. bells . . . . xx.d Itm̄ fore Mr. Weste thobbett v. belles . . . . iiij.s Itm̄ fore Mr. Wygston thobbet v. belles . . . . iiij.s Itm̄ fore Mr. Drake thobbet iiij. bells . . . . xx.d Itm̄ fore Richard ffenes obbet iiij. belles . . . xx.d Itm̄ Rec fore Mr. Cloughe obbet v. bells . . . iiij.s	xvij.s

Caxton's *Liber Festivalis*, as quoted by Dr. Rock (*Church of our Fathers*), "First, if a man asked why Sherethursday is called so, ye may say that in Holy Church it is called 'Cena Domini,' our Lord's Supper Day: for that day he supped with his disciples openly, and after supper he gave them his flesh and his blood to eat and to drink, and said thus, 'Take ye this and eat it for it is mine own body,' and anon, after he washed his own disciples' feet, showing what meekness that was in him, and for the great love that he had to them. It is also in English called Sherethursday; for in old fathers' days the people would that day sheer their heads, and clip their beards, and poll their heads, and so make them honest against Easterday. For on Good Friday they do their bodies no ease, but suffer penance, in mind of Him that that day suffered his passion for all mankind. On Eastereven it is time to hear their service, and after service make holy day. On Sherethursday a man should do poll his hair and clip his beard, and a priest should shave his crown, so that there should nothing be between God and him; for hairs come of superfluity of veins, and humours of the stomach; and they should pare their nails of hands and feet, that comen of superfluity of filth without forth, and shrive him, and make him clean his soul as without; and thus make him clean both within and without."—Fo. xxxii. b.

M

buryalls	Itm̃ Rd of leoñd procter for ye buryall of hys Wyffe dew the laste yere for v. bells	v.s iiij.d	xix.s
	Itm̃ for Jõhn Scherwyn dewe the laste yere for iiij. bells .	xx.d	
	Itm̃ for Sr. John Red buryall ye vij.ti day of Aprell for v. bells & lynge in the churche .	xij.s .	
gylde obets	Itm̃ Rd at thobbet of Mr. Swyks for iij. bells	viij.d	v.s iiij.d
	Itm̃ for Mr. Daũ iij. belles . .	viij.d	
	Itm̃ for Mr. bely iiij. belles . .	xx.d	
	Itm̃ for Mr. Hurste iiij. belles .	xx.d	
	Itm̃ for Mr. Whytwell iij. belles .	viij.d	
	Itm̃ for Mr. lyle iiij. belles . .		
	Itm̃ for Mr. ꝑsons v. belles .		

Sm: pagine . xxviij.li xj.s vij.d

Itm̃ for ye buryall Mr. Clought v. bells & lyenge in ye churche .	xij.s
Itm̃ Agnys brown iiij. belles .	xx.d
Itm̃ Best Wyffe iij. belles .	viij.d
Itm̃ ij. chyldren of Wiłłm Mābres thon iij. bells & ye thodr. iiij. bells . .	ij.s iiij.d
Itm̃ Mr. gyllotts doughtr. iiij. belles	xx.d
Itm̃ ij. children of Anthony Heires iij. bells . .	viij.d
Itm̃ Thomas byerd iij. bells .	viij.d
Itm̃ Wiłłm Hewts maid iij. belles	viij.d

buryalls	Itm̃ Willm Mābres maide iiij. belles . . .	xx.[d]	xlix.[s] iiij.[d]
	Itm̃ byards Wyffe iij. bells .	viij.[d]	
	Itm̃ John Hurdweke iij. bells	viij.[d]	
	Itm̃ Edwarde Howet v. bells	v.[s] iiij.[d]	
	Itm̃ Mr. Burton v. bells & lyenge in ye churche .	xij.[s]	
	Itm̃ John tymsons wyffe iij. belles . . .	viii.[d]	
	Itm̃ Sr. John Massye iiij. bells	xx.[d]	
	Itm̃ for one of John tymson chyldren iij. bells . .	viij.[d]	
	Itm̃ for a nother of ye same Johns chyldren . .	viij.[d]	
	Itm̃ for Thomas Renell & hys Wyffe in pte of paymet	v.[s]	
	Itm̃ Rd of ye chāberlayns as appereth by a oblygacyon . .		xx.[s] viij.[d]
buryalls	Itm̃ so remayns vnp[d] for Thomas Renell & hys Wyffe .	v.[s] viij.[d]	paid xvij.[s] iiij.[d]
	Itm̃ one of Thomas Renell chyldren iij. bells . .		
	Itm̃ for ye buryall Mastres staples v. bells & lyenge in the churche . .		
	Itm̃ for Mr. Wylcoks made v. bells . . .	v.[s] iiij.[d]	
	Itm̃ for ye buryall of Mastres Cresse v. bells & lyenge in ye churche . . .	xij.[s]	

hurdells Itm̄ R[d] for y[e] Hurdells that were bought for y[e] skaffold sold for viij.[d] . . viij.[d]

Sm̄ pagine iiij.[li] viij.[s]
Sm̄ total: xxxij.[li] xviiij.[s] vij.[d]

Payments.

ffees — lix.[s] viij.[d]

Imp[r]imis paid to Sr Wiłłm borow for hys quart[r] ffe at mydsom̄ . . viij.[d]
Itm̄ to frances clerke for his quart[r] wages at y[e] same tyme . ij.[s]
Itm̄ to Thom̄s Skypton for hys quart[r] wage at y[e] same tyme viij.[s] iiij.[d]
Itm̄ to Rob̄t Sexston for hys quart[r] wage at y[e] same tyme ij.[s] viij.[d]
Sm̄ xiij.[s] viij.[d]
Itm̄ at michalmes quarter as much in lyke man̄ . . xiij.[s] viij.[d]
Itm̄ at ꝑstmas quarter in lyke case . . . xiij.[s] viij.[d]
Itm̄ at thannunciacion of o[r] lady in lyke wyse . . xiij.[s] viij.[d]
Itm̄ to the glasiar for hys fee at Ester . . . . xx.[d]
Itm̄ to y[e] sexstons Wyffe for washenge y[e] churche clothes iij.[s] iiij.[d]

Ester — ij.[s]

Itm̄ p[d] to y[e] ꝓphete & for ale on palme sonday . . ij.[d]
Itm̄ for a stryke of chercole on Ester even̄ . . . ij.[d]
Itm̄ to Robt Sexton for skowrynge y[e] churche stuffe at Ester xx.[d]

Whytsontyd	Itm̃ p[d] fyrste for paper pyñes & poynts at Whytsontyde iij.[d] Itm̃ for bred & ale kakes in the churche . . . xiiij.[d] Itm̃ for the costs & charges of all the reste & ꝑcession . xi.[s] i.[d] Itm̃ to y[e] somners on Whytsonmonday . . . viij.[d] Itm̃ to y[e] prests of o[r] churche of the offerynge . . vj.[d]	xiij.[s] viij.[d]
ChurcheWorke	Itm̃ pd in expencs ij. dais at covẽtre when we sold the plate there for owr horses & owre selves . iij.[s] j.[d] Itm̃ pd for a pece of tymbre of xx.[ti] foot longe for the church Ile . . ij.[s] viij.[d] Itm̃ for vj. sparres x. foot longe a pece for the same iij.[s] Itm̃ for iij. bords of ix. foot longe a pece at y[e] same tyme . . . ix.[d] Itm̃ for one sparre of xx.[ti] foot longe . . x.[d] Itm̃ to Wiłłm Manby for iiij. peces of tymbre . ix.[s] viij.[d] Itm̃ for cariage of the same to y[e] churche yerd . ix.[d] Itm̃ for cariage of all the other vj.[d] Itm̃ for bords naylls & od[r] stuffe to Jõhn Heyrek as a apperith by hys byll . vij.[s] j.[d] ob.	xxxiiij.[s] ob.

	Itm̃ for a dosen Hurdells to the skaffold . .	xviij.[d]	
	Itm̃ for ropes to the skaffold	x.[d]	
	Itm̃ for a lode of lyme . iij.[s]		
	Itm̃ for a lode of sande	iiij.[d]	

Sm̃ pagine v.[li] ix.[s] iiij.[d] ob̃.

Church worke	Itm̃ for vj. lods of freston to Mr. Beyle bought at the freres. Rate aft[r] xix. the lode . . . ix.[s]	vj.[d]	xiij.[s] viij.[d]
	Itm̃ for a gable rope to lat down the same stone .	xx.[d]	
	Itm̃ for cariage of all the same to sent m̃tynes churche yerd . .	xviij.[d]	
	Itm̃ in expencs iiij. or v. tymes goynge to Mr. Beillies & to the freres to se & by the same stone for Mr. Vicare & myselfe & Henry Mabley & od[r] tymes to get workmen therto . . .	vj.[d]	
	Itm̃ to Frances More for wrytenge of ij. bylls for thassurance of y[e] churche money Recevyd at Couentre for y[e] plate sold ther	iiij.[d]	
	Itm̃ to Sr. Wiłłm borow for alterynge & wrytenge new ageyn the same by cause ye lyked them not .	vj.[d]	

Workmen	Itm̃ payd to Robert Crofte & Riĉ Symson for the whyle the were aboute ye Ile cōtenynge ix. dais worke in all. Rate after vij.^d the day to eyther of them sm̄ . . . . . ix.^s vj.^d Itm̃ to ye Robt & Riĉ for od^r v. days worke aboute ye skafold v.^s x.^d Itm̃ to ye mason of Greate for battelynge of the same Ile . xx.^s	xxxv.^s iiij.^d
Workemen	Itm̃ to Robt Sexton for helpynge the same Wryght ye mason, ye plumer, the laborers, while the sayd Ile, skaffold, mason worke, & gutters laying w^t tymbre, & poyntynge ye walls aft^r the mason, & for mēndynge ye churche florthe in dyv̄s places cōtenynge in all xxix^ti days. Rate after iiij.^d the day .	ix.^s viij.^d
laborers	Itm̃ to ye mason & od^r iiij. laborers on day takyng down ye ston . xxij.^d Itm̃ to ye same mason & od^r v. laborers the next daye . ij.^s ij.^d Itm̃ to iiij. laborers for carynge ye ston w^t out ye fre gate . xij.^d Itm̃ to iij. laborers ye next day to helpe to lode ye same ston ix.^d Itm̃ for ye cariage therof. Rate after iij.^d ye lode . xviij.^d Itm̃ to Thomas M'shall & ij. od^r laborers iiij. days & an halfe to set up y^e skafold Rate aft^r iij.^d y^e day . iiij.^s ij.^d ob.	x.^s v.^d ob.

Sm̄ pagine . iij.^li ix.^s j.^d ob.

laborers	Itm̄ to ij. laborers ij. days worke helpynge y^{e} mason w$^{t.}$ Robt Sexston . .	vj.^{d}	iij.^{li} xviij.^{s} ij.^{d}
	Itm̄ to iiij. laborers iij. days worke to draw up the ston . .	iij.^{s}	
	Itm̄ to iij. laborers for takenge down ageyne of the skaffold & berynge awey the tymbre where it was borowed . .	ix.^{d}	
	Itm̄ to iiij. mō for bryngenge the great leder .	ij.^{d}	
	Itm̄ for mēdynge of ij. spowts & for a pond of sawder thereto .	ix.^{d}	
	Itm̄ paid for cariage of xx. ¢ weight of led bought ye last yere of Witłm Manbe . .	xx.^{d}	
	Itm̄ to ye plūmer for xlvij. ¢ weight of led castenge and laynge. Rate aft^{r} xvj.^{d} the hundreth sm̄ .	iij.^{li} ij.^{s} viij.^{d}	
	Itm̄ for ij. bays laynge w^{t} old led. Rate aft^{r} iiij.^{s} the bay . . .	viij.^{s}	
	Itm̄ for cariage of xl. ¢ led to the plūmers house .	viij.^{d}	

odr. chargs	Itm̃ pd for the gable rope to the chyme . . .	xv.d	xxiij.s iiij.d ob.
	Itm̃ for smythe worke of one of ye chyme hamrs & sprynte . . .	vj.d	
	Itm̃ for smythe worke at anodr. tyme of one of ye hamers . . .	ij.d	
	Itm̃ for mẽdynge of a box for ye pyx & for the sylur therto	xij.d	
	Itm̃ for mẽdynge of Mr. Vicares surples . .	iij.d	
	Itm̃ for clensynge the churche guttrs in ye great snowe .	ij.d	
	Itm̃ to Robert Sexton for mẽdynge the bell bawderykes	vj.d	
	Itm̃ to ye same Robt for mendynge ye holly watr stocks & for spryncles .	iij.d	
	Itm̃ paid for ryngenge for ye masse peny & to ye belman at my lord a hũtyngdons obbet . .	xj.d	
	Itm̃ for a bell rope . .	xij.d	
	Itm̃ for a rope for the gret plũe of ye clocke . .		
	Itm̃ for halfe an hyde of whyt leddr for ye bell bawderyks	xviij.d	
	Itm̃ to Wiłłm Mãby for ij. new englyche ꝓcessioñs bought ye last yere	vj.d	

Itm̃ for iiij.[li] wax & pond & halfe weke y[t] to for a torche & y[e] makĕg . . .	ij.[s]	vj.[d]
Itm̃ for iiij.[li] tallow cãdles for y[e] lantorne in y[e] churche att wyntr . . .		v.[d] ob.
Itm̃ for one pond grat cãdles one ꝯstonmas day . .		ij.[d]
Itm̃ delyꝰ to Mr. Maire for repacion of y[e] well at y[e] churche style . .	ij.[s]	
Itm̃ to leoñ procter for the subsyde as apereth by hys byll	x.[s]	
Itm̃ for a quyttans for y[e] same		ij.[d]
Itm̃ for thered for y[e] sepulcre ij. yere . . .		i.[d]

Sm̃ pagine . . v.[li] xviij.[d] ob.

From this transcript it will be seen that the income of the Churchwardens for the year 1545 amounted (irrespective of an unusual receipt from the sale of Church plate) to £8 : 13 : 9, which was composed of offerings made quarterly at the altar by the parishioners, payments for the use of the Church bells at obits, for their use at burials, and for the privilege of interment within the Church. The account is full of interesting entries, and will be frequently referred to in these pages. It should be observed that it is headed with the sacred monogram J. H. C. The placing of a sacred name or monogram at the head of a document was not at all unusual at the period now under notice, nor indeed at a much later date. Thus we have here J. H. C. interlaced: at the head of the accounts of the Churchwardens of Melton-Mowbray, made viii. December, 3 Edward VI., is the word "Jesus;" and, not to multiply instances, the accounts of the Chamberlains of the Borough of Leicester for the year 1578–9, and several subsequent years, are headed "Emanuell." This custom is curiously referred to by Shakespeare in his Henry VI. (part ii. act 4, sc. 2) :—

> "*Jack Cade:* What is thy name?
> *Clerk:* Emmanuel.
> *Dick:* They used to write it on the top of letters. . . ."

Whether the use of these sacred devices and words was to attest the truthfulness and correctness of what followed, whether they were used as a kind of benediction by the writer, or whether their use is only an instance of the blending of the religious and secular, which was so prominent a feature in all the relations of life in past times, is a question now difficult of solution.

SECTION IV.

UPON the accession of Edward VI., Cranmer, with the hearty concurrence and assistance of the Protector Somerset, speedily set to work to carry out those plans for the re-arranging and for the reformation of the National Church which had been delayed by the restrictions laid upon him by Henry VIII. The young king, who had been brought up a Protestant, backed by such guides as Cranmer and Somerset, gave, as is well known, a great impetus to the Reformation. One of the first acts of his reign was to issue Injunctions addressed, "To all and singular his Loving Subjects as well of the clergy as of the Laity," in which "intending the advancement of the true honor of Almighty God, the suppression of Idolatry and Superstition throughout all his Realms and Dominions, and to plant true Religion, to the extirpation of all Hypocrisie, Enormities, and Abuses," he gave many and explicit directions as to the removal of certain appendages of the churches, the explanation to be given of those allowed to remain, and referred to other important changes to be effected. Thus he exhorts the clergy not to set forth or extol any Images, Relics, or Miracles, and commands that such Images as were or had been abused with Pilgrimages or offering of anything made thereunto should be forthwith taken down and destroyed; and that from thenceforth no Torches, Candles, Tapers, or Images of wax should be set before any image or picture "but only two lights upon the High-Altar, before the Sacrament, which for the signification that Christ is the very true Light of the world" were suffered still to remain. The clergy were to admonish their parishioners that images served for no purpose but to be a remembrance. It was further commanded that they should provide within three months next after that visitation "one Book of the whole Bible of the largest volume in English," and within twelve months a copy of the "Paraphrasis of Erasmus, also in English, upon the Gospels," and the same set up in some convenient place within the church, whereat their parishioners might most commodiously resort unto and read the same. Every Parson, Vicar, Curate, Chauntry Priest, and Stipendary, being under the degree of a Bachelor of Divinity, was to provide and have of his own within three months a copy of the New Testament in Latin and English, with the Paraphrase upon the same by Erasmus, and diligently study the same, conferring the one with the other. In the time of High Mass the Epistle and Gospel were to be read in English, in the pulpit, or in such convenient place as the people might hear the same; and every Sunday and holy-day one chapter in the new Testament was to be distinctly read in English at matins, and one chapter from the Old Testament at Even-song.* Processions about the churchyard

* The Rubric in both the first and second Prayer-books of Edward VI. directs, "And (to the end the people may the better hear) in such places where they do sing, there shall the lessons be sung in a plain tune after the manner of distinct reading, and likewise the Epistle and Gospel."

were ordered to be discontinued, "but immediately before High Mass the Priests, with others of the choir, should kneel in the midst of the church, and sing or say plainly and distinctly the Litany which was set forth in English, with all the suffrages following, and none other Procession or Litany was to be used but the said Litany in English." It was strictly enjoined that they should "take away, utterly extinct, and destroy" all shrines, covering of shrines, all tables, candlesticks (excepting the two lights upon the altar) trindils or rolls of wax,* pictures, paintings, and all other monuments

* Trindles of wax were probably cakes of wax, which being round were called trindles or wheels. When wax was extensively used in the churches, it was not unusual for offerings of it to be made at the altars. This having been previously taken from the hive, would be melted down and allowed to cool in vessels, the shape of which—generally circular—it would assume and retain, and so when offered would be in the form now so frequently seen in the shop window, namely circular, or not unlike a wheel or *trindle*, or perhaps more exactly a *trundle*. (See Halliwell's *Archaisms*, 889; *Notes and Queries*, 3d Series, iii. 309.) The wax so offered was passed (when needed for use in the church) into the hands of the chandlers, who formerly did not only, as now, buy wax or tallow to make up into tapers or candles for sale, but also made up the wax, etc., of other people, charging them a fixed sum per pound for so doing. There was a curious regulation passed in Leicester at a Common Hall—or, as we now say, a meeting of the Council—held 11th January, 4 and 5 Philip and Mary, which is thus entered in the Hall Book preserved in the Muniment Room: —"At the same Comon Hall it is ordeyned & agreyd . . . That no man shall worke wax nother in tapers nor candells to be sold, but these that be wax chandelers or wylbe come of their companye. Pvydyd that non of the seid occupacōn shall take for the makying other tapers or other candell above a peny a li." Dr. Rock, in his *Church of our Fathers*, gives some curious information respecting Trindles or Rolls of Wax. He says it was not unusual for our forefathers to make a vow when sick to offer to the church in case of recovery a wax candle of their own height, or of that of the diseased limb from which they were suffering. Sometimes, again, a thin taper sufficiently long

of feigned miracles, pilgrimages, idolatry, and superstition; and that no memory of the same should remain on walls, glass windows, or elsewhere within churches or houses; and the Churchwardens, at the common charge of the parishioners, were to provide in every church a comely and honest pulpit, to be set in a convenient place within the same for the preaching of God's word. A strong chest with a hole in the upper part, and locked with three keys, was to be provided in each church and placed near the High Altar as a receptacle for the alms of the Parishioners for their poor neighbours.* One

to measure the bed on which the sick lay was offered. This from its thinness could be coiled up when offered, and would afterwards be cut into pieces short enough for tapers for use at the altar and about the church. This he says not unlikely was the kind of Trindell or Roll of Wax forbidden by Edward VI. to be placed in churches.

* An interesting and valuable paper upon Offertory Boxes, by Mr. M. H. Bloxam, will be found in the first volume of the Publications of the Associated Architectural Societies, p. 13.

This chest was called the Poor Men's chest. Bishop Ridley, in his visitation Injunctions for the Diocese of London, 1550, had the following curious "Item" in reference to it:—

"*Item,* That the minister in the time of the Communion, immediately after the offertory, shall monish the Communicants, saying these words, or such like, *now is the time, if it please you, to remember the poor Men's Chest with your charitable Almes.*"—Burnet's *Ref.* ii. part ii. 288.

There are several entries in the Churchwardens' Accounts showing the existence of a chest or coffer of this description in S. Martin's Church: for instance, in 1550-1 I find:—

Itm̃ pd to Thomas Kerbe for to
keys for ye pore man's chest viij.^d^

This chest was opened as necessity required, and money given to the poor, in the presence of certain of the parish:—

1550-1.
Itm̃ gyven to the p^r^soners at the
sight of Mr. Nic̄his Herek,
Mr. John Herck, and Mr.
Vycker . . . . . xx.^d^

1549-50.
It. pd upon good fryed: out of
the Comōn box at the com-
aundement of the pyshe to
be dalt among pore peopyll ix.^s^ iij.^d^

of the Homilies set forth by authority was to be read every Sunday, and a Register of Weddings, Christenings, and Burials was to be kept.*

These Injunctions were strengthened by others specially addressed to the Bishops, in which they were exhorted to see that the former were put into execution in their several dioceses; and they were commanded themselves to preach at least four times a year and to give Orders to none as their chaplains but those who could preach God's word and would labour oft at it.†

Notwithstanding the many changes here sanctioned and commanded, and notwithstanding the anxiety to carry on the Reformation, great care was taken not to push it forward with undue haste, or in anywise to give countenance to licentiousness or irreverence. These changes were to be made by ecclesiastical authority only, and not, it was expressly stipulated, "by private persons." The clergy were diligently to provide that the Sacraments were duly and reverently ministered in their churches, and at all times (as they had leisure) were to hear and read somewhat of Holy Scripture, and to have always in mind that they ought to excel all other in purity of life, and should be examples to the people to live well and christianly.‡

These injunctions were quickly received in Leicester, being probably delivered, in person, by the Chancellor of the Bishop of the Diocese, who preached in S. Martin's Church in this year (1546-7) :—

> Itm̃ pd for a gallon of wyne for my lord of lyncolne chanceller when he prechyd at Sent M̅tyns . xij.[d]

* Sparrow's *Col.* p. 1-12. † Burnet's *Reformation*, ii. p. 53.
‡ Sparrow's *Col.* (1684 ed.), p. 5.

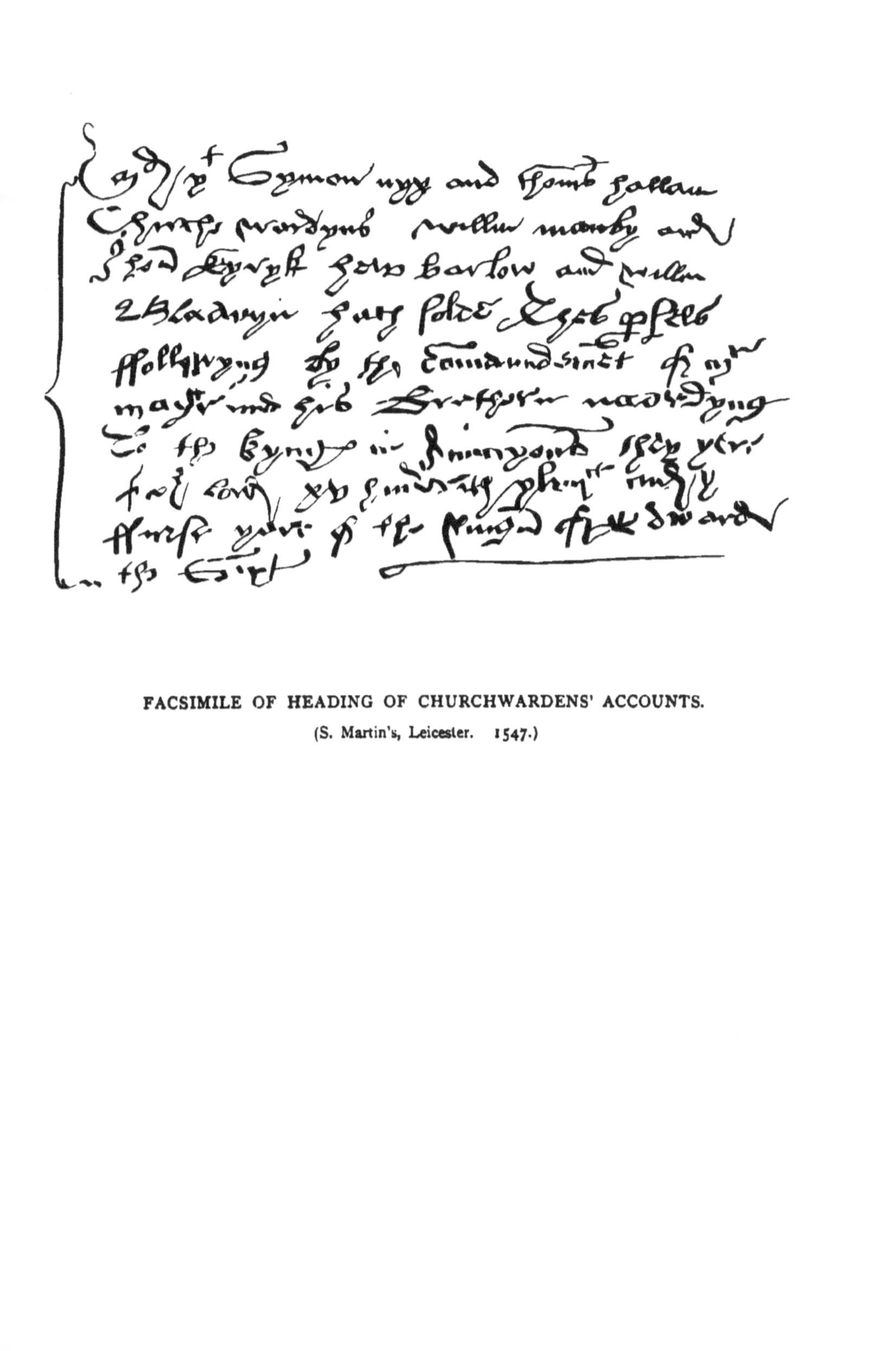

FACSIMILE OF HEADING OF CHURCHWARDENS' ACCOUNTS.

(S. Martin's, Leicester. 1547.)

and with reference to this church were acted upon by the Churchwardens and other influential persons in the parish, under the direction of the Mayor and Corporation, as appears from the following copy of the original memorandum now preserved in the Churchwardens' accounts :

> Md. y^{t} Symon Nyx and Thom̄s Hallam Chirche Wardyns Wiłłm Manby and Jhon Eyryk Hew Barlow and Wiłłm Blacwyn hath solde Thes ꝑsels ffollowyng by the com̄aundemēt of M$^{r.}$ Mayr and his Brethern accordyng To the kyngs Injuncȳons they yere of o$^{r.}$ Lord xv. hundrith xlvij. and y^{e} ffurst yere of the Raign of Edward the Sixt.*

ffurst Solde vij. Clothis that hengyd beffore the Roode Loffte price	iij.^{s}	viij.^{d}
Solde to Nȳchis Eyrike a tabernacle .	ij.^{s}	viij.^{d}
Sold to Willm Tayler Smyth a nother tabernacle .		xij.^{d}
Sold to Willm Cloughe ij. tab^{r}nacles .	v.^{s}	
Sold to Hew Barlow a tabernacle . . .	iij.^{s}	
Solde to Henry Mayblay the hors y^{t} the Georg Roode on Pryce		xij.^{d}
Solde the olde Irn waying a C a qr and vij.^{li} Price	vj.^{s}	ij.^{d} ob.
Solde to Thom̄s Hallam a Tabernacle .		xij.^{d}
Solde to Roger Pott a Tabernacle . . .		xij.^{d}
Solde to Jhon Tayler of Stonghtō grange as muche alamblasꝰ. as comyth to . . .		xx.^{d}

* I am indebted to the courtesy of the Chairman of the Museum Committee of the Corporation of Leicester and to the President of the Leicester Literary and Philosophical Society for the loan of the copper-plate—now the property of the Town Museum—from which the accompanying facsimile of the heading of this account is printed. The copper-plate was once the property of Throsby the historian, and an impression from it is given in his *History of Leicester*, p. 246.

Solde to Mast$^{r.}$ Gyllatt s̄rten allamblast$^{r.}$			x.^{d}
Solde to Mast$^{r.}$ Daueport ffor a tabernacle .		iij.^{s}	iiij.^{d}
Solde to Jhōn Eyryke y^{e} organe chamb$^{r.}$ . .		viij.^{s}	vj.^{d}
Solde to Symon Nyx the florth and the vente that the George stood on		iij.^{s}	x.^{d}
Solde to M$^{r.}$ Newcome* iiij. hundrith and a qr of bras at xix.^{s} the hundrith Summa . .	iiij.^{li}	ix.^{s}	
Solde to the Pott$^{r.}$ iij. C. and iij. quartarns of bras at xix.^{s} the hundrith	iij.^{li}	xj.^{s}	iij.^{d}
Solde to Wittm Tayler a hundrith of bras . .		xix.^{s}	
Sold to Ryč. Raynford the Sepulcre light waying iij. score and xv.^{li} at iij.^{d} ob̄. a li. . .		xxi.^{s}	x.^{d} ob̄.
Sold to Willm Tayler Smyth viij.^{li} wax at iij.^{d} ob̄. price		ij.^{s}	iiij.^{d}
Sold to Willm Mābу xxix.^{li} of wax at iij.^{d} ob̄. a pound		viij.^{s}	v.^{d} ob̄.
Sold to M$^{r.}$ Newcoome l. pound waight of the organe pypes		xvj.^{s}	
and so all the whole y^{t} is all redy sold comyth to .	xiij.^{li}	ij.^{s}	ij.^{d} ob̄.

A large dole was made to the poor from the proceeds of this sale, there being preserved a list of eighty-four "pore peopyll" who received sums varying from two pence to twenty pence each. Among the recipients are found—

Itm̄ gyven to pore Yssabell . .	iiij.^{d}
Itm̄ gyven to Jane Owckhm̄ lyenge bedreyd . .	xij.^{d}
Itm̄ gyven to iiij. marryners y^{t} had the kyngs brod seall	xij.^{d}
Itm̄ gyven to a fatherless chyld . .	ij.^{d}

A considerable quantity of plate had been previously disposed

* He was a bell-founder.

of to the Mayor of Coventry; but of this, unfortunately, no inventory has been discovered. It is thus noticed:

1545-6.

Plate solde — and R[d] of M[r.] Tallance then maire of Couetre the xi. day of Auguste for ẜten plate sold to hym as apperith by hys ꝑticuler byll therof xxiiij.[li] v.[s] x.[d]

and under the payments:

"Itm̃ pd in expencs ij. dais at Covetre when we sold the plate there for owr horses & owr selves . . iij.[s] j.[d]

This money was principally expended for work done about the "ile of the church." The stone was brought from the "freres."* The masons had sevenpence, the labourers threepence a-day.

It will be seen from the foregoing that the first steps towards carrying out the King's Injunctions in S. Martin's Church consisted in the removal of hangings from before the Rood-Loft; Images, which appear to have been made of alabaster, and their tabernacles or niches of wood or stone; large quantities of brass, being probably decorative work; and, it is to be feared, monumental effigies (there is many a matrix still remaining telling a sad tale of needless spoliation);† a

* Probably the Grey Friars, whose house formerly stood on the south side of S. Martin's Church, near the present residence of Dr. Shaw. It had then recently been surrendered to Henry VIII., and a portion at least of the buildings would thus appear to have been demolished, and the materials used in the repair of the parish church. The present Friar Lane takes its name from the Grey Friars, the grounds of whose house, according to Throsby, extended from the upper end of the market-place to the Friar Lane meeting-house.

† At the dissolution of the abbeys the monumental brasses were sometimes

considerable weight of taper wax, it being now comparatively useless; the sepulchre light, both it and the sepulchre being abolished; and the "horse that the George rode on," which has been already referred to as being elevated in the chapel of the Guild of S. George.

Among the payments connected with this first movement are:—

> Paid to Robt Sextin and his fellow for takyng down tabernacles & Images . . . . xxij.[d]
>
> P[d.] to Robt Crofte ffor takyng down a tabernacle and to Wiłłm Payrs . . . iiij.[d]

A second list of articles sold shows how the changes in the Ritual of the Church progressed, and also the richness—as before remarked—of the vestments and hangings formerly in use:—

noted down with the vessels of the altar as part of the plunder. In the list of goods belonging to the abbey of Merevale, valued in the time of Henry VIII., is found—

> It vj. grave stones wyth brasse in them. 0 5 0

—*Mon Ang.* v. 484.

The Accounts of the Churchwarden of Walberswick, county Suffolk, show by the following curious entries how the monumental brasses in our churches were destroyed by the Puritans in the time of Charles I:—

1644.

Ap. 8, paid to Master Dowson that came with the troopers to our church about the taking down of images, and brasses off stones.	0	6	0
Paid that day to others for taking up the brasses of grave stones befor the officer Dowson came	0	1	0
Rec. this 6 Jany 1644 (5) from out the church 40 pounds weyght of brasse at threepence halfpenny per pound .	0	11	8

Nichols' *Illus.* p. 191.

The ꝑcells of the goods that was sold forthe of the church of Sent M̄tyns the xx. day of m̄che in the fyrst yēr of the reygne of o[r.] sov[r]aigne lord Edward the Sext by the grace of god &c. before Mr. Randal Wood then beyng mayre Mr. Gyllot Mr. Reynold Mr. Cotton Mr. . . . Mr. Davp̄ort Mr. Cort Mast[r.] Manbe Mr. John Herek w[t] others

Itm̄ rec. of Mr. Mayre for old gere . . . . v.[d]
Itm̄ receyd of Willm Tayllo[r] for one vest & an awbe [*alb*]* xij.[d]

* The Alb was a garment worn by Bishops, Priests, and Deacons under their other vestures in the celebration of the Eucharist. It was usually of white linen as its name implies (*alba*—white) reaching down to the feet. It had sleeves, and was confined at the waist by a girdle or zone. This is probably the vesture referred to in the accounts of the Churchwardens of Melton-Mowbray in 1553:—

Itm̄ payd to W[m] Hawley for a vestment & a Gyrdle . . ij.[s] ij.[d]

The stole was sometimes passed under the girdle, as is shown in the curious monumental brass of Henry Martin, in Upwell church, Norfolk—A.D. 1435—figured in Mr. Boutell's *Monumental Brasses of England*.

On Festivals and great occasions, however, the albs worn in the larger and more wealthy churches were of richer and more costly materials—velvet, silk, and cloth of gold, frequently richly embroidered. In the list of those belonging to Peterborough, already given, will be found :—

Thirty albes of old cloth of Bawdkyn.

And there was then belonging to the same monastery in addition—

One alb of white silk with orfers of red.—*Gunton*, 63.

At its dissolution, the Priory of S. Martin, Dover, possessed—

v olde aulbes one of redd velvet wrought wth roses and leaves embrodered.—*Mon. Ang.* iv. 542.

The "orfers" mentioned as being on the alb at Peterborough were probably the embroidery or other ornamentation more usually called the *apparels*. Of these the alb had usually four, sometimes six—namely, two small square ones sewed one at the end of each sleeve just above the hands, two at the lowest parts of the skirts, one before over the insteps, the other behind at the heels of the wearer; two were sometimes hung, one in the front on the breast, the other on the back between the shoulders. The apparels of the alb were frequently made to match the chasuble or vestment with which it was worn.—See Rock's *Church of our Fathers*, i. 443.

Itm̃ recevyd of Mr. Davenport for ii. vestments .	vj.[s]	viij.[d]
Itm̃ rec. of Mr. Cotton for ij. hangyngs for the hye alt̃ of whyt damaske & purpyll vellvet . . .	xxxiiij.[s]	
Itm̃ rec[d] of Mr. Vyker for an old vest of gren . .	ij.[s]	ij.[d]
Itm̃ rec of Mr. Manb[e] for alt̃ clothes . .	xij.[s]	
Itm̃ rec. of the same for a organ case .	iij.[s]	
Itm̃ rec of Mr. Davenport for alt̃ clothes . . .	xij.[s]	
Itm̃ rec. of the same for alt̃ clothe of Redd velvet & whyt damaske	xvij.[s]	
Itm̃ rec of Ric. Davy for ij. vest: of blew velvet .	xxix.[s]	
Itm̃ rec of the same for ij. yellow copps* [*copes*] .	xiij.[s]	
Itm̃ rec of the same for a blew velvet coppe	xviij.[s]	
Itm̃ rec of Mr. Manbe for iij. whyt cops .	xvij.[s]	
Itm̃ sold to Mr. Reynolds one canope .	xx.[s]	
Itm̃ sold to the same one vest of red . . .	vj.[s]	viij.[d]
Itm̃ sold to Mr. Cotton one pall of blew velvet . .	xiij.[s]	iiij.[d]
Itm̃ sold to Thomas Hallam one gren copp* of brydgs sattyn [*Bruges satin*] & one alt̃ cloth of the same	ix.[s]	
Itm̃ Willm Odam for the rode lyght . . .	vij.[s]	viij.[d]

Sm̃a £11 : 2 : 3[d]

* The cope was a priestly vestment somewhat resembling a large cloak reaching nearly to the feet, without sleeves or arm-holes, and open in the front. Down each edge of the opening was the orphrey, a border generally embroidered or ornamented, and it was held together and fastened on the breast by a clasp called a morse or pectoral. A hood hung behind. The cope was worn at most of the services of the mediæval Church excepting by the celebrant at Mass when he wore a chasuble. It was made (as shown in a previous note (p. 35) of the most costly materials of various colours, gorgeously adorned. It will be observed, as before stated, that the colours of the altar-clothes and of the vestments here mentioned were various, and that they were worn to mark the recurrence of the different seasons of the Church's year. Colour, like the manner of performing the service of the church, varied slightly in different places, or followed a different "use," but probably the custom of the Pre-Reformation church in England in

It must not be supposed that in thus carrying into effect one portion of the Injunctions of the King, the other, providing for the better instruction of the parishioners of S. Martin's, was neglected. Under date of 1547-8 is (after a payment for a new surplice for "Sr. Willm the pīshe prest"):—

Itm̄ pd for an Homyle for Sr. Willm the pīshe prest xij.[d]

In the next year's accounts are:—

Itm̄ pd to Mastr. Manbe for the praphrasye of erasmus x.[s]
Itm̄ pd for ij. chenes & naylls for the bybell . . v.[d]

The church probably possessed a copy of the Bible in English, provided in obedience to the former command of Henry VIII., which was now "set up in some convenient place within the church" whereunto the people might resort

this matter was not much dissimilar to the practice of the Roman Catholic church now, which is, according to its ritualistic writers, this:—

White—on the Feasts of Our Lord, the Virgin Mary, the angels, and saints who were not martyrs.

Red—on Pentecost, Invention, and Exaltation of the Cross; Feasts of Apostles and Martyrs.

Green—on most of the Sundays.

Purple—in Advent, Lent, Ember-days, and Vigils.

Black—on Good Friday and Masses for the dead.

Other colours were used probably for Processions, in which the cope was the proper vestment.

It is possible that occasionally, by special permission, Mass was said in copes; for instance in the Ecclesiastical Kalendar prefixed to the Customary formerly in use in the Church of the Monastery at Peterborough is found in the month of March—

"The Abbot said Mass.

"In this month there was *Missa matutinalis cum cappa* for the souls of the Fathers and mothers etc. of all the monks of this monastery."

And Robert Lyndesey, Abbot of that house in the beginning of the thirteenth century, ordained the celebration of three Feasts in copes—viz. the Transfiguration of our Lord, the Translation of S. Thomas, and the Birthday of S. Hugh.—Gunton's *Peterborough*, 295, 325.

It is, however, clearly doubtful whether the cope was in this case worn by the celebrant, or only by the monks over or instead of their cowls.

to read the same; and it was, as was customary, chained to the desk or lectern upon which it rested.

A Register had been previously provided, for in 1547-8 is found:—

> Itm̃ pd for wryttynge new of the churche boke for crystinynges Weddyngs & buryengs . . vj.[s] viij.[d]

The removal of Images and Pictures on the walls from the churches was variously received in different parts of the country. The Injunctions of Edward VI. provided for the removal of all such as had been "abused with Pilgrimages or offering of anything made thereunto." This caused great disputes among the people as to the necessity or not of removing the images in their parish churches, some affirming they had been superstitiously abused and ought to be removed, whilst others as stoutly asserted the contrary. This caused the Council—in order to the quieting of those disputes—to issue an order on the 21st February 1547-8, addressed to Cranmer, for the general removal of all Images, requiring him to give commandment that all such remaining in any church or chapel within his diocese should be removed at once, and that he should signify the same order to all Bishops in his Province, who in their turn were to promulgate the same within their respective dioceses.*

There is an entry in the Churchwardens' accounts for 1547-8 which probably points to the receipt of this order at S. Martin's Church by the hands of the visitors:—

> Itm̃ pd to the vysyters clerk for makyng a byll . . xij.[d]

* See the order quoted by Burnet (*Reformation*, ii. part ii. 182).

However this may have been, there is immediate evidence that the order of Council was speedily acted upon in our church, for in 1548-9 the church was "white limed" at a cost of £6 : 4 : 5; thus obliterating all superstitious paintings from the walls, and many changes were effected in the arrangement of the chancel, as appears by charges about the "new quere" (choir). The Rood Loft, or more probably the figures upon it, were taken down,* and many other circumstances show that the Injunctions of the King and the last-mentioned Order of Council were carried out gradually, but effectually, in S. Martin's parish. Down to the year 1548 no change was made in S. Martin's Church in the mode of administering the Holy Communion: it was still what was called by the Romish Church "the Sacrifice of the Mass," and was given to the people in one kind only. Reference is made to this in order to call attention to a custom indicated in the Churchwardens' accounts which has seldom been noticed by writers upon the usages prevalent in the English Church at the Reformation. Under date of 1547-8 are several charges for the "Holy Loaf:"—

Itm̃ pd for the Holly lof the forthe day of Mc̃he iij.[d]
Itm̃ pd for the holly lofe on Palme Sonday iij.[d]

with several similar entries.

This "Holy Loaf" was quite distinct from the consecrated bread or wafer of the Holy Eucharist, and was not distributed

* "Itm̃ pd to John Wyntseale Robt. Sekerston and Rog[r] Johnson for takyng down the Rode Loft . . . . xviij.[d]

The Loft, however, was painted in the year 1550-1.

Itm̃ pd to Yonge for payntyng of the rode lofte xl.[s]

until after Mass was over. As soon as that office was ended a loaf of bread was blessed (not consecrated), and then with a knife, probably set apart for that purpose, cut into small slices for distribution among the people, who went up to the altar and received it from the priest, whose hand they kissed.* The giving of this Holy Loaf, or Eulogia as it was called, was adopted by the Church at a time when the number of communicants had diminished from the whole body of the faithful, who communicated in primitive times at each celebration of the Holy Communion, to a very few, or scarcely any, recipients; and appears to have been given to all the people at the close of the Liturgy, to preserve a semblance of that unity and communion which existed in earlier times.†

This is explained and confessed in the Article "of Rites and Ceremonies" signed by many Bishops, Abbots, etc., in or about the year 1536, thus:—

"Giving of holy bread to put us in remembrance of the sacrament of the altar, that all Christen Men be one Body Mystical of Christ, as the Bread is made of many grains, and yet but one Loaf, and to put us in remembrance of the receiving the holy Sacrament and Body of Christ, the which we ought to receive in right Charity: which in the beginning of Christ's Church, men did more often receive than they use now-a-days to do."

And in certain Injunctions given by the King's visitors to the clergy and laity within the Deanery of Doncaster towards the close of the reign of Henry VIII. the priest was directed to say distinctly and plainly, before dealing the Holy

* Dr. Rock's *Church of our Fathers*, i. 135. † *Origines Liturgicæ*, ii. 154.

Bread, "*Of Christ's Body this is a Token, which on the Cross for our sins was broken; wherefore of his death if you will be partakers, of Vice and Sin you must be forsakers.*"

Its use was continued in S. Martin's Church, as we have seen, down to the year 1548.

In 1547, however, Convocation had declared that the Holy Communion ought to be administered in both kinds. This decision was ratified by Act of Parliament, and a number of Bishops and learned divines * were appointed to draw up an "Order of the Communion," which was printed and brought into use the following year (1548), and which tended much to settle the minds of the people, and to strengthen the Church. No one can read the Proclamation prefixed to this "Order" without being struck by the reverent spirit which dictated it, and by the ardent longing for Christian unity, and the sincere desire to avoid anything like excess or impetuosity in the changes then being introduced, which breathes in every line. "We would not," it concludes, "have Our Subjects so much to mislike Our Judgment, so much to mistrust Our Zeal, as though we either could not discern what were to be done, or would not do all things in due time: God be praised, We know both by what His Word is meet to be redressed, and have an earnest mind, by the advice of Our most dear Uncle, and other of Our Privy Council, with all diligence and convenient speed so to set forth the same, as it may most stand with God's glory, and edifying and quietness of Our people: which we doubt not, but all Our obedient and loving Subjects will quietly and reverently tarry for."

* Among whom was Dr. Robertson, Archdeacon of Leicester.

The Rubric at the end of this Communion Service provides that the consecrated "Breads" should be broken into two pieces at the least, and the wine consecrated "without any levation or lifting up."*

This Order for the Holy Communion, though in the first instance published alone, was, with some emendations, incorporated with the Book of Common Prayer, which was compiled by the same hands, and submitted to Convocation and Parliament in the same year.† During the year following (1549) the two united were put forth by authority, and commanded to supersede every other Form. It was in consequence introduced into S. Martin's Church, as is evidenced by the following extract from the Churchwardens' accounts for the year 1549–50:—

> "Itm̃ pd to Mr. Manbe for a boke of S̃rvyce for y[e] churche . iiij.[s] viij.[d]"‡

Almost immediately after the introduction of the Reformed

* Sparrow's Canons, etc., pp. 18-24, ed. 1684.

† It may be well to note the order given in the rubric to the Communion Service in this First Prayer-Book of Edward VI. as to the vestures of the Priest:—"Upon the day, and at the time appointed for the ministration of the Holy Communion, the Priest that shall execute the holy ministry shall put upon him the vesture appointed for that ministration; that is to say, a white albe plain, with a vestment or cope. And where there be many Priests or Deacons, there so many shall be ready to help the Priest in the ministration as shall be requisite, and shall have upon them likewise the vestures appointed for their ministry; that is to say, albes with tunicles."

‡ In order to encourage the use of the Book of Common Prayer by the Laity in their worship in church, it was ordered by Council "that no maner of person do sell this present booke unbounde above the price of ij. shyllynges and ij. pence the piece" (or, according to some copies, two shillings and sixpence

Liturgy and Common Prayer a new visitation was appointed, and "Articles to be followed and observed according to the King's Majesty's Injunctions and Proceedings" were issued. These Articles—among other Orders—gave special instructions that the ceremonies formerly in use in the office of the Mass should be abolished, and not counterfeited in the Holy Communion, which some ministers had been in the habit of doing—that none should pray upon beads—that Common Prayer upon Wednesdays and Fridays should be diligently kept—"that no man should maintain Purgatory, Invocation of Saints, the six Articles, Bedrolls, Images, Reliques, Lights, Holy Bells, Holy Beads, Holy Water, Palms, Ashes, Candles, Sepulchres, Paschal, creeping to the Cross, hallowing of the Font of the Popish manner, Oil, Chrisme, Altars, Beads, or any other such abuses and superstitions, contrary to the King's Majesty's Proceedings."* Upon the apprehension of the Protector Somerset, an impression became prevalent that the Reformed Liturgy would be abrogated and the old services restored. To contradict this, a letter was written on Christmas-day 1549 by the Council to the Bishops, assuring them that the King intended to carry forward the Reformation,

each copy); "and the same bounde in paste or in boordes, not above the price of three shyllynges and viij. pence the piece" (or, according to some copies, four shillings and eightpence each copy, the price given as above by the Churchwardens of S. Martin's).

And in the Preface to the First Prayer-Book it is said, "Furthermore by this Order the curates shall need none other books for their public service but this book and the Bible: by the means whereof the people shall not be at so great charge for books as in time past they have been."

* Quoted in Burnet's *Reformation*, vol. ii. part ii. 230.

and gave the following Order, which is here quoted, as showing the various Office-books used in the Church in the reign of Henry VIII. :—

"That immediately upon the receipt hereof you do command the Dean and Prebendaries of your Cathedral Church; the Parson, Vicar, or Curat, and Churchwardens of every parish, within your diocese, to bring and deliver unto you or your Deputy, any of them for their Church or Parish, at such convenient place as you shall appoint, all Antiphonals, Missals, Graylles, Processionals, Manuels, Legends, Pies, Portasies, Journals, and Ordinals, after the use of Sarum, Lincoln, York, or any other private use." These were to be defaced and rendered unfit for future use.*

Archbishop Cranmer had previously—in 1548—issued Articles of Visitation for the Diocese of Canterbury; the Bishop of Lincoln probably did the same in this diocese, for the Churchwardens of S. Martin's charge eightpence in 1548–9 for "makyng ye inventory of ye church goods;" and in 1550 Bishop Ridley did the same for the Diocese of London, enquiring whether the Injunctions of the King were strictly carried out.† Soon after which Orders from Council were sent to the Bishops commanding that all the altars in every church should be taken down, and that a table should be set up in some convenient part of the chancel to serve for the administration of the Blessed Communion.‡ How these orders were obeyed in S. Martin's parish is thus shown :—

* Quoted in Burnet's *Reformation*, vol. ii. part ii. 267.

† Sparrow's *Canons*, etc., pp. 25 and 35. Ed. 1684.

‡ Bloxam's *Gothic Architecture*, p. 444. Ed. 1860.

1549-50.

Itm̃ pd to Thoms Wylmore for hys qrt wags for rynging of the day bell . . . . . xx.[d]

Itm̃ rec. for a sellyng [*ceiling*] of Sent Dunstons alr sold to Mr. Cort . . . . . . xvj.[d]

Itm̃ for a voyte [*an ornamental canopy*] of sent Katterns alr sold to Will Clough . . . xij.[d]

Itm̃ recd of Willm̃ Allert for the table [*picture*] that stode at sent Katryns alr . . . . . xij.[d]

Itm̃ rec of Mr. Overend for the holly watr stoke . xvj.[d]

Itm̃ rec of Thom̃s Allan for a grey cope of brydgys satten . . . . ix.[s]

1550-1.

Itm̃ rec. of Mr. Overend for ye. table [*picture*] in ye rode chappell . . . . v.[s]

Itm̃ rec. of Ric. Mable for the table in our lady chappell . . . . vj.[s] viij.[d]

Itm̃ rec of Thomas Dauson for a payntyd clothe and a beyre clothe . . . . . . xvj.[d]

Itm̃ rec. of Thomas . . . for the vowte of sent george autter . . . . . . ij.[s] viij.[d]

Itm̃ rec for ij. candelstycks ij. holly watr stoks & vj. lyttell bells weyng c. & d. [*a hundredweight and a half*] . . . . xxxvij.[s] vj.[d]

Itm̃ rec of Ric . . . . for a grave ston . . . v.[s]

Itm̃ pd to Robt Sekerston & his fellow for a weks worke for takyng downe the altr in or lad's [*lady's*] quere . . . . . . iiij.[s] ix.[d]

Itm̃ pd to Robt. Crofts for cutting downe ye quere . viij.[d]

Itm̃ pd to Mr. Wylcoks for bords yt went to ye table [*the new communion table*] . . . . iiij.[s] iiij.[d]

Itm̃ pd for posts for the same table to A beadmore iiij.[s] iiij.[d]

Itm̄ pd to Marrye for makyng the same table for . xij.[s] iij.[d]
Itm̄ pd for naylls that went to the seats . v.[d]
Itm̄ pd for glew for the same table . vij.[d]

1551-2.
Peyd for matts to be abowght ye tabull ij.[s]

With the altars and their decorations were also removed, as we see from these extracts, the tables or pictures near to them.*

In the year 1650-1 is

Itm̄ rec. of Willm Tayllo[r.] Smyth for y[e] pastall stock (*the stock for the Paschall candle before referred to*) . iiij.[d]

* In the year 1549-50 and 1550-51 are the following :—
Itm̄ rec of Will[m] Tayllor Srgant (?) in ernest of the iij Catche coppe bells aft̃ xxv.[s] a hundryth . . . . . . xij.[d]
Itm̄ p[d] to Rob[t] Sekerston and Rog. Johnson for takyn downe the iij. Catche Coppe bells . . . xij.[d]
Itm̄ rec of Mr. Lambt̃ (?) & Mr. Herek for the leyst Catche Cope bell . . . . xxvij.[s] xj.[d]
Itm̄ rec of Will[m] Tayllor & Willm Syngylton for tow of the same bells . . . . iij.[li] xj.[s] viij.[d]

Of catch cope bells no explanation is here attempted. It has been here suggested (*Notes and Queries*, 2d series, vii. 466) that a catch cope bell is *cache-corps* —*i.e.* a funeral or a passing bell. This cannot explain the case before us, inasmuch as there were three bells. Again it is said (*Notes and Queries*, 3d series, ii. 439) that they were probably the three bells contained in the small belfry or campanile on the gable end of a church, because *cope* signifies an arch or hill, or the top of a wall, and that this belfry, standing in that position might well have been called "catch"—*i.e. cache cope* from its covering the top of the wall: neither can this explanation, it is thought, be accepted in the case of the three bells at S. Martin's. That they were suspended and rung by means of ropes is, however, clear from the only other entry relating to them :—

1547-8.
Itm̄ for iij. bell ropps one catche cope rope . . iij.[s] iiij.[d]

and in the following year (1551-2) there are several entries showing the gradual development of the Reformation. Thus among the receipts are :—

Itm̃ rec. of Richard Mabley for a presse . . xxiij.[s] iiij.[d]
for a crowne of wode kyverd wt. sylṽ & ij. croses of wode kyverd wt. sylṽ & a notte of copper . . . . . iij.[li] vj.[s] viij.[d]

and among the payments :—

Peyd to Wylm for ryngyng ye daye belle . xx.[d]
Peyd to Wylm for knolyng ye belle to ye lectr. vj.[d]
Peyd to goodeman Hore for settyng up ye letterne one ye pulpytte . . viij.[d]

There is a considerable charge in the same year for mending windows, owing probably to the removal of "superstitious pictures" therefrom :—

Peyd to ye glasyer for mẽdyng ye glasse wyndowes in ye chyrche . . . . . xviij.[s] vj.[d]

The performance of Miracle Plays, before alluded to as being a common mode of conveying instruction and amusement to the people previous to the Reformation, was not disallowed under Edward VI., although doubtless the tendency of those now permitted to be performed in churches was to show the Romish system in dark colours, and to help forward the national movement as much as possible.

There is an interesting entry in the accounts of the Churchwardens of S. Martin's for the year 1546-7, referring to a character either in a Miracle Play performed in the church (probably that known in pre-Reformation times as "The Slaughter of the Innocents"), or to one of the personages in the Processions already described :—

Item p[d] for makynge of a sworde & payntyng of the same for harroode* . . . . viij.[d]

There is also a curious instance of a Play being performed —it may almost be said with certainty—in S. Martin's Church in 1551, attended with circumstances showing most indisputably the great attraction these performances had for the good Burgesses of Leicester, and consequently the great power they were likely to exercise in moulding the opinions of the time. In that year "my lady of Huntingdon"† sent to the Corporation, as a mark of her favour or as a token of her friendship, a buck, which, in accordance with the good practice of those times, the "company,"—that is, the members of the Corporate body—resolved to cook in the most approved fashion, and to have a venison feast in the Guild Hall. Accordingly the buck was prepared for the table, "the ale, flower, and pepper" having been provided, but all was forsaken by the worthy

* Herod—I am indebted to Mr. William Kelly for calling my attention to this singular entry.

Since preparing this Chronicle for the press Mr. Kelly's excellent work "Notices of Leicester" has been published. In that work he quotes this entry from my manuscript volume with the following remarks :—"In the 'Widkirk,' or, as they are more commonly called, the 'Townley Mysteries,' the play (the 'Slaughter of the Innocents') is entitled 'Magnus Herodes' as being the piece in which he rants and swaggers the most—traits, indeed, by which the character continued to be so well known down to the time of Shakespeare as to have given rise to his saying in Hamlet of 'out-Heroding Herod' . . . ." (page 18).

† Probably the mother of the first Earl of Huntingdon. She had a residence in the Newarke, Leicester.

members of the local parliament to witness the Play which was then being performed in the church. The circumstance is thus quaintly told by the Chamberlains of the year in their accounts :—

1551.

Itm̃ p[d] for expences that went to the buck that my lady of Huntingdon gave to the xlviij.[ti] whych was ordeyned at the hall for the Company, and they came not because of the play that was in the churche ; whych wth bred, alle, flower, pepper, bakyng, and other charges, amountyth to the some of . . x.[s]

It was not, however, merely to witness Plays that the Mayor and Corporation (or, to use the phrase then in use, "the Mayor and his Brethren,") visited S. Martin's Church, but, as is well known, they in bygone days honoured God, and consequently did not disgrace themselves, by attending public worship there dressed in their robes and bearing with them the insignia of their office. There was formerly a seat set apart for the Mayor in that church; and in the Chamberlains' accounts for 1551-2 we find the following allusion to it :—

Itm̃ p[d] to John Wryght for payntyng in M[r.] Meres (Mayor's) Chappell for the mace . . . . . xij.[d]

Itm̃ p[d] to Robert Hore for an yrone to hange the mace in ther . . . . iij.[d]

In the same year (1551-2) the Chamberlains paid twenty pence "to the Kyng's . . . . for bryngyng a Com̃yssyn for the church goods."

This commission was probably a warrant inquiring as to the carrying out of the Injunctions of the King and the Orders from Council. And in the following year (1553) visitors were sent to examine what plate was still remaining in every church. They were instructed to leave one or two chalices of silver, with linen for the Communion Table, and for surplices, in each church; to take in other things of value to the Treasurer of the King's Household, and to sell the remainder and give the proceeds to the poor.* The effects of this visitation are apparent at S. Martin's, for shortly after we find a further sale of vestments and appendages, some of them extremely curious inasmuch as they refer to matters connected with the Processions which, as we have seen, formed so important a part of the church ceremonies before the Reformation :—

1552-3.

Recevid of nycoles Gossim of nottyingam for ij coppes j vessment & ij tenakyles of clothe of tesshew j vessmēt & ij tenkylys of cloth of silver & ij coppes & j vessment of blew velvet† . . . . xviij.

* Burnet's *Reformation*. "Commissioners were dispatched into every part of England in the last year of Edward, to gather such gleanings as were still left in the shape of chantry-lands unsold, and furniture of churches. They were themselves, however, commonly forestalled by the people; so that, according to Heylyn, 'many private men's parlours were now hung with altar clothes, their tables and beds were covered with copes instead of carpets and coverlids, and many made carousing cups of the sacred chalices, as once Belshazzar celebrated his drunken feast in the sanctified vessels of the Temple.'"—Blunt's *Reformation*, 244.

† The Tunica or Tunicle was a garment worn by the sub-deacon over the albe in the office of the Mass; it was frequently made (like the Cope and Chasuble) of rich and costly material. It had rather wide sleeves, and reached below the knees. In shape it appears to have been very like the Dalmatic, or vesture worn by the deacon, only somewhat smaller in its dimensions: indeed, according to a manuscript list of objects used in the service of the Church, written in the fourteenth century and now pre-

Recevid of Richarde Dane for a corporas casse* & viij shets j towell j auter clothe & the Rowd cowt† . . . . . xxxiij.[s] iiij.[d]

served in the Town Library, Leicester, the Tunicle and Dalmatic were really the same garment:—

Hec tunica, e . . . a tunikyl,
Hec talmatica, e . . . idem.

Perhaps called the latter when worn by a deacon, the former when worn by a sub-deacon.

* "Hoc corporale, *a corporas*" (MS. fourteenth century, Leicester Town Library). A Corporas case was the case or box in which the Corporale was kept; the Corporale (from *corpus*) being a square piece of fine linen which was spread on the altar previous to the consecration of the Host, and which was said to be used as a symbol of the linen clothes in which the body of our Saviour was wrapped when taken down from the cross. Thus in a memorandum at the end of the accounts of the Churchwardens of Melton for the year 1562 I find:—"Item in the hands of Robert Odam . . . . A Corpus Case & Clothe."

The Corporal was sometimes made of richer material than linen and richly ornamented. In the Nunnery of S. Martin, Dover, before the Dissolution, were "vij. olde corporacs of dis̄s cullors silke, w[t] vij. kurches to the same" (*Mon. Ang.* iv. 542). And belonging to Lincoln Cathedral, *temp.* Henry VIII., were "a red case with one corporas with pearls" and "a corporas case and the corporas of gold pyrled and crimson velvet."—*Mon. Ang.* vi. 1279.

In the Rubric to the Holy Communion, "commonly called the Mass," in Edward VI.'s first Prayer Book, the minister is directed to "take so much bread and wine as shall suffice for the persons appointed to receive the Holy Communion, laying the bread upon the *Corporas*, or else in the paten, or in some other comely thing prepared for that purpose." The Corporas is not mentioned in Edward VI.'s second Prayer Book, 1552.

† The Rood Coat is seldom mentioned in documents relating to the church furniture of the pre-Reformation period. It was probably the cloth with which the large rood, or cross upon the rood-loft, was covered on Passion Sunday, and which remained upon it until Good Friday. This idea is strengthened by the entry of the final sale of what was most probably the Rood Coat belonging to S. Martin's Church, soon after the accession of Elizabeth, in which instance it is called a *Rood Cloth*:—

1561-2 Rec. for a Rode Clouthe. viij.[d]

It is nevertheless possible that a real garment of that name *may* be intended

Recevid of Master nycoles renoled for a vessment of blew velvit	x.[s]
Recevid of master mayer for a coffer . . .	v.[s] iiij.[d]
Recevid of Raffe Clarke for a lytell coffer . .	xvj.[d]
Recevid of nicoles goldesmithe for ij. sherts y[t] was for seynte nicoles & a hold towell . . .	iij.[s] iiij.[d]

in the above entry of the sale of the Rood Coat, and that occasionally the figures upon the Rood Loft—the Mary and John, or the Patron saint of the church—were habited in real clothing, for in 1503, John Andrew, of Henley-on-the-Thames, said in his will: "Also I bequeath to our Lady's Coat, in the chapel of Henley, a gold ring, the which was William Wylde's, to hang on the said coat;" and the custom is referred to by Foxe in his *Ecclesiastical History* (vol iii. p. 104), in which, after describing the replacing, with much ceremony, of the Rood in S. Paul's Church, "anno 2nd Mariæ," concludes his account thus:—

"Not long after this, a merry fellow came in to Paul's, and spied the Roode, with Mary and John, new set up; thereto, among a great sort of people, he made low courtessie, and said—'Sir, your Mastership is welcome to Towne. I had thought to have talked further with your Mastership, but that ye be here clothed in the Queene's colours. I hope ye be but a Summer's bird, in that ye be dressed in white and green.'" And so again, in a list of ornaments once belonging to the church of the Holy Trinity, Milford, these coats are enumerated:—

"*Coats belonging to our Lady.*"

1. "A coat, for the good days, of cloth of tissue bordered with white; and for her son another of the same, in like case.
2. "A coat of crimson velvet, and another for her son in like case.
3. "A coat of white damask, and another for her son in like case, bordered about with green velvet."

—*Notes and Queries*, 3d series, iii. 19, 137, 179.

It is possible, however, that these latter were used in Processions, and not for the figures on the Rood Loft. This decking or dressing of Images was strongly reproved by some of the Bishops in the English Church in the time of Henry VIII. Nicholas Shaxton, Bishop of Salisbury, issued Injunctions to the clergy in that diocese in the year 1538, in which he directed:—

Item That ye suffre no . . . . Decking of Ymages with Gold, Silver, Clothes, Lights, or Herbs; nor the People kneel to them, nor worship them, nor offre Candles, Otes, Cake breed, Chese, Wolle, or any such other Thinges to them, etc. etc.

Recevid of Rychard Hewis for corporas case & sente martens cowt * & a towell of dyap † worke . ij.[s] viij.[d]
Recevid of Jon̄ Wryght for xiiij. banar clothes . iiij.[s]

The Proceeds of the sale of these now useless vestments and "properties" was expended in the purchase of the following articles for use in the services of the church, the cost of which the Churchwardens charge in the same year :— ‡

1552-3.

Payde to raffe clarke for ij. sawlters y[t] they say y[e] salmes one in y[e] chyrche at mattins & at evensonge . xx.[d]
Payde for a boke of the preaffrasys [*of Erasmus*] . vij.[s]
Payde for a boke of the newsarvis . . . v.[s]
Payde to Rychard Parear for a bocke conserning the rebellys w[c] was rede in y[e] chyrche . . iiij.[d]
Payde to thomas Carver for y[e] tymber that y[e] ij. lectarynes stand one in y[e] chyrche . . xvj.[d]
Payde to Horre for ye ij. lectarnys of yerne . . vj.[s]
[These two Lecterns of iron were for the Bible and the Paraphrases of Erasmus.]
Payde to Edwarde Brownes wyfe for makyng tow ratchetts for y[e] clarke . . . . vj.[d]

* This was the coat with which the figure of S. Martin was clothed either when it stood upon the Rood Loft or was carried in the Processions already referred to. It was not unusual, as we have just seen, to make offerings of various kinds to these images, which offerings, when their nature permitted, were affixed to them or their clothing. Thus the nunnery of S. Martin, at Dover, possessed, at its dissolution, "one cote for an Image of Saint Thomas, garnysshed w[t] dĩṽs broches, rings, and other juells." —*Mon. Ang.* iv. 543.

† Diaper.

‡ In 1552 the Articles of Religion—forty-two in number—were published "to root out the Discord of Opinions, and establish the Agreement of True Religion."—Sparrow's *Col.* 41.

The book of the "new service" here referred to was the one issued by authority in 1552, in which considerable alterations and additions were made in the different Offices and in the Rubrics as they appeared in the Book of Common Prayer set forth three years previously. The price of this, like the first book, was fixed: "In Queres for two shillynges and sixe pence, and not above; bound in Parchement or forell for three shillynges and iiij. pence, and not above; and bound in Lether, in Paper Boordes or Claspes, for foure shillynges, and not above." The General Confession and Absolution were added in the Second Book; Common Prayer beginning in the First Book with the Lord's Prayer.

It has been before remarked that the dawn of the Reformation was ushered in by a Leicestershire Priest—Wicliffe. Now we find Latimer, the son of a Leicestershire yeoman, aiding in establishing it, and finally bearing the strongest possible testimony to the truth and holiness of its principles, and to the sincerity of his own convictions, by dying a martyr's death rather than repudiate the one or stifle the other. After resigning his bishopric and suffering imprisonment in the reign of Henry VIII., Latimer regained his liberty upon the accession of Edward VI. He then, however, refused to be reinstated in his bishopric, but spent much of his time in preaching both before the court and in the country. He made frequent journeys into the latter, preaching usually twice a day. Many of these Sermons are extant. It is an interesting fact connected with the local history of the period that we can trace the presence of the great Reformer and Martyr in Leicester, where, in all probability, he preached in our church of S. Martin. In the accounts of the Chamberlains of the Borough of Leicester for the year 1552-3 is :—

> Itm' p^d for a gallon of wyne & peyres gyven to M^r. Latym^r. & M^r. Lever . . . . ij.^s

That "Master Latimer" was the usual designation of the Martyr at this time is evident from an entry in Machyn's Diary, p. 57, where, under date of 1553-4, "the Archbysshope of Canturbere Crenmer, the bysshope of London was Rydley, and master Lathemer Condam" (that is *quondam* bishop of Worcester) are mentioned. From Leicester Latimer appears to have gone to Melton-Mowbray (or he came here from thence), where he undoubtedly preached, for in the Churchwardens' accounts of that parish for the year 1553 are found the following entries :—

> Itm̃ payd to John Hynmane & to Robert Bagworth for rynginge of ye great bell for master latimore sarmon . . . . ij.^d
>
> Itm̃ payd for master latymer chargs . . . ij.^s viij.^d

SECTION V.

AND now after a reign of six years Edward VI. finished his "short but saintly course." His death had been for some time expected with far different feelings by different parties in the state. The favourers of the Reformation looked with extreme anxiety and sad foreboding into that future which, to the eye of the partizan of Rome, promised so much. The former had much to lose, the latter everything to gain by the death of a prince whose successor might adopt a policy exactly opposite to his own in religious matters, and attempt to force back upon the people the dogmas and ritual of a hierarchy the infallibility and supremacy of which they had just repudiated. And events proved these forebodings to be true; for upon the death of Edward, and after the failure of the ill-judged attempt to make the Lady Jane queen, Mary, the well-known and honest, though bigoted and harsh devotee of the Romish Church, ascended the throne, which was undoubtedly hers by right of succession. The great object of her ambition and desire was to re-establish the Papal ecclesiastical supremacy in England, and to effect this she exerted all her strength to crush the leaders of the Reformation and to trample under foot the newly-acquired liberties of the English Church. In attempting this she was, however, the unconscious instrument in God's hands of eventual good to the

Reformed Church. But for her accession to the throne the spoliation of the Church as to its temporalities, which had not only been begun under Henry VIII., but had been continued under Edward VI., might have gone on until, by the withdrawal of its proper temporal supports, the learning and the independence of its ministers would have been much imperilled, and its consequent power for good in succeeding time much weakened. Mary at once checked the further alienation of church property, and though she could not prevail upon her Parliament to order the relinquishment by their then possessors of the confiscated lands of the dissolved abbeys, still she herself set a not ignoble example by at once restoring those lands which had been attached to the Crown from such sources. With these she also gave up those first-fruits and tenths which, after they had been again resumed by the Crown, were eventually and finally restored to the Church by Queen Anne, and now form the fund known as Queen Anne's Bounty. And if we believe that tribulation and a scourge are oftentimes God's instruments for the good, not of individuals only, but of communities and nations, then we shall, by a careful study of the dark page of the Church's history in this country opened before us by the accession of Mary to the throne, not fail to trace the finger of God in those fiery persecutions which then tried the faith of so many holy and good men even to the death; for surely the oft-quoted line "the blood of the martyrs is the seed of the Church" was well verified in the martyrdom of such men as John Rogers, Hooper, the learned Cranmer, Ridley, and our own honest, plain-spoken countryman, Latimer. The death of these men was a more effectual homily against Popery, a more powerful advocacy of truth, than they could have delivered from their pulpits had their lot been cast in less troublous times.

It would be beyond the purpose of a Chronicle of S. Martin's Church to attempt to record the many Statutes now passed or revived, and the various means employed by Mary and the favourers of Roman Catholicism to restore it to its high place and power in this country. Some of these, so far as they affected the appearance of our churches, will come under our notice in tracing their results in the parish of S. Martin. With reference to very many other important proceedings of the Queen and her advisers in Church and State, it can here only be generally said that the policy of the late King and his Council was completely reversed as to ecclesiastical matters; most of the statutes, such as the Act of Uniformity, the Act of Supremacy, the Act forbidding appeals to Rome, Mortmain, and other similar enactments of Henry VIII. or Edward VI. in favour of the Reformation in religion, were repealed, and sought to be for ever erased from the Statute Book.

There is no mention in the Records of S. Martin's Church of the death of Edward VI. The only announcement we have from them of the fact is in the heading of the Churchwardens' accounts for the year 1553-4, where, instead of describing the year as being in the "raigne of or sovagne lord Edward the sext by the grā of god of England ffraunce & Ireland Kyng def of the feyth & on erth of ye church of England & also of Ireland the supm̄e head," we have the significant change to "the fyrst yere of the reygne of or most drad & grȳous (gracious) soṽaigne lady quene Mary by the gc̄e of god &c."

Down to the very death of Edward VI. the sale of the appurtenances of the Romish ritual continued. Thus the first entries of moneys received by the Churchwardens in the year 1553-4, the year in which Edward died and in which Mary ascended the throne, are—

Itm̄ rec. for an olde blak vestment & a tunycle	x.[s]
Itm̄ rec. of Roods the viij. day of June for a Cofer	iij.[s] iiij.[d]

Judging from the very gradual way in which the vestments of the ministers and the ornaments and vessels of the Church of S. Martin were disposed of, it is fair to surmise that either the sale was difficult, owing to the market being glutted, or there was a lingering affection in many for the outward signs of their ancient worship which rendered them loth to lose them until almost forced to do so. The latter surmise is probably the correct one. Many would look with distrust and suspicion upon the changes effected, and would adhere outwardly as long as possible to the ritualistic customs they had been accustomed to from their infancy; and when outward conformity was impossible or unsafe, would still secretly exert their influence to prevent the entire eradication of those ceremonies and those outward appliances of a form of worship which they hoped to see again restored to them. And very many again, whilst repudiating some of the doctrines of the Romish Church, would still cling to a gorgeous ritual associated so intimately with all their past lives, the lives of their fathers, and with their past history for so many generations.

The course to be adopted by the Queen as to the mode of conducting the public services in the churches* was quickly notified to the parishioners of Saint Martin's by the arrival among them of Commissioners sent down to see that the customs and ceremonies of the Romish Church were at once restored, and that the Wardens and parish provided all things necessary for the proper celebration of public worship in their church, according to the ritual and teaching prevalent in England before the changes effected by Henry VIII. and Edward VI.

The first and most important thing to be done, in the estimation of the Commissioners, would be to remove the wooden Communion Table placed in the chancel by command of Edward VI. for use in the Sacrament of the Lord's Supper, and to restore in its stead the stone High Altar to its former position there. The High Altar in the Romish Church consisted of an unbroken slab of stone or marble, called the Altar-stone, which rested upon a mass of masonry somewhat in the form of a tomb, in which it was usual to enclose particles of the Eucharist or consecrated wafer, and, when procurable, the relics of a saint. The Altar-stone, however large the altar upon which it rested,† was always one unbroken slab of suffi-

* The Queen sent a Letter, with Articles for his guidance in ecclesiastical matters, to the Bishop of London in March 1553-4. These without doubt are but samples of those sent to all the other Bishops at the same time. In them the Bishop was directed that the Holy-days and Fasting-days, the honest and laudable ceremonies observed and kept in the time of Henry VIII., should thereafter be used and observed. The Processions were to be continued after the old order of the church in the Latin tongue.

† The altar-stone belonging to Bradwell Priory (Bucks) is described in an

cient size to allow of its projecting a few inches beyond the body of the altar on three of its sides. The entirety of the slab was supposed to represent the unity of belief in the church. The slab when placed upon the altar at the dedication of a church was solemnly consecrated by the Bishop with holy oil, and incense* was burned upon it at the four corners and

inventory taken of its goods prior to its dissolution, *temp.* Henry VIII., as "an awter ston nygh iiij. yards longe."—*Mon. Ang.* iv. 510.

* It would appear from the following extracts that incense has been frequently used in the Church of England since the Reformation :—

1603.—Two pounds of frankincense were burnt in the Church of Augustine, Farringdon Within, London.—Malcolm's *Londinium Redivivum*, ii. 88.

1626.—"Paid for frankincense 2[d]."—*Churchwardens' Accounts of Great Wigston, Leicestershire.*

1631.—The country parson takes care . . . secondly, that the church be swept and kept clean without dust or cobwebs, and at great festivals strewed and stuck with boughs, and perfumed with incense.—George Herbert's *Priest of the Temple*, chap. xiii.

Temp. James I.—"A triquertral censer, wherein the clerk putteth frankincense at the reading of the first lesson. The navicula, like the keel of a boat, with a half-cover and foot, out of which the frankincense is poured."—Furniture of Bishop Andrewes' Chapel, *Canterbury's Doom*, p. 122.

Temp. Charles I.—"In Peter House there was on the altar a pot, which they usually called *the incense pot* . . . a little boat out of which the frankincense is poured, which Dr. Cosins had made use of in Peter House where he burned incense."—*Canterbury's Doom*, pp. 74, 123.

Ibid.—"Upon some altars there was a pot called *the incense pot.*"—Neal's *Puritans*, ii. 224.

1683.—In the accounts of St. Nicholas, Durham :—"For frankincense at the Bishops' coming 2[s] 6[d].—Surtees' *Durham*, iv. 52, fol. 1840.

1684.—See Evelyn's *Diary*, March 30, 1684.

1760.—In the coronation procession of George III. appeared the King's groom of the vestry, in a scarlet dress, holding a perfuming pan, burning incense, as at previous coronations.—Thomson's *Coronation of George III.*—*Notes and Queries*, 3d series, viii. 11.

It would, however, it is thought, be difficult to show that in any instance the incense was used *symbolically* in any *parish church* in post-Reformation times. It was used simply for purposes of fumigation.

in the middle, where five crosses—to signify the five wounds of Christ—were marked.*

The altar-stone, which had thus been consecrated perhaps centuries before, and used during the succeeding years as the resting-place of the sacred vessels of the Church, and more especially as bearing upon it what in the eyes of the devout Roman Catholic was the actual presence, in tangible form, of the body of his Saviour, would be regarded with extreme reverence, and its desecration viewed, and justly so, with the utmost abhorrence.

The Mayor of Leicester at the time the Commissioners would reach the town, or by the time the commands of the Queen would be received and acted upon, was Mr. Thomas Davenport, who was elected to the mayoralty in 1553, most probably on the 21st September (the feast of S. Matthew), that being then the customary day for such election. Resting upon a few brief entries in the Churchwardens' accounts, it is scarcely stepping from the hard and dry statement of an antiquary's fact to the province of surmise and conjecture, to presume that he was one of the class just referred to, who secretly, during the late reign, clung to the form of worship he had been used to from his childhood, and who now rejoiced at

* Dr. Rock's *Church of our Fathers*, i. 244. A few of these ancient altar-stones escaped destruction at the Reformation.—Vide *Glossary of Architecture*.

its restoration. For it will be remembered that it was "Master Davenport," who in the first year of Edward VI. purchased a Tabernacle; afterwards we find him paying for two vestments, an altar-cloth of red velvet and white damask, and some other altar-clothes; and now, when the High Altar is again to be erected in his parish church (for he was a parishioner of S. Martin's), we find he had also secured the consecrated altar-stone, and had preserved it in his house, from whence it was fetched to be again placed in its original position :—

1553-4.

Itm̄ pd for the carryeng of the alt^r ston for Mr Mayres house to the churche . . . . iiij.^d

Itm̄ p^d. to Robt Sekerston for settyng upp the Alter & mendyng of the churche . . . . . . xij.^d

Itm̄ pd for a busshell of lyme for the alt^r . . . . x.^d

Itm̄ pd for ij. men ij. days for beryng ston to ye alt^r . xvj.^d

Itm̄ pd to Rowland Wayght for ij. days work about the alt^r xvj.^d

The Table, or picture, which formerly was placed near, or over the High Altar, was now restored to its place :—

Bowght of M^r. Lamberd the table at the hye alter whyche ys yet unpaide . . . . xx.^s

A pix was purchased to place upon, or over the altar, in which to reserve the Host for the sick :—

Itm̄ p^d for a pyx for the Sacrament . ij.^s vj^d

over which a canopy was fixed :—

Itm̄ p^d for a yarde & a quart^r. of red sey to cover the canopy ov^r the sacrament . . . . . xvij.^d

Several other articles pertaining to the altar were also provided: a sacring bell, being a small hand-bell rung at different parts of the service during mass :—

Itm̄ pd for a sacrynge bell . . viij.[d]

two candlesticks and a cross—probably a crucifix :—

Itm̄ pd for ij. candylstykes for the alter . . . ij.[s]
Itm̄ pd to Synglton for a crosse . . . . xx.[s]

and a holy-water stoup and a chrismatory are mentioned :—

1554-5.
Itm̄ pd to Synglton for a holywat[r.] stock . . . v.[s]
Itm̄ pd to Robt Huseley for oyle & creme & mendyng
of the crysmatorye . . . . . xij.[d]
Itm̄ pd to Robert goldsmyth for a pattyn of a challyce xj.[s] vj.[d]

Also—

Itm̄ pd for iij. corporas casys . . xij.[d]

The costly vestments of the priests were again provided, indeed some of those sold in the late reign were repurchased, and that in one case apparently from the Queen's Commissioners :—

1553-4.
Itm̄ for ij. coops & a vestment of blue velvet . xx.[s]
Itm̄ pd for a whyet sattyn cope . . . x.[s]
Itm̄ p[d.] to the quenes commissioners for the cops
of tyssue that were solde . . . viij.[li]

Itm̃ pd to Mestrys gillot for a vestment & an albe and all that belongyth therto* . . xiij.^{s} iiij.^{d}
Itm̃ p^{d} to y^{e} Comyssyoners for ij. press† . . iij.^{s} iiij.^{d}

The Rood-loft was again adorned with the figures of the Virgin Mary and S. John :—

1555-6.

Itm̃ pd to Rob$^{t.}$ Croft for mendyng the Rode loft . ij.^{d}
Itm̃ pd to Willm Tayllo$^{r.}$ for turnyng of the standers in the Roode loft . . . . . . xj.^{d}
Itm̃ pd for ix. taper dysshes for the Rode loft . ix.^{s}

1557-8.

P$^{d.}$ to Davy for makyng the Roode Marye & John . xiij.^{s} iiij.^{d}
P$^{d.}$ to John Barber for gyldyng of the roode Mary & John . . . . xxij.^{d}
P$^{d.}$ for heks & staples to hang theym upon . . vij.^{d}
P$^{d.}$ to John Barbers wyffe for gyldyng the rode Mary & John . . . . xiij.^{d}
P$^{d.}$ to Ric Reynford for the rode lyght . . iiij.^{d}

"Gatherers for the roode lyght" were now appointed,

* The "vestment" here, as elsewhere, was a chasuble, that garment being usually called a vestment in the pre-Reformation church. Both that and the Alb have already been described. The "all that belongyth therto," probably comprised the apparels, the girdle, and perhaps the stole and the amice, the latter being an oblong piece of fine linen or richer material, spread over the shoulders: indeed this payment appears to have been for an entire suit of vestures as worn by a priest at High Mass.

† Two Presses in which to keep the vestures of the clergy. Throsby (Ed. 1777) mentions the existence then of a press called an ark, in the vestry of S. Mary's Church, Leicester, which contained "seven cranes" for the purpose of hanging vestures upon.

William Taylor and Thomas Barker filling that office in 1557-8. A Rood Coat was purchased :—

1553-4.
Itm̃ pd for a Rood cote . xx.[d]

The Lectern of Brass—which appears to have been sold—was replaced in its old position :—

Itm̃ pd for the brassyn lectarne xx.[s]

This Lectern, as we know from other references to it, was in the form of a brass Eagle—

1555-6.
Itm̃ p[d] for scowerynge of the egyll xvj.[d]

a form common in the church before the Reformation, for the desk from which the Epistle and the Gospel were read.*

* The "brazen Eagle" for the lectern has been used in the English Church for many centuries :—" Another lettorn of brasse . . . with an Eagle on the height of it, and hir winges spread a broad" is mentioned in the *Ancient Rites, &c., of Durham* (*Glossary of Arch.*) ; indeed this form would appear to have been formerly the common one, for we are told that previously to the great Rebellion most village churches possessed their own Eagle, desk, or lectern of brass or wood, whence the lessons were read to the people. With regard to this symbol an ancient expositor observes, that "the church flies on the pinions of Holy Scriptures through all ages, and into all lands, so that the two wings of the great Eagle are the two Testaments of the Incarnate Word, who ascended on the clouds of heaven and carries His children thither, like the Eagle described in Scripture, 'spreading abroad his wings' and mounting with his young upon them." This form may, however, have been adopted in reference to S. John, whose especial symbol is the Eagle.

The constant use now of this and the other symbols of the Evangelists in our churches appears here to call for remark. Their appearance in stained-

The service-books required in the various Offices of the Romish Church now took the place of Edward VI.'s Book of Common Prayer, and means were taken to make the

glass windows, on monumental brasses, in carvings of wood and stone, indeed in every possible way in church decoration, must be familiar to every one, and that not in ancient work only, but also in modern. They appear in the eastern window of S. Martin's chancel, on the modern brass upon its floor; and there is, I think I may venture to say without an examination, scarcely a church in Leicestershire, where much modern ornamentation has been attempted, where they are not represented.

The types now employed to signify the Evangelists do not appear to have been those used in the early ages of the church, but as they are now the only usual ones, their forerunners need not engage our attention here. The Man, the Lion, the Ox, and the Eagle were adopted (as I have attempted to show in the *Historical Collector*, ii. 70) from Ezekiel's Vision (Ezekiel, i. 5), and the Revelation of S. John (Rev. iv. 7).

Adam of S. Victor (writing in the twelfth century), after speaking of Ezekiel's Vision, says, referring to that of S. John:—

"Round the Throne, 'midst angel natures,
Stand four holy living creatures,
Whose diversity of features,
Maketh good the Seer's plan.
This an Eagle's visage knoweth,
That a Lion's image sheweth,
Scripture on the rest bestoweth
The twain forms of Ox and Man.
These are they, the symbols mystic,
Of the forms Evangelistic,
Whose four Gospels, streams majestic,
Irrigate the church of God."

S. Matthew is represented by the creature, which "had a face as a man," because he begins his Gospel with "the book of the generation of Jesus Christ," that is, his human generation; or, according to some writers, because he brings forward the human nature of our Lord more prominently than the divine.

To S. Mark is given the Lion, because he "sets forth the royal dignity of Christ," even in his opening verse describing him as the Son of God, and because, as the historian of the Resurrection, this is a fit symbol, there being in mediæval times a belief that the young of the Lion was born dead, and after three days was called into life by the roar or by the breath of its progenitor: the Lion again is said to have been assigned to S. Mark, in allusion to his description of the mission of the Baptist —"the voice of one crying in the wilderness." One of the mediæval poets says: "Mark roars a lion in a desert place."

The Ox represents S. Luke, because

musical portions of the services as efficient as possible: the organs were repaired, and the choristers were rewarded:—

1553-4.

Itm̄ p^d. to S^r. Wiłł Burrows for a salter a ꝑcessyoner a manuell & a cowcher . . . . . . vj.^s viij.^d

Itm̄ p^d for a manuell to wed crystyn & burrye wth all iij.^s iiij.^d

Itm̄ p^d to Wiłł Ward for a masse boke & a cowcher . x.^s

Itm̄ pd to S^r. Wiłł burrows for canvass & packthred for the orgayns . . . . iiij.^d

[For mending the organs vj.^s]

Itm̄ more p^d. for a grayll to syng in the church on* . x.^s

he dwells more fully upon our Lord's Passion, the ox being an emblem of sacrifice, and he also "of priestly deeds indites."

S. John has the Eagle—

"John, love's double* wing devising,
Earth on Eagles' plumes despising,
To his God and Lord uprising,
Soars away in purer light."
Adam of S. Victor.

The Eagle is symbolical of S. John, because he towers to heaven in his contemplation and enunciation of the divine nature of our Lord; and probably the dignity and sublimity of the Book of the Revelation, that terrible and glorious vision, would point to this as his fitting type.

Whatever may have been the origin of the form of the Eagle for the lectern, from which the Epistle and Gospel were read in the pre-Reformation church, and from which the lessons from Holy Scripture are now read, the idea of supporting the Holy Gospels in this way is very significant of the glad tidings of salvation being borne, as it were, on Eagles' wings to all nations; and it is hoped that few will regret the re-introduction into S. Martin's Church of this ancient form of lectern from which to read the lessons, in the carved oak Eagle which has lately been presented to the church, to commemorate the erection of the new tower, and as a successor to the Eagle of brass which we see adorned its choir so many years ago, and which was sold in 1568-9 for the paltry sum of £4 : 18 : 0.

"Receyved of Mr. Morres for the Egle . . . . iiij.^li xviij.^s
—*Churchwardens' Accounts.*

* Love to God and love to man.

* The Psalter contained, as its name implies, the Psalms of David pointed for

1554-5.

Itm̄ p[d.] to Fraunc̄s Caynesworth for syngyng . . vj.[s] viij.[d]
Itm̄ p[d] to Ric. Lyllyng for playng of the organs . v.[s]

chanting, and in some cases also hymns from the Old and New Testaments.

The Processioner or Processionale contained the Litanies, etc., used in Processions.

A Manuel comprised the various Occasional Offices of the church which a priest could minister. A Mass-book or Missal contained the Office of the Mass.

The Grayle contained the Graduale, which was a part or the whole of one of the Psalms chanted between the Epistle and Gospel, and so called from the custom which once prevailed of singing it on the steps (*Gradus*) of the Ambo or Pulpit in which the Epistle used to be recited. The *Antiphonary*, which contained the anthems or verses for the beginning of the Communion, the offertory, etc., was also often called *Graduale.*

In addition to the Service-books mentioned above as purchased for S. Martin's Church in 1553-4 there were others in general use in the churches—such as the *Collectarium* or Collect Book, the Book of Legends, the *Homilarium* containing short addresses or Homilies, etc. Of this latter there is—if I mistake not—a curious example now preserved in the Town Library, Guild Hall, Leicester. It is an ancient manuscript volume, written in English upon vellum, labelled on the back "Misale in MS." This is clearly a mistake, as it contains Homilies for the different Saints' days and Sundays in the year, but whether it was set forth by authority or was the production of a single person I cannot say. The title-page—if it originally had one—is gone. There is also now preserved in the same Library a number of Miscellaneous Manuscripts on vellum, of the thirteenth and fourteenth centuries, bound together in one volume, one of which is a List of Latin terms used in the Service of the church with equivalent English words. This is valuable for the purpose of this note as showing the service-books then in general use. I find the following:—

"Missale . . a mes bok.
Ordinale . . Ordinari bok.
Gradale . . a Gradalle.
p'secionale . presecōnal bok.
porteform̄ . a portos.
legēdarm̄ . . a legent.
martilogm̄ . a martilog̅.
Caladm̄ . . a calonder."

That is, a Mass-book—an Ordinale or book of rules, showing what lessons should be read, responses sung, or commemorations made, etc. (Dr. Rock states it is another name for the Pye or Directory, the number and hardness of the rules of which are mentioned in the Preface to our Book of Common Prayer)—a

Some at least of the minor altars were re-erected, though neither they nor their chapels regained their former amount of decoration :—

1553-4.

Itm̃ p[d] for dressyng & . . . . sent georgs harnes . vj.[s] viij.[d]

Itm̃ p[d] to John barbor for payntyng in the churche & dressyng the alters . . . . ix.[s]

1554-5.

Itm̃ p[d] to Rowlande Mason for makyng the auter in o[r.] lady chapell. . . . . . xviij.[d]

Itm̃ p[d] to John Barbo[r] for . . . . a cloth for o[r.] lady's aulter . xxij.[d]

Graduale as last explained—a Processionale—a Portos or Breviary—a Legendarium or book of Legends—a Martyrology and a Calendar.

The Breviary appears to have been formed out of all these books; it was differently arranged in different places, and it underwent various revisions at different times. The difficulty attending the use of so complicated a liturgy must have been—as noticed in the Preface to our present Prayer Book '*Concerning the Service of the Church*'—very great, and this difficulty was increased by a different "use" or mode of "saying or singing" the service being adopted in different churches. Thus there was Salisbury Use, Hereford Use, the Use of Bangor, York, and Lincoln. That of Sarum, however, prevailed to a great extent over England—the Bishop of Salisbury now is always precentor of the College of Bishops—and it was probably that mode of conducting the service of the church which was in use at S. Martin's before the Reformation. There is now preserved in the Town Library, Guild Hall, Leicester, a "Missale ad Usum Ecclesie Sarum, 1519," printed in black letter, rubricated, and in beautiful preservation: the Canon of the Mass—which is almost the only part showing the effects of much use—is printed upon vellum, the remainder of the volume being on paper. This may probably have formerly belonged to a church or religious house in Leicester: the soiled condition of the Canon of the Mass and a few corrections in ink show it, I think, to have been used by a priest. It is marked on the title-page "*The booke of Francis Higginson*," with the price at which he purchased it apparently second-hand.

and probably for the same altar :—

Itm̃ pd. to Nic̄his Lawson for a pattyn of the challyce . xvj.d
Itm̃ pd to Syngelton for a crosse & sencers . . v.s iiij.d

1555-6.

Itm̃ pd to the sextyn for mendyng a hole in the Roode Chappell . . . . . iiij.d

In common with the other appurtenances of the altar in the Mediæval Church, the Gospels and the Office-Books there used were frequently of the most costly and beautiful description both as regards their caligraphy and their binding. Those used in our Cathedrals and Monasteries before printing was invented, and even long afterwards, were written upon vellum superbly illuminated and coloured ; for—as I have remarked elsewhere — transcription and illumination held an important place among the arts of the middle ages. Sitting day after day, year after year, in the Scriptorium of his Monastery, many a monk devoted the whole of his life to produce a few of those exquisitely written and illuminated manuscripts which are still the pride and ornament of our public and private libraries. That the man so employed was very frequently a true artist must be evident to all who have given even a cursory glance at the products of his skill and manipulation still left to us, so many examples of which were gathered together in the splendid collection of antiquities in the Loan Museum, South Kensington, and exhibited there during the year 1862. It was required of a man to be a good illuminator (in addition to the possession of a perfect knowledge of the mechanical portion of his art) that he should be an observant lover of nature, for did not the initial letters and the borders of his manuscript abound with copies of her most beautiful works? There

"Angels round His glory throne,
Stars His guiding hand that own,
Flowers that grow beneath our feet,"

found a place ; there animals and grotesques, possible and impossible, were introduced in postures and positions graceful or ludicrous ; and there his fellow-man, in all the various phases of his existence, from the sleeping infant and innocent child to the crowned monarch and mitred abbot, were impressed to aid his decoration, and to give grace and beauty to his handywork. Neither were it the initial letters and borders of his manuscript only which showed his artistic skill and inventive genius : the text which followed—whether the burning words of prophet or seer, the sweet psalm or canticle, the record of Evan-

Shortly after this date collections were made towards the expense of dressing the altars. In the receipts for 1557-8, the churchwardens credit their account with 11.[s] 11½.[d] Received "at the gatheryngs for the aulters."

A Paschal stock was provided, and the sepulchre again set up at Easter tyde :—

gelist, the message of Apostle, the Service of the Church, or the legend of saint or martyr, showed the hand of a master penman, and rivalled in its exactitude and precision the regularity and evenness of the modern block and type.

Many of the monasteries possessed libraries of considerable magnitude. Gunton gives, in his *History of Peterborough Cathedral*, a long list of works formerly belonging to that house before its dissolution ; and it is but true to say that in many cases the Bible was the first book provided. Thus one of the first acts of the first abbot of Croxden Abbey, near Uttoxeter, in Staffordshire, was to transcribe the greater portion of the Holy Scriptures for the use of the monks. Another abbot of the same house purchased for their use a Bible in nine volumes, with notes by the Archdeacon of Leicester, the price of which was equal to £533 : 6 : 8 of our present money (*Transactions of Leicester Arch. Socy.* i. p. 147) ; and though in later times the simple truths of the Bible were sadly overshadowed by the teaching of the church, and its pure doctrines and precepts sadly neglected and forgotten, a veneration for the material Gospel was still shown—as stated at the head of this note—by enshrining it in the most costly bindings ; plates of gold or silver encrusted with precious stones clasped the richly-illuminated altar-books of our cathedrals and monasteries—at Winchester Cathedral was "a book of the four Evangelists written all with gold and the outer side of plate of gold"—whilst those possessed by our parish churches were scarcely inferior in costliness and beauty. In the neighbouring church of S. Mary de Castro, Leicester, were copies of the Gospels bound in silver—it was not uncommon to bind each evangelist separately.

1512.

"Paid for binding the silver Gospel book and covering the back with leather	0	0	4[d]
For binding the Gospel book covered with silver: the dean paid as much	0	0	4[d]

—*Churchwardens' Accounts*, quoted by Nichols.

1554-5.

Itm̃ pd to M^r. Tayllo^r. for the pascall stock . . viii.^d
Itm̃ pd for payntyng of the pascall stock . . xiiij.^d
Itm̃ pd to John Molp (?) for tymber & for makyng of the sepulcre . . . . v.^s
Itm̃ pd for naylls for the sepulcre . . iiij.^d
Itm̃ pd for the sepulcre lyght . . . . iiij.^s
Itm̃ pd to John Barbo^r. for payntyng the Sepulcre &c xxij.^d

To próvide for the cost of keeping the light burning before the sepulchre, officers were appointed to collect donations from the parishioners, who were called "Gatherers for the Sepulcers lyght." In 1554-5 they paid to the churchwardens four shillings, and in 1557-8 these officers were Richard Chettle and . . . Thompson, who, at the close of that year, had remaining in their hands four shillings and one penny half-penny in money and eleven tapers.

The annual procession to Saint Margaret's Church was revived, and is thus noticed :—

1553-4.

Itm̃ pd for xij. banner clothes . ij.^s

1554-5.

Itm̃ pd to John Barbo^r for the banners . . . iij.^s
Itm̃ pd for the offerynge that lackyd at Sent m̃gyts at Whytsonday & drynck ther for the v^rgyns . . xij.^d

In the following year, 1555-6, we find, in addition to payments for banner-poles :—

Itm̃ pd for alle & Caks at sent m̃gytts xviij.^d

Again, in 1557-8, are :—

Pd for iij. galons of ale & iiij.[d] in kaks at seynt m̃garetts	xix.[d]
Pd for beyryng of the Crose & banners . . .	xiiij.[d]

And lastly, in 1558-9, the last year of Queen Mary's reign :—

Pd for the chargs of the pc̃ession to seynt m̃geretts	. iij.[s]	
Pd the same tyme for other offeryngs to the alters	. ij.[s]	ij.[d]
Pd for ale & cakes the same tyme		x.[d]

There is one trace of the performance of a Miracle Play in S. Martin's Church during the reign of Queen Mary, she having partially revived the custom. In the year 1555-6 is the following charge by the Churchwardens :—

Itm̃ pd to the iij. shepperds at Whytsontyde . .	vj.[d]

The three shepherds were the principal, and sometimes the only characters in the then well-known Play "the Adoration of the Shepherds."

In 1557-8, the Bishop's attendance at the visitation in this Church is thus noticed :—Pd one gallon of ale & to the ryngers at the comyng of my lord byshop . . . . ij.[d] ob.

When Mary ascended the throne she gave an assurance "that she meant graciously not to compel and constrain men's consciences" in religious matters; and in her public proclamation she declared that "she minded not to compel any of her subjects thereunto—*i.e.* to the religion she had professed from her infancy—until such time as further order by common assent might be taken therein." This toleration was not, however, long observed: not content with making the many alterations already referred to in the laws affecting ecclesiastical matters, and with a compulsory return in the public worship of the church to the ceremonies and to the ritual of Rome as indicated in the above extracts from the Churchwardens' Accounts, the bigotry of the Queen was goaded by her ecclesiastical advisers into a persecution of those holding the tenets of the Reformation, which resulted in the martyrdom of so many, under circumstances which have rendered the short reign of Mary a dark and fearful page in the history of this country and of humanity. It was in 1556 that Dr. John White, the Bishop of Lincoln, held a visitation in Leicester, under the authority of a mandate from Cardinal Pole, the Papal Legate, the chief purpose of which appears to have been to inquire into the orthodoxy of the inhabitants, for on the 21st of April in that year Thomas More was summoned to appear before the Bishop to answer various charges of heresy brought against him. He accordingly presented himself before the prelate in the churches of S. Martin and S. Margaret, and being examined touching his belief in the doctrine of transubstantiation, replied: "This is my faith, that in the sacrament of the Altar is not the body of Christ, no more than if I myself should give one a piece of bread, and say, Take eat, this is my body; meaning my body within my doublet." He was convicted as a heretic and condemned to be burnt, which sentence was carried into effect in Leicester in the month of June following.*

The revival of a belief in the efficacy of prayers for the dead, and of the means resorted to before the time of Edward

* Nichols' *Leicestersh.* vol. i. 560. According to Fuller, More was the only person within the diocese of Lincoln who perished at the stake for religious opinions during the reign of Mary.

VI. to secure the performance of certain religious services for the benefit of the soul of the testator after death, is curiously illustrated by the following copy of the Will of a parishioner of S. Martin's dated about this time :—

"In the Name of god Amen The xxv.[ti] day of October in the yere of o[r.] Lord god a thowsande fyve hundreth fyftie & seven I Henry Perke of y[e] Towne of Lecester paynter beynge sycke in bodye but in good & ꝑfect Remembraunce prayse be to god make this my last will & testament in forme followynge, fyrst I bequeth my soule to almyghtie god my maker & Redemer & to o[r.] Ladie Sent marie & to all the Blessed cōpanye of heav̄e and my bodye to be buryed in y[e] churche yard of sent saynt* Martyn in Leic̄ aforsayd. Itm̄ I bequeth to y[e] mother churche of Lyncolne—iiij.[d] Itm̄ to the high aulter of sent Martyn in Leic̄ aforsayd my pīshe church—iiij.[d] Itm̄ I gyve & bequeth to Alic Pelton my wyves god daughꝰ my tenement at y[e] cankewell to have & to holde the sayde tenement w[th] y[e] app[r]tenances to y[e] sayd All: her heyres & assignes for ever, after the Decease of me the sayd Henry & Ellyn my wyffe *payinge yerelye out of y[e] same tenement to y[e] churche of saynt Martyn aforsayd* —iii.[s] iiij.[d] *to be prayed for w[th] all my frends* & *all x̄pen souls.* Itm̄ I bequeth to John Sturge my kynsman xxx[ti] kyndds. Itm̄ I gyve & bequeth to Jane Harvye my goddaughꝰ the thycke brasse pott, the Residew of all my goods my Debts & funerall discharged I gyve & bequeth to Ellyn my wyfe whom I ordayne & make my full & sole executryx of this my last will & testament, Also I make suꝑvisor of the same Willm̄ Harvye to see y truely ꝑformed in all thyngs accordynge to y[e] tenor of y[e] same. These beynge witnesses John Sturge, Richard Tayler & others."†

* So in original.

† Copy preserved at the end of the Churchwardens' Accounts of S. Martin's Parish for the year 1571-2. This annual gift to the church I find to have been received by the churchwardens so late as 1641.

Neither had the good old custom of providing by will for some addition to the decent furniture of the Church entirely disappeared at this time; for, under date of 1558-9, the death of a priest—Sir Thomas Burrowes—is recorded amongst the receipts for the use of the bells at funerals :—

rec. for iij. bells for S^r. Thomas Burrowes	viij.^d

and by various payments in the same year we learn that he gave, or left by will, an altar-cloth to the Church :—

pd for soyng the alter cloth that S^r. Thoms gave	ij.^d
pd for ij. yards of Canbyse to lyne the same .	vj.^d
pd for ij. yards of canbyse to ley ov the same alter	vj.^d

Among the receipts by the churchwardens in the reign of Queen Mary are several entries by "Lincoln Farthings." These and "smoke farthings" were identical. The "smoke farthings" appear to have been in some cases an ancient ecclesiastical impost collected throughout the diocese for the use of the cathedral, and in consequence were frequently called after the name of the mother church; so the smoke farthings collected in this town would be called "Lincoln Farthings," Leicester being at that time within that diocese. Mention of this tax is made in the Register of William Alnewick, Bishop of Lincoln (fo. 48), by which it would also appear that occasionally the smoke farthing or Lincoln farthing was for a time conceded to any church in the diocese in which expensive works of building were going on, and where extraneous help was therefore necessary.*

* The paragraph referred to (translated), is as follows :—"Smoke farthings. —Commission of the lord bishop to levy the smoke farthings, otherwise called

Lincoln farthings, from our faithful lieges of our Archdeaconry of Leicester, to be converted to the use of our mother church of Lincoln our spouse: the said smoke farthings are granted for the construction of a campanile (bell-tower), to the prebendal church of Saint Margaret, Leicester, 1444."

The same custom prevailed within the diocese of Ely, where (as early as the twelfth century), every person who kept a fire within the diocese was obliged to pay one farthing yearly to the altar of S. Peter in the cathedral church. This tax at a later date was collected by the churchwardens, and was called "Elie farthings or smoke farthings."—*Notes and Queries*, 1st series, ii. 345; ix. 513.

The Lincoln farthings were collected in S. Martin's at Whitsuntide, as is shown by the entry of their receipt by the churchwardens, 4 and 5 Philip and Mary:—

rec. in lyncolne ffarthyngs at Whytsontyde . . . iij.[s] x.[d] ob.

There are only four entries relating to them, the last being in the first year of Queen Elizabeth:—

Rd. for lincolne farthings ij.[s] ij.[d] ob.

I find no charge in the accounts to show that these sums were paid to the cathedral church. Perhaps they were, by permission of the Bishop, appropriated towards the discharge of the necessary expenses incurred by the churchwardens.

The following curious entry in the accounts of the churchwardens of Minchinhampton, Gloucestershire, for the year 1575, may throw a different light upon the origin of smoke farthings:—

Paid "to the sumner for peterpence or smoke farthynges sometyme due to the Anthecriste of roome . x.[d]"

SECTION VI.

THE death of Queen Mary and that of her principal adviser, Cardinal Pole, occurred close to each other. She ended a life embittered by domestic neglect and public dislike on the 17th November 1558; he died on the following day. Little time was lost in proclaiming Elizabeth as the new Queen, and the announcement was received in London and throughout the country with unusual marks of approbation and joy. The fact is thus noticed in the accounts of the Churchwardens of S. Martin :—

1558-9.

Pd for ale to the Ryngers when the quenes grace was ꝑclamyd . . . . . viij.[d]

Although Elizabeth was well known to be a favourer of the Reformation, her movements upon her accession to the throne were all marked by that extreme caution and freedom from precipitancy which had always been strong traits in her character, from the time when her brother Edward called her his "sweet sister Temperance," through that eventful period of her life—the reign of her sister Mary—when a hasty word or an incautious action would, in all probability, have sacrificed her life. Her first policy was therefore to make her throne secure, and not wilfully to estrange any party in the state from her by hasty changes in the Laws Ecclesiastical or in the Ritual of the Church, until such time as she could well reckon on the support of her people, and be in a position to cope with any attempt made by the Romish party to overthrow her government or subvert her wishes. She formed her Council of both Romanists and Protestants, making the latter, however, her chief advisers. The re-introduction of the Reformed Liturgy, and the final overthrow of the Romish system, were accordingly proceeded with step by step, and every care was taken to curb the impatience and false zeal of those who, by hasty and unlawful proceedings, would have brought odium upon the Reformation which they professed to serve. The first change permitted was the reading of the Epistle, the Gospel, the Decalogue, the Lord's Prayer, and the Creed, in the churches, in the English tongue; in all other matters the Roman rites and customs were to be followed until further orders were given, and all religious controversy was strictly prohibited. The administration of the Holy Communion in both kinds, the consequent abolition of the Office of the Mass, and the restoration of the English Liturgy, however, quickly followed. The two great Acts of Uniformity and Supremacy, which had been repealed in the late reign, were then revised by Parliament. The revised Act of Uniformity, after stating that the original Act, passed in the 5th and 6th years of Edward VI., had been "repealed and taken away by Act of Parliament in the first year of the reign of our late sovereign Lady Queen Mary to the great decay of the due honour of God, and discomfort to the professors of the truth of Christ's religion," proceeds to enact, That the Prayer-book set forth by Edward VI. in 1552 (with certain specified alterations) should be used from and after the feast of S. John Baptist then next, and that the Form of Common Prayer should be used exclusively by the clergy, under heavy penalties and eventual deprivation of spiritual promotions, with imprisonment for life. The laity were commanded to attend their parish churches to hear it, under pain of ecclesiastical censure and pecuniary penalty. With regard to the ornaments of the Church and its ministers, it provided that such should be retained as were used by authority of Parliament in the second year of Edward VI., until other orders should be taken therein by the authority of the Queen, with the advice of her Commissioners appointed and authorised under the Great Seal of England, for causes ecclesiastical, or of the Metropolitan. And that in case any contempt or irreverence should happen in the ceremonies or rites of the Church, the Queen should have power, by the advice of the Commissioners or Metropolitan, to ordain and publish any further ceremonies or rites tending to God's glory, the edifying of his Church, and the due reverence of Christ's holy mysteries and sacraments. And lastly, all laws whereby any other Service, Administration of Sacraments, or Common Prayer were established or set forth to be used within the realm, were declared thenceforth utterly void and of none effect.*

The Queen now also (in 1559) issued her Injunctions to the clergy and laity of the realm. These Injunctions were the same—with some additions and alterations—as those already referred to as being set forth by Edward VI. in the

Sparrow's *Col.* 110.

first year of his reign. Among the additions, the clergy were ordered to use and wear such seemly habits, garments, and such square caps as were most commonly and orderly received in the later part of the reign of King Edward VI., in order that they might be known to the people in all places and assemblies, both in the church and without, and thereby to receive the honour and estimation due to the special messengers and ministers of Almighty God. The laity were commanded to attend their parish church, and overseers were appointed to see that they resorted thither every Sunday and holiday, and that they stayed during the whole of the service; transgressors, after being admonished, were to be reported to the ordinary. Litany and Prayers were to be said in church every Wednesday and Friday. Whenever the name of Jesus should in any Lesson, Sermon, or otherwise in the church be pronounced, due reverence was to be made by all persons, young and old. With regard to the altars, it was ordered that although their removal was "no matter of great moment, so that the Sacrament be duly and reverently ministered," yet for the sake of uniformity throughout the whole realm, and for the better imitation of the law in that behalf, it was ordered that no altar be taken down but by oversight of the Curate of the church and the Churchwardens, or one of them at the least, wherein no riotous or disordered manner was to be used. The Holy Table was to be placed in every church where the altar formerly stood, excepting during the administration of the Holy Communion, when it was to be placed in the most convenient place in the chancel. The Sacramental bread was to be made without any figure thereon, and somewhat larger and thicker than the wafers formerly used in the Private Mass. The form of Bidding Prayer closed the Injunctions.*

Visitors were dispatched through the country with these Injunctions, to whom the Churchwardens of every parish were commanded to deliver "Inventories of Vestments, Copes, and other ornaments, Plate, Books, especially Grayles, Couchers, Legends, Processionals, Manuals, Hymnals, Portuesses (or Breviaries), and such like appertaining to the church."

The visitors in due time arrived at Leicester and inspected our Church of Saint Martin. The Churchwardens' accounts attest both this and the changes which followed :—

1559-60.

P[d] to the visytors for ther dewties		xij.[a]
P[d] for an Injunction boke		iiij.[d]
P[m] to W[m.] Shynglton for a bible & a parapheasis .	iij.[s]	iiij.[d]
P[d] for a sarvis boke	v.[s]	iiij.[d]
P[d] for iij. sawters	v.[s]	j.[d]
P[d] for a ꝓsessioner		ij.[d]
P[d] for a sawter to John Yng		xx.[d]

This Processioner probably contained the short service, directed to be said by the Curate during the Perambulation of the Parish at the time accustomed.

1560-1.

P[d] to John Ynge for ij. chenes & ij. staples for the byble & paraphrasis . . . . ix.[d]

The altars were again, and finally, removed :—

1559-60.

P[d] for drink to iiij. men at tayken downe the alter stones . iij.[d]

* Sparrow's *Col.* 67-85.

Several entries referring to some of the customs peculiar to the Romish system are found curiously intermingled with these marks of change and Reformation. Thus, in 1559-60, are :—

Pd. for a strike of charkolle for hollied fier . . .	iiij.d
Pd. for the offering at SainctÆgetts . . .	ij.s ij.d
Pd. for iij. gallons of ale & ij.d in kakes .	xj.d

The performance of Miracle Plays, already referred to as having been superseded in the reign of Edward VI. by dramatic exhibitions tending to further the Reformation and to throw ridicule upon the superstitions of the Romish system, had been partially revived under Queen Mary. The drama does not, however, appear to have flourished in any form under her gloomy shadow, for whilst in the reigns of her immediate predecessor and successor many visits of players to Leicester are recorded, in the reign of Mary, according to Mr. Kelly,* one visit only of the Queen's players to this town can be authenticated. Upon the accession of Elizabeth stringent measures were adopted against the performance of Miracle Plays and other exhibitions calculated to retard the progress of the Reformation. She, however, as is well known, greatly encouraged dramatic performances, and probably many of those brought before the people in the early part of her reign were of a religious character. Her Majesty's Company of Players visited Leicester in 1560, when they were liberally rewarded by the Corporation.† This was probably the same occasion as that referred to in the following entry in the

* *Ancient Records of Leicester*, 18. † *Ibid.* 19.

Accounts of the Churchwardens of S. Martin's for the year now under notice (1559-60) :—

P[d.] to ye plears for ther paynes . . vij.[d] ob.

Whether this Company performed within the walls of our Church, or whether the Churchwardens added the sum just quoted to the reward bestowed upon the performers by the Chamberlains of the Borough after an exhibition in the Guild Hall, is not clear. It may, however, be stated in favour of the first of these probabilities, that we have already seen that such performances did take place in the Leicester Churches only nine years earlier, and that we know at a much later period (1602) the practice had not entirely ceased ;* added to which the Churchwardens of S. Martin's appear to have been possessed at that period of certain appurtenances or "properties" required in these performances, which it is fair to presume were sometimes used in our church, inasmuch as we find they were occasionally lent, or rather let out, by the Churchwardens to their country neighbours. In 1560-1 they credit their account as having "Rec. for serten stufe lent to the players of fosson vj.[d]"

Whatever may have been the nature of the play performed by the "plears," and for which they were rewarded by the Churchwardens, there is little doubt that the Church of S. Martin was still used (as had been customary in earlier times) for purposes ill suited to the uses for which it was erected. There are two entries, the first in 1559 :—

Recd for the Mawrys daunce of chyldren . . . iij.[s]

* "Paid to Lord Mordens players, because they should not play in the church, xij.[d]"—*Syston Parish Register*, quoted by Mr. Kelly, *Ancient Records, Leic.* p. 18.

The second in 1560:—

Recd of Basforde for the lord and the lady xxj.^{d} ob.

which remind us of the performance of Robin Hood's play probably within the walls of the church.*

There is little to show that many changes were effected in S. Martin's Church during the year 1560-1, beyond some work done in the choir, and to the seating of the church as required for the proper performance of, and participation in, the Reformed Liturgy. There is, however, evidence that Injunctions—probably from Bullingham, the new Bishop of Lincoln, then just consecrated by Archbishop Parker—were received at S. Martin's towards the close of 1560 or early in 1561:—

1560-1.

P^{d} for a Iniunction bocke iiij.^{d}

which appears to have been acted upon in a manner hinting that the parishioners were not in a hurry (as indeed is shown by the very few changes effected in 1560-1) to again get rid of the vestments and other outward appurtenances of the Romish

* For an account of Robin Hood's play see Mr. Kelly's *Notices of Leicester*, 57. We find entries of the Morris dance connected with many parish churches: the Churchwardens of S. Helen's, Abingdon, charge in 1559:—

For two dossin of Morris belles . . . 0 1 0

In the Church Books of Great Marlow, Bucks, we find:—

1593.—Item payde to one for careying of the Morrys coats to Maydenhed 0 0 4

1612.—Item received of the Churchwardens of Bysham, Loane of our Morris's coats and bells . . 0 2 6

—Nichols' *Illus.* 142, 135.

ritual which they had been forced to purchase only a few years previously. Nor was that singular when we recollect the stormy and changeful times in which they lived. Soon after the last-quoted entry the purchase is shown, as already mentioned, of the chains and staples for the Bible and Paraphrase which, until then, apparently, had not been replaced openly in the Church. Soon, however, hesitation seems to have passed away, and the Churchwardens proceeded to carry out the Injunctions of the Queen issued in 1559, and those of their new Protestant Bishop, which it is surmised they had now received, for under date of 1561-2 are the following receipts :—

Rec. of Wylliam gyllot for a suit of vestements .	xlij.*s*	vj.*d*
Rec. of Rycharde blacwyn for sertyn stufe sollde to is father	xx.*s*	
Rec. of Mr John Heyrycke for sertyne stufe shollde to hym by ye Parreshe	viij.*s*	vj.*d*
Rec. of John Yng for benner clouths . . .	ij.*s*	

The Rood Loft was taken down :—

Rec. of Robarde butler for ye Rode loufe . . .	xij.*s*	
Rec. for a Rode clouthe		viij.*d*
P^d.^ to Boddeley for takyn up ye bordes in ye Roode laufe		iiij.*d*
P^d.^ to John Wyntershells and is man . . . . and to make up ye holes where ye baymes was in ye Rode looft		xx.*d*

The Parishioners were not satisfied with carrying out a portion only of the Instructions sent to them; they set about repairing their church and adapting it to the wants of the

Reformed Worship; and here we meet with the first appearance in the existing Records of the Church of a levy, assessment, or Church Rate. The "high" or nave roof requiring a new beam, the Churchwardens credit themselves with :—

Rec. of a sessmente made for ye laying in of ye bayme
in ye hey Roofe . . . . vij.*li* x.*s*

This beam was purchased of "Mr. Templle" for fifteen shillings, and was fetched from the "freers"—probably the Grey Friars which formerly stood on the south side of S. Martin's Church. The seating of the church, too, received much attention, and many seats were fetched from the ancient church of S. Peter, Leicester, which was then standing :—

It' pd to Robarde Butler for hymsellfe and is iij mene
ij dayes about ye fetchyng of ye setes frome sent
Peters and makyn ye Colletters sete . . v.*s* iiij.*d*

The Mayor's seat was "beautified":—

It' pd to hym for garnyssyng of Mr. Mayre's sete xvj.*d*

The Ten Commandments were painted and set up in the Church :—

Itm̃ pd for a tabyll of ye Commandments and a Kal-
lynder . . . . . . xvi.*d*
It' payd to Harre Brynbyster for y frame to y^e^
Commandments . . . . . xiij.*d* ob̃.
P^d^ to Wyllam basforde for wrytyng ye ten Com-
mandments . . . . . . ij.*s*

The "Kallynder" referred to was that set forth by authority

in 1561, showing "the order how the rest of holy scripture (besides the Psalter) is appointed to be read."*

The "brasyn Lactorne" was scoured, "ij. psames bokes w^t^ notts" were purchased, the Priests' and Clerks' surplices were mended, and the choristers had a Christmas dinner:—

Pd for a dynner that wast bestode upone ye Clerkes y^t^ kepe ye qeyre at Crssonmes . . . . vj.^s^ viij.^d^

Means were now also taken by the Corporation to compel the attendance of the householders at the Wednesday and Friday services in the Parish Churches, and to secure the decorous observance of Sundays and holidays. At a Common Hall, on the 20th of February 1562, it was ordered that one person from every house in the town should attend at every sermon on Wednesdays and Fridays, under a penalty of four pence; that no victualler should keep open his door during the service times on Sundays and Holidays, and tradesmen were commanded not to open their shop windows and doors at those times.

The payments by the Churchwardens in each succeeding year show the gradual development of the Reformation in the carrying into effect the Injunctions of the Queen and the Bishop. There are frequent incidental references to changes in the arrangements, and in the fittings of the church, which

* In the Churchwardens' Accounts of S. Helen's, Abingdon, under date 1561, is found:—

"For a table of Commandments and a Kalender, or rewle to find out the lessons and psalmes and for the frame . . . . 2^s^ 0^d^

—*Archæologia*, i. 17.

exemplify this in an unmistakeable manner. Thus in 1562 is found :—

Itm̃ payd to Olevar Carvar for makynge the commvneon table frame . . . . . . ij.[s] viij.[d]

The slab or actual table was frequently loose—as appears to have been the case here—and not attached to the frame upon which it rested. Many of the Tables were so made in the reign of Edward VI., by those who were wishful to express their denial in a belief in the sacrificial character of the Sacrament, and who by so doing kept away from their loosely-formed Tables the stability and character of an Altar. Moreover Tables thus formed would be more easy of removal for use in the administration of the Holy Communion according to the Injunctions. In 1553 we are told John Austen, with others in the church of Adesham, Kent, "tooke up the table, and laid it on a chest in the Chancel, and set the tressels by it."* This kind of Table was specially commanded to be used shortly after the date now under notice (1562) in certain "Articles for Doctrine and Preaching" set forth for due order in the Public Administration of the Holy Sacraments.† A copy of the Office of the Holy Communion was now purchased for use at "God's Board," as the movable altar or table was frequently called :—

1562-3.
Itm̃ payd for a commveneon boke . iij.[s]

The quantity of wine required in the administration of the

* Fox's *Martyrology*, quoted by Bloxam. † Sparrow's *Col.* 121.

Holy Communion at Easter in the same year contrasts forcibly with the Office of the Mass lately suppressed, in which the cup was denied to the laity:—

1562-3.

Itm̃ payd for wyn for the commvneon at Estur iij. quartes of mamse and ix. quarts of claret wyne . iiij.^{s} vj.^{d}

Very considerable repairs were now made in the windows of the church, rendered necessary, probably, by the wanton havoc lately made in the stained glass under colour of demolishing subjects repugnant to the doctrines of the Reformation, and perhaps by the then further removal of such "superstitious pictures:"—

1562-3.

Itm̃ payd for ix. sheyfe of glasse for the Reprations of the glasse wyndowes abowte the chorche . . xxvij.^{s}

Itm̃ payd to Wyllyam Basforde for mendyng the glasse windows abowt the chorche . . . . xx.^{s}

[several other charges about the windows]

It must not however be supposed that these great changes in the Ritual and the Ceremonies of Religion, nor the stringent measures now adopted to enforce the attendance of all at the Sermons preached in the Churches on Wednesdays and Fridays, as well as at the Services on Sundays and Holidays, drove away all festivity and merry-making from among the inhabitants of ancient Leicester. Before leaving the year 1562-3, there is one more entry in the Churchwardens' Accounts which shows this was not the case. It claims our notice, not because it refers to anything specially connected with our

Church—for the custom to which it refers is not even mentioned—but because it recalls one of these holiday scenes which broke the monotony of every-day life in Leicester in the early years of Elizabeth's reign :—

1562-3.*

Itm̄ payd to the Ryngars on blak monday at the commavndemente of mastur mere . . . . . vij.[d]

Black Monday is an old name for Easter Monday.† On that day the Mayor of Leicester and his brethren, attired in scarlet gowns—"Easterday and Blacke munday" being the seventh of the occasions on which scarlet was appointed to be worn—and attended by their proper officers, went to a close bordering upon, or parcel of, Leicester forest, then, and still known as "Black Annis's Bower-close," to take part in a mock hunt of the hare. The custom, according to Throsby, originated probably out of a claim by the Town of Leicester to the royalty of the Forest; and it was managed in this way :—The morning was spent in various outdoor amusements and recreations; about noon a dead cat, which had previously been dressed with anniseed, was fastened to the tail of a horse, and trailed over the ground in a zigzag direction, then through the principal streets of Leicester, and eventually to the door of the Mayor's residence. Shortly after that the dogs—which were lent for the occasion by various county gentlemen, whose huntsmen received gratuities from the Corporation—were

* A high wind appears to have done damage to the Churcht his year—"Itm̄ payd to John Ynge for the nels to nele downe the Leddes that was blone up in the tempaste . . . . xvij.[d]"

† Halliwell's *Dict. Archaisms.*

taken to the spot where the cat had first touched the ground; the hounds of course followed the trail, after them at full speed the huntsmen, who, after chasing the imaginary hare through all the windings of the trail, dashed through the town streets to the Mayor's door, who upon that, as on many other occasions, gave a liberal feast to his friends, which was enlivened by the presence of the Town Waits, who attended dressed in their scarlet gowns, and wearing their silver badges, one of which is now to be seen in our Museum. Now although it is evident from this description that his worship the Mayor did little damage to the game on the Dane's Hills on Black Monday, still upon one occasion at least his worship wished to encourage an idea that a considerable slaughter had taken place, for in the Chamberlain's Accounts for the year 1671 is found the following:—

> Itm̄ pd to two and twenty men that brought and carried hares before Mr. Maior and the Aldermen by Mr. Mayor's order."

The auditors do not appear to have considered this outlay as necessary to support the dignity of the Mayor, or as desirable as a precedent, for the payment was not allowed. Throsby relates that this custom began to fall into disuse after the year 1767, but traces of it existed for many years, and still in a trifling degree exist, in the annual holiday held on the Dane's Hills and the Fosse Road on Easter Monday.*

It was, then, in celebration of this annual holiday that the Mayor (whose close official connection with S. Martin's Church

* Mr. Kelly's *Records of Leicester*, 42.

must have been observed throughout the perusal of these pages) commanded the bells to be rung on Black Monday.

Much diversity now existed among the clergy as to their dress, and the use of other things indifferent in themselves, but a uniformity in the use of which always tends to that decency and order which, from the foundation of the church, has been commended to its members, and specially to its ministers. The Archbishop of Canterbury and some of the Bishops accordingly met, and on the 25th January 1564 were issued "Advertisements partly for the due order of the public administration of the Holy Sacrament, and partly for the apparel of all persons ecclesiastical," the objects of which were to knit together the "state ecclesiastical in one perfect unity of Doctrine . . . in one uniformity of Rites and manners in the ministration of God's Holy Word, in open Prayers and ministration of Sacraments . . . and in one decent behaviour in outward apparel." After several articles for Doctrine and Preaching, are those provided that the Common Prayer be said or sung decently and distinctly in such place as the ordinary should think fit; that the Homilies should be read without any gloss or addition; that the Holy Communion should be administered in Cathedral churches and Colleges upon the first or second Sunday in every month at the least, the principal minister to wear a cope "with Gospelles and Epistoler agreeably, and at all other prayers to be said at that Communion Table, to use no copes but surplices. . . . . That every minister saying any public prayers, or ministring the Sacraments or other Rites of the church, should wear a comely Surplice with Sleeves to be provided by the parish. That the parish should provide a decent Table standing on a frame for the Communion Table, which was to be covered with a Carpet, Silk, or other decent covering, and with a fair linen cloth at the time of ministration. The ten commandments were to be set upon the East wall over the said Table. That the font should not be removed, nor the curate baptize in parish churches in Basons. That when any Christian Body was in passing, the bell should be tolled, and the curate * specially called to comfort the sick person. Many articles follow giving minute directions as to the dress of the clergy.†

These "advertisements" were probably communicated to the Vicar of S. Martin's through his Bishop. There is no entry in the Churchwardens' Accounts notifying the fact, but there are many showing that changes continued to be made, and that therefore the articles just quoted and the Injunctions previously received were, to some extent at least, obeyed: for example, the pulpit and the seats were again repaired :—

1563-4.

Paid to John Inge for neles for mending the little pulpit and the seates	iiij.[d]
P[d] to robert Seckerston for mending of the little pulpit .	iiij.[d]
P[d] to Bodeley for a day worke aboute the seates & formes	viij.[d]

There is nothing in the Records of the Church to give certainty to any opinion respecting the kind of seating used within it down to this date. Although, very generally, the

* That is, the minister of the Parish, whether Rector, Vicar, or stipendiary Curate ; each and all of these were 'Curates'—had the cure of souls. We pray in our Common Prayer for "all Bishops and Curates."

† Sparrow's *Col.* 123

seats in our parish churches down to the close of the sixteenth century were fixtures with low backs and open at the ends, similar to those now in use in S. Martin's Church, still it is thought that at the time of the Reformation the greater proportion at least of the seats in this Church were movable benches without backs, and with low ends finialed, similar to the one or two ancient specimens still preserved in the North Porch. This notion is founded on the fact that whilst the "seats" in the church are often mentioned, at this date appropriated seats or pews are but seldom referred to—we have only "Mr. Mayor's seat" and "Mrs. Mable's seat" mentioned—nor any mention of seat doors or backs; and, besides this, there are two curious entries which it is thought refer to the fixing of the previously movable benches within a kind of ground framework similar to that now in use. Amongst many entries for expenses incurred about the seating are the following, in

1568-9:—

Payd to Webst[r] & hys man for a days worke & a halfe in ground sellyng* ye seats in the Churche . . xxij.[d]
Payd to Bodelay for syllynge ye seates in the Church . vij.[d]

Several years after this (in 1586-7) when "the Mayor's brethren's chapel" was seated, we find more explicit information respecting the seats. There are charges "for a Deske borde to lay there bookes on" . . . . "for too peeces to leane ther bakes to" . . . . "for a seat dore"—then first mentioned—and "a payre of hingels for the same" . . . . "for too square peces of timber of tenn foot long the pece and

* Ground-sill—the Threshold of a door.—Halliwell's *Archaisms*.

vj. inches square for sleepers and sills." These seats were covered with "green flannell at xj.*d* the yard" set on the same with red leather nailed with "vj. hundred of white tax."

This looking forward so many years is, however, transgressing the Chronicle form of these pages. In coming back to the date at which we have now arrived (1563-4), a claimant for a fixed pew is found in the person of the Earl of Huntingdon, who now or shortly after became a parishioner of S. Martin's, and doubtless often attended the services in the parish church :—

1563-4.

P[d] to thomas Oliver for a day worke & a halfe aboute my lorde's seate	x.*d*
P[d] for a skin of red lether and halfe a thousand red neles for mi lorde's seate . . .	xvj.*d*
P[d] for mattes for my lorde's chappell* . .	iiij.*s* iiij.*d*

This seat, like that just noticed as being prepared at a later date for the Mayor's brethren, was lined with green flannel.†

* *Query*—Was the word chapel then used for an enclosed pew? It might be so used from a supposed similarity in the enclosed space to a small chapel divided from the body of the church by parcloses.

† Bloxam, speaking of Pews, remarks: About the commencement of the seventeenth century, our churches began to be disfigured by the introduction of high pews, an innovation which did not escape censure; for, as Weaver observes, "many monuments of the dead in churches in and about this citie of London, as also in some places in the countrey, are covered with seats or pewes, made high and easie for the parishioners to sit or sleep in; a fashion of no long continuance, and worthy of reformation." . . . . In the directions given on the primary visitation of Wren, bishop of Norwich, A.D. 1636, we find an order "that the chancels and alleys in the church be not encroached upon by building of seats;

The Earl of Huntingdon (says Mr. Thompson, in his *History of Leicester*)—who, for several years, was directly connected with this town by his residence here, and in consequence of its contiguity to the castle of Ashby-de-la-Zouch and several of his estates—was the eldest son of Francis, the second Earl of Huntingdon. He was born about the year 1535, and at eighteen years of age was married to a daughter of John Dudley, Earl of Northumberland. A year or two after that date (1557) he obtained a grant of the office of steward of the prince's fee in Leicester. He was one of six brothers, some of whom embraced the Roman Catholic, and others the Protestant religion: his views were puritanical, and he became the leader of that party in the country, as the Earl of Leicester was at Court. He was, in short, a zealous puritan.

In the year 1569 he purchased a house in the Swinesmarket (now called High Street) from John and Ralph Eaton, gentlemen. This building became his residence in Leicester, and was therefore called the "lord's place" or the "great house." It was there he was wont to entertain his friends; and persons of the highest rank were frequently his visitors. The lofty towers of the edifice (of which one still remains) betokened that it was the residence of a man of rank, and rendered it a place of importance in the estimation of the

and if any be so built, the same to be removed and taken away; and that no pews be made over high, so that they which be in them cannot be seen how they behave themselves, or the prospect of the church or chancel be hindered; and therefore that all pews which within do much exceed a yard in height be taken down near to that scantling, unless the bishop, by his own inspection, or by the view of some special commissioner, shall otherwise allow."—*Gothic Architecture*, p. 465-6.

townspeople. It was to that building that the authorities often conveyed their presents of wine and confectionary, when the Earl's noble friends were staying with him, or when he found an asylum for the numerous "hot-headed" puritan preachers, whom he is said to have supported. The Borough Accounts of the period bear ample testimony to the fact that these zealous teachers were on many occasions supplied by the townspeople with presents of malmsey, claret, muscadine, and Gascony wine.* The Lord's Place is referred to once about this date in the Churchwardens' Accounts, thus :—

1567-8.

Payde to the men that brought the churche lether from my lordy's place . . . . ij.^{d}

To return to the Church, we find a Book of Homilies was purchased :—

1563-5.

P^d to robert Wilcockes for a booke of Homelies . iij.^{s} iiij.^{d}

The presence of the poor man's chest is attested in the same year :—

P^d to John Harte for a key for ye poore man's cheste . iij.^{d}

and again, in the following year :—

Pade for mendinge of ij. lokes of the pore man's chast . viij.^{d}

which in obedience to the Queen's Injunctions would be placed in "the most convenient place" in the Church for the reception of alms for the poor.† In the same year one—pro-

* *Hist. Leic.* 256.

† The Poor Man's Chest was usually provided with three locks and keys, one being kept by the Clergyman, the other

bably a offertory box—was purchased with a lock and key to place on the Communion Table :—

1564-5 :—

Pade to Harrie Bringester for a box to set on the Com̄-vnion tabil . . . . xij.[d] (?)

In the year 1563-4 the Churchwardens paid to "Thomas a lester for a booke of Prayers viij.[d]" which was probably a copy of the Form ordered to be used twice a week, and an order of pûblic fast to be used every Wednesday and Friday during the time of the Plague, which then appeared: and again shortly after, they paid fourpence "for a booke of Prayers, being the Form of Thanksgiving to God" set forth in 1564 for the ceasing of the Plague. *

two by the Churchwardens: thus, in the Visitation Articles of the Archbishop of Canterbury, in 1576, is mentioned "a strong chest or box for the almose of the poor, with three locks and keys for the same." Hogarth introduces an alms-chest in one of his pictures, with the aperture covered by a cobweb, thus showing the desuetude into which it had fallen in the eighteenth century.

* The Starlings were the greatest plagues the Churchwardens had to contend with at this period: constant charges, like the following, are found in the accounts :—

1563-4.

P[d] for gunpouder to beate ye starlings from ye churche . ij.[d]

P[d] for lime roddes for the same . . . . ij.[d]

1564-5.

Pade for iiij. boltes for to shoute a starlins . . . . . . vj.[d]

Pade to Mr. Clarke for halfe a pounde of gonpouther for to sheut at starlins a (and) Harte to sheute at am . . . . . ix.[d]

1565-6.

Itm̄ payd for Lyme to catche ye sterlyngs in y[e] churche . . . vij.[d]

1568.

Payd to Edward Pynnar for settynge of lyme rodys abowte the churche wyndows . . . . iij.[d]

A further sale of Brass is referred to :—

1563-4.

Rec. of Willm Shingleton for xxix. pound of brasse . vj.^s

and the following notice of the ancient church of S. Peter is found in the same year :—

Receaved of robert Johnson for ye rent of Sainct Peters church yard this yeare . . . . v.^s

The Cope being, in the advertisements just quoted, limited in its use to Cathedral and Collegiate churches, the churchwardens of S. Martin's now sold the only remaining one in their possession, and with it some albs, the last relics of the gorgeous vestures of the clergy in the church before the Reformation :—

1564-5.

Recetes for chorch Goodes.

Receved of M^r. Gellat for a Kope and ij. obes .	xxvj.^s	x.^d
Receved of Robert Rodes for iiij. towels . .	ix.^s	
Receved of M^r. Darker for a nobe . .	iiij.^s	viij.^d
Receved of John Stanford . .		iiij.^d
Receved of John Wylne for a towill . .		xij.^d

In addition to the Ten Commandments at the eastern end of the Chancel, texts of Scripture were painted upon the walls in various parts of the church, towards the cost of which some of the parishioners subscribed in the following manner :—

1564-5.

Recetes tourd the ritinge of the scripture in chorch.

Receved of Thomas bamford . . .	vj.^d
Receved of William iacson sumakar . .	iiij.^d
Receved of Thomas Robinson . . .	vj.^d

Receved of Harrye Newbolde . iiij.^{d}
Receved of Misteris Asbie . . v.^{d}
Receved of Easter . . . . ? . . . . iiij.^{d}
Receved of fraunsis gellat . . . . iiij.^{d}

It may fairly be presumed that the walls were considerably ornamented with various colours, for the outlay was large :—

1564-5.

Pade to William Bassforde & William Hovit for ritinge ye cripture . . . . . xj.^{s} vij.^{d}
Pade to M^r. Manbie for collers that the penter occapidd aboute the chorche . . . xxiij.^{s} vj.^{d}

In the following year (1565-6), the sale is mentioned of what is the last-mentioned relic of the processions which formed, as has been shown, in earlier times, so important a feature in the church ceremonies :—

1565-6.

Receyved of M^r. Eyrycke for a banner poll . . iiij.^{d}

A new service-book was purchased :—

Itm̃ payd to M^r. Viccor for a servis booke . . viij.^{s}

and several payments in connection with the organ or organs are notified about this time : thus in 1562-3 there is a payment "for polling downe the orgyn chambar;" in 1565-6 William Smyth is compensated "for helpyng aboute ye organs;" but now in 1566-7 the organ was taken down and sold :—

1566-7.

Receyd of Mast^r. Manby for the orgayn pypes and the case and all (things) thereto belonging . . . . v.^{li}
It' payd to Raffe Clarke for makeyng a bylle of the sale of the orgaynes to M^r. Manby . . . . . ij.^{d}

The carved work or coloured decoration upon the pulpit was defaced or destroyed :—

1566-7.

Itm̃ payd for puttynge out the Imageyse out of the pulpyte iiij.*d*

and as if to be rid of even the least outward memorial of the Office of the Mass, the ancient Chalice was sold, and a Communion Cup purchased for use in its place :—

Md. sold by Mr. Willm Manbye by thassent of ye p̄ishe one Chales weyinge xv. ounce 3 quarters aftr v.*s* iiij.*d* the ounce wch comyth to iiij.*li* iiij.*s* iiij.*d* ; and also bought by the sayd Mr. Willm Manbye one Communyon cupp wth a kever duble gylte wayinge xxj. ounce & a halfe at vj.*s* the ounce wch comyth to vj.*li* ix.*s* so yt there remaynythe to be payd unto ye sayd Mr. Willm Manbye over and above ye pc̄e of ye Challs. by ye p̄ishe the some of xliiij.*s* viij.*d*

anno domini, 1567.

It was the custom in the Church of England for the officiating priest in his stall in the Choir to turn towards the people in those parts of the service especially addressed to them, as in the Absolution and in the Lessons, but the other portions of the Service were said by him with his face towards the east; "and very reasonable was the usage," says Bishop Sparrow, "for when the people was spoken to, it was fit to look towards them, but when God was spoken to it was fit to turn from the people." This custom, however, was not found conducive to a proper participation by the people in the Reformed Liturgy, and it was enjoined by some of the Bishops that to the intent the people might the better hear the morning and evening prayer when the same was said by the minister, and be edified thereby, that a decent low pulpit should be erected, and made in the body of the church, wherein the minister should stand with his face towards the people when he read prayer.* This change appears to have been effected in S. Martin's Church about the same time that the Chalice was exchanged for the Communion Cup :—

1567-8.

Payd to Mr. Heyryck for nelys when the mynystars seate was turned . . . . iiij.d

Payd to Robart Krafftys and Wyllm Krafftys for one days worke abowte the seatys where the mynystar and the clark syttyth . . . . . . xx.d

Payd to Edward Dakynge for a mat for ye mynystar and the clark to stand upon at the lecture . . iij.d

The sermon had now undoubtedly become a more important part of the service than formerly, and there is a gentle hint that it had also become longer :—

1567-8.

Payd for a kandlestycke to hange upon the pulpyt . iij.d

This led to the necessity of providing well for the sitting accommodation of the parishioners. S. George's Chapel was now for the first time fitted with seats :—

1567-8.

Payd to Willm Symson & hys man for halfe a dayes woorck abowt the seatys in the church . . viij.d

* Bloxam's *Gothic Architecture*, 461-2.

1568-9.

Itm̃ payd to Rychard Symson & hys son for settyng y[e] seats in Saynt George Chappell for ij. days worke aft[r.] x.[d] ye day for hymselfe and viij.[d] ye day for hys son iij.[s]

Itm̃ payd to Henry Brynghurst for makynge y[e] seats in y[e] churche and other Repacy̅ons in y[e] Churche . . iij.[li]

These alterations, and the increased accommodation provided for the congregation, entailed a considerable expense upon the Churchwardens, who sold their Brass Eagle Lectern to assist in discharging their liabilities :—

1568-9.

Receyved of M[r.] Norres for the Egle . . . iiij.[li] xviij.[s]

Having sold the Eagle upon which the Bible or Service-books had rested for perhaps several centuries, and which some may think might well have been preserved as an outward recognition in the furniture of the Church of that inward bond which united the Church of the Present with the Church of the Past, almost the next entry in the Churchwardens' Accounts goes to show that it was not the desk only upon which the Bible rested which they had ceased to value, but that they neglected to provide a copy of the Bible itself for the perusal of the parishioners, and that they had to pay a fee to the Bishop's Commissary in consequence :—

1568-9.

Itm̃ payd to Meast[r.] Comyssarye for a byble . . xxiiij.[s]

Itm̃ payd to M[r.] Comyssarye when we was suspended for Lackynge a byble and to hys offycers. . . xxiij.[d]

The copy that was lacking was, as just stated, the one commanded to be placed in some convenient place in the Church for the people to resort unto to read, and not the copy for the use of the minister during Common Prayer which our church of course must then have possessed.

This year a list was made of all the Communicants in the parish :—

> Itm̃ to Mr. Browne son for wrytynge all ye names of them yt receyve ye comũnion in ye pꝛshe . . iiij.d

The parishioners in the following year (1569-70), as was usual, made their offerings towards the expenses of the church :—

> Receyved of the yonge people for there churchworke ix.s ob.
> Receyved of the housholders for the whoolle yeere for there churchworke as apperethe . . xlvij.s vij.d

and in that year were removed the remains of the large Cross which until the Reformation stood within the church, and from which the building was, as before mentioned, in earlier times frequently called "S. Cross :"—

1569-70.

> Payd to bodeley for Caryinge ye stones & Ramell away where ye Crosse stoode . . . . . viij.d

In 1570-1 the besom of destruction again passed through the church :—

> Payd unto Wylyame Symsome and Robert Craftes for takynge downe ye thynge over the funt . xij.d

"The thing" was probably a canopy.

> Payed unto Rychard Sympsome and Robert Craftes for a dayes worke for takynge downe of the pertyssons abowt they chansyle . . xx.d

The partitions would be the screen work or parcloses dividing the Chapels of S. Catharine and S. Dunstan from the Chancel.

Payed unto Yreland for cuttynge downe the ymages hedes in the Churche . . . . xx.[d]
Payde unto hyme for cuttynge downe a borde over the funt . . . . xiiij.[d]
Payd unto hyme (Robert Jonson) more for takynge downe the Angels wyngs (&c. &c.) . . xij.[d]

After this use of "axes and hammers," and destruction of the "carved work," the church—as if to obliterate the marks of their destruction—was whitewashed :—

Payed unto Robert Jonson for whyt lymynge of the churche xl.[s]

The necessary money was this year raised as follows, in addition to the ordinary receipts for the use of the bells, etc.—

Receved of M[r.] Manbey for certen wood & a chest . xxx.[s]

The "certain wood," without doubt included the partitions just removed from the Chancel.*

Receved of Thomas Tyers for they toppes of the asshes in the churche yeard . . . . vj.[s]
Receved for churchworkes as apprethe by a booke . xlj.[s]
Receved of the servantes and mens chyldren . . vj.[s] ix.[d]
Receved of y[e] towne for v. mvlyns for genensbrowe wyndoe . . . x.[d]

* Whether the screen dividing the Chancel from the Nave was removed at this time cannot be shown. That there was no intention or wish to remove the screens so placed, when the Rood-lofts over them were ordered to be destroyed,

The Gainsborough was a place of confinement in the south-east part of the market-place, and consisted of a dungeon under ground for prisoners, shops on the ground-floor, which were let to traders, and over them an upper room wherein the justices met.

Receved of the meres brethen for a leave (levy) for the commvnyon cupe & whyt lymyng of the churche xxvj.^{s}
Receved of the eyght & fortey wthin this paryshe for the same . . . . . . xxv.^{s}
Receved of commenets in thys paryshe for ye same . xj.^{s} x.^{d}

The Communion Cup here referred to was the one purchased, as we have seen, in 1567. Among the payments is :—

1570-1.
Payed vnto Mr Manbey for that he were not payed for that that lacked of the Comvnyon cupe as doth appeare by the booke of the accompts . . xliij.^{s}

It was about this time (in 1569) that Archbishop Parker inquired in his Visitation Articles "whether they do minister in any prophane cups, bowls, dishes, or chalices, heretofore used at masse, or els in a decent Communion Cuppe provided and kept for the same purpose only." Archbishop Grindal, in 1576, a few years later, inquires "whether you have in your Parish Churches and Chapels a fair and comely Communion Cup of Silver, and a Cover of Silver for the same, which may serve also for the ministration of the Communion bread."

is evident from the Visitation Articles of Archbishop Parker, A.D. 1569, and those of Archbishop Grindal in 1576, quoted by Mr. Bloxam in the last edition of his *Gothic Architecture*, p. 453.

From this it appears the cover of the cup was to be used as the Paten.

Having thus swept out of the church not only all "superstitious pictures," but apparently almost every work of art or interest, with the almost barbaric ruthlessness which unfortunately usually accompanies great National Religious or Political Revolutions, and from which it were wellnigh a miracle had the Reformation of our church been entirely free,* there is little in the Records of the Church during the remaining earlier years of Elizabeth's reign to call for special remark; indeed there seems to have been so little for the churchwarden to do congenial to the feelings of the times, or rather perhaps so many things for him to do of an unpleasant nature, that we find in the year 1570-1 it was necessary to pass an order for the infliction of a fine upon such as should refuse to take the office when elected thereto. This is notified in

* That this stripping of the Churches of all comeliness and beauty was, as is well known, contrary to Queen Elizabeth's own feelings and wishes, is shown by the following remarks in a letter written by her to the Commissioners for causes ecclesiastical in the year 1560: "In sundry churches and chappels where divine service, as prayers, preaching, and ministration of the sacraments be used, there is such negligence and lacke of convenient reverence used towardes the comelye keeping and order of the said churches, and especially of the upper parte called the chauncels, that it breedeth no small offence and slaunder to see and consider on the one part the curiositie and costs bestowed by all sortes of men upon there private houses, and the other part the unclean or negligent order or spare keeping of the house of prayer, by permitting open decaies, and ruines of coveringes, walls, and wyndowes, and by appointing unmeet and unseemly tables, with fowle clothes for the communion of the sacraments, and generally leavynge the place of prayers desolate of all cleanlyness and of meet ornaments for such a place, whereby it might be known a place provided for divine service."—Bloxam, 451.

the following quaint memorandum at the close of the Accounts for that year :—" Further y[t] y[s] agreed by M[r.] Mayor & hys brethren yf anye man doe refuse to be churchwarden when he y[s] elected shall paye for the fyrst tyme x.[s] and the money to y[e] use of y[e] churche ;" and in the following year, 1571-2, we find two parishioners were accordingly fined for refusing to fill an office which every churchman ought to consider it an honour and a privilege to undertake.

Among those unpleasant duties would be the subjection to the annoyances arising from the extreme watchfulness of the ecclesiastical authorities. " The people were not merely superintended, but were teased and irritated by perpetual visitations and inquiries often about trifles." One of the disagreeable duties of the Churchwarden of S. Martin, too, in the reign of Elizabeth, was probably to note the attendance or non-attendance of the inhabitants, or a proper proportion from each house, at the Wednesday and Friday sermons, and to report defaulters. This compulsory attendance was again more stringently enforced by the Corporation a few years later, for at a Common Hall held on the 18th November in the eighteenth year of Elizabeth's reign, during the mayoralty of Mr. Richard Davye, it was agreed :—

> "That there shall upon evỹe wensdaye and evīe ffrydaye in the weeke come to the Churche of S[t.] M'tins to the Sarmond twoe or one att the leaste of evye howsholde w[th]in this Towne & subbarbe, and there to tarrie duringe the tyme of the s[r]mond uppon payne of xij.[d] for evye defalte to the vse of the Poore." *

* *Hall Book*, vol. ii. 260, in MS.

Shortly after this (which shows incidentally that S. Martin's was then considered the principal church in the town) the Corporation again directed no one to drink or tipple in ale-house or inn on Wednesday, Friday, or Sunday, during divine service.*

A few entries more may be quoted significant of the times, and then this Chronicle must—having arrived at the period limited in the title—be brought to a close. To pursue the subject further would be to trench upon another important era in the History of our Church—an era marked by the gradual development of that schism, the seeds of which were sown in Zurich and Geneva, and the fruits of which were the overthrow in this country of the externals of the National Church, and the rebellion against, and eventual execution of, the King :—

1573-4.

P[d] to Edward Howet for making a fote for the beare (bier) . . . . ij.[d]

1575-6.

Payd for an houre glasse . . iiij.[d]

This was to place upon the pulpit to regulate the length of the sermon.

1581-2.

Paid for an Homyley booke called Bullingers decades viij.[s]

1583-4.

The Mayor's seat was "trimmed" etc., at a cost of 8s. 6d.

* *Hall Book*, vol. ii. 260, in MS.

This year the Churchwardens received certain Interrogatories respecting the state of the church :—

Paid for ye bishop interagotories vj.^d^

to which they made a presentment, upon which they had of course to pay another fee :—

Payd to ye bishop clark ffor his hand to o^r.^ presentment iiij.^d^

At the end of this year's Accounts is the following Inventory of goods belonging to the Church :—

So remayneth to the churche at ye fote of y^is^ accompt xlix.^s^ iiij.^d^ Also a Comūnion Cupp of sylver wth a kever and the same dubble gyld wth a napkyn. And bullyngers Decades and the injuncksons.

A Carpet for y^e^ Comn̄yon Table
ij. g^t^ bybells
an old Tabell Clothe
and a new
a surples
vij. cushins

SECTION VII.

GUILDS.

THE Anglo-Saxon word from which "Guild" or "Gild" is derived signifies "to pay," and a Guild was an Association formed for specific purposes, towards the attainment of which all the members contributed their proper and fixed payments in money. The date of the origin of Guilds or of their introduction into England is unknown, but it is evident that they were extensively founded in Anglo-Saxon times, and long before any existing Charter or License for their foundation was granted.

Guilds were of two kinds, Religious and Secular. The former embracing men of various trades and occupations, banded together for their common spiritual benefit in this life and after death, and for their decent and orderly interment at their decease; the latter comprising men all of one calling, united chiefly for the purpose of watching over the interests of their particular craft. These Secular Guilds subsequently merged into the Trade Companies.

In the Middle Ages almost every church had one, some several, Religious Guilds connected with it. Thus in Leicester—whilst S. Mary's Church had its Guild of the Holy Trinity, S. Margaret's its Guild of S. Margaret and S. Catharine, S.

John's Chapel that of St. John, All Saint's Church the Fraternity of the Assumption of the Blessed Virgin Mary—S. Martin's Church had its Guilds of Corpus Christi and S. George. On the entry of a brother—women as "sisters," were also admitted—into the Religious Guild, he promised to be faithful to the Brotherhood, and to pay all due respect to its superiors. After the payment of his Guild dues, his Deed of Admission, signed by the master and wardens, and sealed with the common seal of the Fraternity, was given to him. His name was also registered upon a tablet at the altar of the Guild Chapel, in order that he—in common with all the living and dead members—should be prayed for by name by the priest every day in his celebration of Mass.* For every Guild—and this, as was before intimated, was the chief object of all Religious Fraternities—possessed its Guild Priest or priests, whose duties were to say Mass every day for the welfare of the living, and for the forgiveness of the souls of departed members and benefactors. Once every year, if not oftener, all the members met and celebrated in their Chapel, Evensong for the dead,† and on the following morning, *Dirige* or Matins for the dead, followed by a High Mass of *Requiem*‡ for their deceased brethren, whose names were all read out of the bead-roll by a priest from the pulpit. On these occasions the members of the Guild appeared in their livery, for each Guild

* In 1514 a Table was ordered to be made with the names of all the brethren and sisters, quick and dead, of the Guild of the Holy Trinity in St. Mary's Church Leicester, and was to stand on the Trinity altar.—*Throsby*, p. 221.

† Called "*Placebo*," because such was the first word of that Service.

‡ *Requiem*, the first word of the Introit.

chose a peculiar livery or dress, which the brethren wore at their meetings, when they walked in procession, assembled for worship before their own altar in the Church, held their annual festival, or paid the last solemn marks of respect to a deceased member at his burial. This dress consisted of a vesture or gown of one, and a hood usually of some other, colour. Each member also wore upon his sleeve, or other prominent part of his dress, a badge or cognizance, called the cognizance of the Guild, generally representing the figure or well-known symbol of the saint under whose special patronage and protection the Guild was placed, and whose name it bore. The principal meeting in the year was upon the Festival of the Titular Saint, when, after solemn processions and attendance at the services in the Church just referred to, the brethren and sisters, attired in their distinctive dress, met and feasted together in the Hall of the Guild, when the Fraternity was rich enough to possess one, or in some other appointed and convenient place. On the following day the members again met for the discharge of the business of the Guild—the arrangement of its finances and the appointment of its officers, which latter were usually a master and two stewards, to which were added, in the richer Guilds, one or more rent-gatherers or collectors. These officers rendered yearly a rental and a statement of receipts and payments, and of the amount of money remaining in their hands belonging to the Guild.*

* The Rules of the Guild of S. Margaret and S. Catharine, Leicester, enjoined . . . "the brethren and sisters, that twice a year they should meet upon the feasts of S. Margaret and S. Catharine, to hear high mass and likewise make offering; and at the feast of S. Margaret, all of the society, who were willing and

Upon the death of a member, as before intimated, the brothers and sisters of the Guild (some Guilds possessed special mourning-gowns for the occasion), walking in procession with torches or lights burning, bore the coffin containing the corpse (over which the Guild hearse-cloth* had been thrown) to the church, and on the following day they again assembled to hear Matins for the dead, when sometimes Mass was also performed and an offering made by all present of the mass-penny for the good of the departed soul. When a member died within a given distance from the town wherein the Guild was founded, the corpse was fetched by the members or met by them at the gates, and attended in the same manner as if the death had occurred within the walls.†

Some of the Guilds in our large towns, being wealthy, had a house set apart for poor members, who were also provided with food and clothing, and who were summoned twice a day to "bid their beads" in the chapel of the Guild for all the departed, as well as living, fellows of their Fraternity. In all Guilds—whether a house was possessed or not—the decayed, aged, or sick members were always relieved so far as the funds would permit.‡ Guilds, too, sometimes assisted in

able, should moreover put on their habits and eat together, and on the morrow should meet for reckoning and discharging the expense."

* See catalogue of Loan Exhibition, South Kensington, for a description of some of these cloths.

† The Guild of S. Margaret and S. Catharine, Leicester, provided that if a member died within the space of twelve leagues around the town he should be brought by his brethren to Leicester, with torches, to the Church of S. Margaret.

‡ The Rules of the Guild of S. Margaret and S. Catharine, Leicester, ordained that "if any brother or sister shall be in poverty by reason of sickness, or by robbers, or through false men, or by fire, or by water, he shall have the assistance of the association."

providing additional priests for the parish church, purchased vestments and requisites for the altar, service books and the like, inserted stained-glass windows, and in other ways provided for the decent adornment of the House of God.*

Such is a scanty outline of the objects for which the Religious Guilds were founded, and of their mode of procedure. These will be shown in some degree by a reference to the original documents, which will be brought under notice presently, relating to the Guilds of Corpus Christi and S. George in S. Martin's Church and parish, and could be abundantly verified by extracts from manuscripts relating to Guilds elsewhere existing in mediæval times. Only one extract need however be here given; it is a curious one, and shows perhaps in as succinct a manner as possible the constitution of these Fraternities, and the benefits, real or supposed, accruing to their members. Stow, in his *Survey of London*,† speaking of the Guild of S. Barbara in S. Catharine's Church near the Tower, gives its Articles as follow:—

"Who so ever by the grace of God is dysposyd to entre into the blessyd fraternyte of the Gylde of our gloryous Savyour cryst Jhũ, and of the blessyd vyrgin and martyr Saynt Barbara foundyd in Saynt Kateryns church next the towre of London, and wyll have the pardon, prevylege and profet thereto graunted and ordeynd: must pay to the seyd fraternyte the some of x.^{s} iiij.^{d} sterlynge at his first enterynge, if

* The brethren of the Guild of the Assumption of the blessed Virgin Mary, in All Saints' Church, Leicester, agreed among themselves, by a subscription of one penny each every Sunday, to raise a fund for the purchase of one vestment, one chalice, one missal, and other ornaments for the altar. See also examples given in Dr. Rock's *Church of our Fathers*, ii. 439.

† Strype's Ed. book ii. p. 7.

he will; or ellys by leaser within the space of vii. yeres; that is to say, at his first entering xii.[d] and every quarter followyng iiij.[d] tyll the seyd x.[s] iiij.[d] be payd in mony, plate or any other honest stufe. And at the first payment he or she that so enteryth in to the seyd fraternyte, whether they be weddyd or single, shall receyve a letter with the seal of the warden collectour, which warden collectour shall receyve his name, and bring it to the auter of the glorious Jhũ and Seynt Barbara in Seynt Kateryns church before seyd, and thereto be regestryde; and there shall be prayd for dayly be name: And when the last payment of the some of x.[s] iiij.[d] is payd, then the seyd brother or syster shall receyve a letter with the common seal of the seyd fraternyte and place with the masters name and wardens therein for the tyme beyng. Whereby he shal have a great commodyte and suerty of lyvyng: that is to sey that yf the seyd brother or syster fall in decay of worldely goods, as by sekenes or hurt by the warrys, or uppon the land, or see, or by any other casualte or meanes fallen in poverte: Then yf he brynge the seyd letter sealyd with the seyd common seal, the master and al the company shal receve him favorably, and there he shal have every weke xiiij.[d] house rome and beddinge, and a woman to wash his clothys, and to dresse his mete: and so to continue yere by yere, and weke by weke, durynge his lyfe by the grace of Almighty Jhũ and Seynt Barbara."

Corpus Christi Guild, Leicester.

However much obscurity may be thrown over the origin of some of the Religious Guilds founded in this country, there is (fortunately for our present purpose) none whatever as to the time when this Guild was commenced in S. Martin's Church, by whom it was originated, nor as to the objects contemplated by its founders in its formation.

By the certificate of Henry de Deby and Thomas Wakefield, Wardens of the Guild in the reign of Richard II.,* is shewn that in 1343 Ralph de Ferrers, Chevalier; John Hayward of Leicester, receiver; Gilbert le Avener; John Porter, clerk; Geffrey de Kent; Roger de Knyghtcote (Knighton?); John Martyn; John de Cliveshall (or Elmeshall); Richard Leverych; Thomas de Deby; John Ive the elder; John de Louesby the elder; and William de Dunstable, determining to establish a Guild in the Church of S. Martin of Leicester, commenced one "in honour of the Precious Body of our Lord Jesus Christ, and his benign mother the Holy Mary and all other saints," upon the articles and in the manner following :—

"In the name of God, Amen. This is the foundation of the Fraternity, begun in honour of the solemn Feast of the Consecration of our Lord Jesus Christ and His Blessed and Precious Body and Blood, and of His Glorious Mother the Virgin Mary and all the Saints of heaven, by the grace of His Holy Spirit, and by the good devotion of the founders who by one [common] assent and one will ordained in amendment of their lives, and for the salvation of their souls and [the souls of] their ancestors, their fathers and mothers and all their friends, and the souls of their successors and all their friends. And the said Fraternity for the time to come must take care that all the articles and ordinances by them made for the sustaining of the said Fraternity be firmly kept and held by them and by their successors without any contradiction for ever. And first this foundation commences at the said feast in the year of our said Lord Jesus Christ one thousand three

* Written in Norman-French and preserved in the Miscellanea of the Tower of London (bundle 308), now first translated and printed from the original document.

hundred forty and three when by common assent and one will agreed to between them, they ordain and grant for them and their successors the articles and these articles of their foundation to keep up and maintain in manner as follows:—

"It is ordained also by the entire assent of all the founders that there shall be a singing Chaplain of the community for all those of the Fraternity, and for all its benefactors, both for the living and dead, and more especially for all those who first shall commence this Fraternity, and for the souls of their ancestors, and for all those who hereafter shall keep up and maintain it. That the names of the founders be written upon a tablet before the Chaplain, and named every day in his Mass. And let the Chaplain whoever he be hereafter have this charge.

"Also it is provided and agreed that each of them (that is, each member of the Guild) have one torch of pure—'*honeste*'—wax to carry in the honour of God and the solemn Feast of the Consecration of the Blessed Flesh and Blood of our Lord Jesus Christ, and that such torch be saved for all the year ensuing. And if it chance that any of the brethren of the Fraternity be summoned at the command of God (that is, die), whatever hour it be, that every one shall come to the *dirige*, and also on the morrow to the mass with his torch.

"It is ordained and agreed also that the founders aforesaid have the sovereign keeping and ordering of things and points touching the said Fraternity throughout all their lives without contradiction of those who hereafter shall be included in the Fraternity: and that at such time as any one of them succumbs to the will of God that the others elect one from the Community who shall be meet and suitable in his place.

"Also it is agreed that if any of the Fraternity fall into poverty or sickness by which he cannot gain his livelihood it is accorded that he be aided out of the common stock so long as it and the company are able to accord it, until he be cured of his malady or poverty, and that they of the brotherhood shall visit him and inspect him severally at their pleasure to be that as is aforesaid.

"It is agreed and accorded also that every one at the Feast of the Consecration shall render account of how much he has received or levied upon the Community, and also of what he shall have disbursed for the Community, and that which may remain shall be at the ordering of the sovereign wardens; and on that day there shall be election made of them who shall be guardians or receivers for the year to come unless they have reasonable cause of impediment that they cannot make election on that day, then at the least within fifteen days after they shall make it.

"Also it is provided and agreed that all those of the Fraternity shall assemble themselves in a certain place according as they shall have notice at three times in the year, to have consultation of their common business, that is to say, at the Feast of All Saints, Christmas, and Easter, and that every one for himself that is of the Fraternity, bring with him his proportion without further delay.

"Likewise it is agreed and arranged that if it occur that any one who is received into the Fraternity be an evil doer or an evil speaker, or a contradictor to the articles of the foundation, and he be twice warned by the sovereigns of the Fraternity and be unwilling to justify himself, and the third time be charged before the company of the trespass, that then he be ousted from the Fraternity for ever; and also the penalty be inflicted on those who three times are warned to come to the common assembly and do not come, if they have no reasonable impediment as is above said."

Then follows an article on the admission of members, by which is shewn that none "from without" were admitted as members of the Guild, without the permission of the majority of the founders or their successors.

Having commenced the Guild and drawn up their regulations for its management, the originators were joined by others, anxious, with themselves, to obtain those benefits which singly they would have found it difficult and expensive to obtain, but which by combination were placed within the reach of all the members. These successful applicants for admission "from without" were William de Humberstone; John de Petlyng, mercer; William de Wakefield; John Ive junior; Richard de Stafford; Robert de Coventre; and Roger del Waynhous de Leycestre. This accession of members, and consequently of influence and income, caused the founders to extend the very modest proposal contained in their first Articles of having one singing Chaplain to "founding one Chantry of four Chaplains to celebrate divine service;" and it now became necessary, in order to enable the founders to purchase and endow the Guild with land and other real property, to obtain from the King a Licence for its formation, and Letters Patent permitting them to purchase lands and rents in Leicester and its suburbs for the benefit of the chaplains and their successors for ever, notwithstanding the Statute of Mortmain then in force.

Application was accordingly made to Edward III. for the desired document, who by Letters Patent, dated at Westminster on the 19th of August in the twenty-third year of his reign (1349), granted to the founders just quoted by name, "of his special grace" and in consideration of forty marks, "to found a certain Chantry of four Chaplains for celebrating divine service [every day for ever] in the honour of the Precious Body of our Lord Jesus Christ and the Glorious Virgin Mary his Mother and all the Saints, in the Church of

S. Martin of Leicester," for his salvation and that of Henry, Earl of Lancaster, Henry de Walton, archdeacon of Richmond, and the founders of the Guild whilst they were living, and for their souls when they should be taken away from this world, and for the souls of their progenitors then "long since deceased." These Letters also gave power to the founders to give and assign to the Chaplains and their successors land, tenements, and rents to the value of Twenty pounds in Leicester and its suburbs, not held by the king *in capite*, to celebrate divine service in the manner just described; and to the Chaplains power was granted to receive and hold the same notwithstanding the Statute of Mortmain touching lands and tenements, etc. etc.*

Almost immediately after obtaining these Letters Patent, the founders purchased six messuages, fifty-three shops (*quinquaginta et tres shopas*), six tofts and a half, and thirty-six shillings of rents, with appurtenances in Leicester and its suburbs, and a valuation of the same was made by inquisition and returned into Chancery by John de Wyndesore, Escheator in the County of Leicester. From this Return it appears that this property—not including the thirty-six shillings arising from rents—was worth sixty-two shillings and eightpence yearly. The king then issued further Letters Patent, dated Westminster, 2 February 1350-1, empowering the Chaplains of the Fraternity and their successors celebrating divine service as before mentioned to hold the same to the value of ten marks per annum, in part satisfaction of the twenty pounds which under the Statutes of the Guild they were permitted

* Miscellanea in Tower, bundle 308.

to receive yearly when the funds would allow of that full stipend.*

Shortly afterwards the property of the Guild had increased to the annual value of £6 : 8 : 7, in addition to thirty-two shillings of rents which it was the intention of the founders to amortise for the support of the chaplains. It, however, was found early in the reign of Richard II. that this had not been done, and moreover that Ralph de Ferrers was the only survivor of the original founders of the Guild. It therefore became necessary to appoint new feoffees. Ralph de Ferrers accordingly infeoffed Henry de Deby, Thomas Wakefield, William Humberstone, Ralph Fisher, John Cook, John London, Adam Shōpp, John Sporiour, Thomas Wynger, and William Turnour, to accomplish the intentions of the Founders, and to carry out the objects of the Guild.

At that time Henry de Deby and Thomas Wakefield were wardens of the Fraternity, and in their Certificate already quoted from† they state that during the first four years the brethren and sisters provided only one chaplain, since which time two chaplains singing divine service had been appointed, and the affairs of the Fraternity had been managed by two wardens. At that time, too, for reasons not given, the property of the Guild had much diminished, for the wardens state that they "have no goods or chattels or possessions, except to the value of twenty shillings, for the sustenance of the beforesaid chaplains." The annual Procession of the members in their gowns, carrying their torches, and bearing aloft the Host, and their feasting together afterwards, was not, however, neg-

* Pat. 25 Edward III. ps. i. m. 37. † See page 185.

lected, for the wardens go on to say: "Also at the feast of the Body of our Lord Jesus Christ, at the observance of the same feast, the said brethren and sisters have used every one of them to carry a torch going in procession with the said Precious Body of our Lord Jesus Christ each time in a company. And after procession so made at the observance of the same feast, each time they have used to be at an eating together, every one paying for their vesture and eating."*

This Certificate of the Wardens of the Guild, which was written early in the reign of Richard II., appears to have been a preparatory step towards a legal recognition of a considerable change in the circumstances of the Fraternity which—through the liberality of two townsmen—was shortly afterwards effected. These two townsmen were William de Humberstone and John Ive Junior, who, wishing to give to the Guild certain property, applied to the king—Richard II.—for permission to do so. This property consisted of eleven messuages, six shops, and eleven pounds six shillings of rents, with appurtenances, in Leicester and its suburbs—a considerable sum of money at that time. The King (in accordance with the legal usage of the period) issued his Writ in the sixteenth year of his reign to Thomas Ralegh, his Escheator in this county, to hold an Inquisition in Leicester to inquire whether the king or the country would suffer damage, should the gift be allowed. Accordingly, on the Thursday next before the feast of S. Lawrence in that year (10th August 1392), the Escheator summoned John Peterburgh and others as jurors before him, who said upon their oaths that it would not be to the prejudice

* Miscellanea of the Tower, bundle 308.

of the king or other men, if he granted permission to William Humberstone and John Ive the younger to give and assign the property just mentioned to the "four chaplains of a certain chantry founded in honour of the Precious Body of our Lord Jesus Christ and the Glorious Virgin Mary and all Saints in S. Martin's Church of Leicester, celebrating divine service every day in the church aforesaid, in manner aforesaid for ever for the welfare of . . . . and of the aforesaid William and John whilst they shall be in life, and for their souls when they shall have been withdrawn from this world," as well as for the souls of those mentioned in former documents, and which were here again quoted by name. The jurors further stated that the property sought to be given to the Guild was worth £19 : 16 : 0 annually, and that the donors possessed other property in Leicester sufficient for the customs and services, and for the performance of dues and all other burdens which they had been accustomed to sustain in suits, views of frankpledge, aids, tallages, watchings, fines, redemptions, amerciaments, contributions, and all other things whatsoever: and further that the donors could still be put upon assizes, juries, and other recognisances, just as they were accustomed to be put before the donation and assignment. This Injunction was sealed by the jurors and returned to Chancery.*

Very soon after the receipt of the information gained by this Inquisition, Richard II. issued his Letters Patent, dated at Beverley on the 7th September in the same year (1392), by which he gave licence to William de Humberstone and John Ive the younger to assign the property with which they

* Inq. ad quod dampnum, classed as Inq. p. m. 16 Richard II. No. 135.

wished to endow the Guild to its chaplains and their successors.*

This increased wealth rendered it important that upon the death of Richard II. and the accession of his successor, the rulers of the Guild should take steps to secure a confirmation of the privileges previously granted to them. They at once applied to the new king, Henry IV., for his ratification of these Letters Patent issued by his predecessor. He did this by granting confirmatory Letters, dated at Westminster the 4th of July in the second year of his reign (1401), in which he stipulated that the chaplains of the Guild should pray for his welfare, and for that of his most dear sons, Henry, Prince of Wales, Thomas, High Steward of England, John and Humphrey, and for his most dear daughters Blanche and Philippa. Some idea may be formed as to the progress made by the Guild by the numbers to be prayed for, mentioned in these Letters Patent, compared with the number mentioned in previous ones. Thus in the Letters just referred to as granted by Richard II. in 1392, are found—irrespective of the king and his friends—nineteen names, and all the benefactors of the Guild; whilst in these confirmatory Letters of Henry IV. sixty-four persons are mentioned, irrespective of the members of the royal family, and the masters, brethren and sisters of the Guild.†

* Quoted in Pat. Roll, 2 Henry IV. ps. i. m. 34.

† Pat. Roll, 2 Henry IV. ps. 1 m. 34. As this document may possess (on account of the names mentioned therein) some interest, a translation from the original is here given :—

"The King to all to whom, etc. greeting. We have inspected letters patent of our Lord Richard, late king of England after

This shows clearly that not only the wealth but the numbers of the Guild had increased rapidly. Indeed, during

the Conquest the Second, made in these words: Richard by the grace of God King of England and France and Lord of Ireland To all to whom these present letters shall come, greeting. Know ye that whereas of late by our Letters Patent we have granted and given licence for us and our heirs in as much as in us is to William de Humberstone and John Ive junior that they should found a certain chantry of four chaplains to celebrate divine service every day for ever in honour of the precious body of our Lord Jesus Christ and the glorious Virgin Mary his mother and all saints in the Church of Saint Martins of Leycester for the welfare of us and the aforesaid William and John whilst in life and for our souls when from this world they shall have departed, and for the souls of our grandfather Lord Edward late King of England and Henry de Walton late archdeacon of Richmond, Ralph de Ferrers chevalier, John Hayward of Leicester receiver, Gilbert de Avenir, John Porter clerk, Geffrey de Kent, Roger de Knyghtcote, John Martin, John de Elmeshale, Richard Leverych, Thomas de Deby, John Ive senior, John de Louseby senior, William de Dunstable, John de Petlyng, mercer, William de Wakefield, Richard de Stafford, Robert de Coventre, and Roper de Waynhous of Leicester, and of all benefactors of the chantry aforesaid, and of all faithful departed, and to give and assign lands, tenements, and rents to the value of £20 per annum with appurtenances in Leicester and the suburbs of the same town and elsewhere which are not held of us in capite; to have and to hold to the aforesaid chaplains themselves and their successors chaplains of the said chantry to celebrate in form aforesaid for its maintenance for ever, the statute of lands and tenements in mortmain etc. notwithstanding as in our letters aforesaid more fully is contained: We willing our grant aforesaid to be freed in due effect have granted and given licence for us and our heirs as much as in us is to the aforesaid William de Humberstone and John Ive junior that they may give and assign eleven messuages six shops and £11 : 6 : 0 of rent with appurtenances in Leicester and its suburbs which are held of us and which are worth per annum in all issues about the true valuation of the same beyond the rent aforesaid eight pounds and ten shillings as by an inquisition thereof taken by our command before Thomas de Reylegh our Escheator in our county of Leicester and returned into our chancery is found: to have and to hold to the aforesaid chaplains and their successors chaplains of the said chantry to celebrate divine service in the church aforesaid for the welfare and souls aforesaid and for the soul of

this, the fifteenth century, it attained to a degree of importance, not only as to its possessions and its numbers, but also as to the

Henry late Earl of Leicester every day in full satisfaction of the lands tenements and rents to the value of the aforesaid £20 per annum for ever. And to the said chaplains in like manner have we by the tenor of presents given special licence that they may receive and hold the messuages shops and rents aforesaid with appurtenances from the aforesaid William de Humberstone and John Ive junior for them and their successors aforesaid in form aforesaid for ever as is aforesaid the statute aforesaid notwithstanding; not willing that the aforesaid William de Humberstone and John Ive junior or their heirs or the aforesaid chaplains or their successors by reason of the premises by us, or our heirs, justices, escheators, sheriffs or other our bailiffs or ministers whomsoever may be oppressed troubled or aggrieved in any way. Saving however to the capital lords of that fee services therein due and accustomed. In witness of which thing we have caused to be made these our letters patents. Witness our self at Beverley the 7th day of September in the 16th year of our reign.

"Now we ratifying the letters aforesaid and all things in them contained, do accept approve and confirm those things as pleasing to us and our heirs, as much as in us is, even as the letters aforesaid reasonably do testify. Willing moreover that the aforesaid chaplains and their successors should pray for our welfare and that of our most dear sons Henry Prince of Wales, Thomas High Steward of England, John and Humphrey and our most dear daughters Blanche and Philippa, as well as of Richard Grey of Codnor chevalier, Henry de Beaumont chevalier, William Ferrers of Groby chevalier, Thomas Rempston chevalier, Thomas Langley clerk, John Elnet clerk, Richard Elnet archdeacon of Leicester, Simon Bache clerk, John Yereburgh clerk, John Neuton clerk, William Wynsseby clerk, Richard Kirkdone clerk, William Decon clerk, William Smyth clerk, Ralph Skefyngton, John Cook and Alice his wife, John Losebay and Agnes his wife, Thomas Wakefield and Avice his wife, Richard Knyghton, Roger Humberston and Margaret his wife, John Chirche and Katharine his wife, Richard Braunston and Agnes his wife, Nicholas Barbour, John London and Elizabeth his wife, Robert Skylington and Johan his wife, Adam Cook and Avice his wife, Thomas Atte Halle and Agnes his wife, John Flekeney and Margaret his wife, Richard Thryngston and Joan his wife, John Monke and Margaret his wife, William Maltby and Margaret his wife, Richard Chaloner and Emma his wife, William Turnour, Margaret Chapman, Emma Humberstone, Cecily Sproddeburgh, John Barbour, Isabella Brown, John Freman,

prominent part which its masters were called upon to take in public matters connected with local government, which rendered it the most influential and conspicuous of the many Fraternities which, as we have seen, abounded in Leicester in mediæval times. This is curiously evidenced by a somewhat long entry in the *Hall Book* of the Corporation of Leicester, made on the 18th of March 1477, which, notwithstanding its length, is here extracted from the original manuscript volume, as giving not only information respecting the position at that time held by the masters of Corpus Christi Guild, but as also giving a curious insight into the management of municipal matters, and into the methods adopted by the mayor and his brethren to uphold their dignity, and to secure the respect and honour which they considered due to themselves and to their office :—

To the Honoure and louing of almyghty god and increce of vnite and worshypp of the Maire and of his Bredeř of the bynke of the Town of leycestr' And further more commendacōn in the fest of Seynt Edward the kyng in the xvij. yere of the regne of oure liege lord kyng Edwarde the ffourth by the assent and agrement of John Reynolds then being maire of the same Town and of all his seid

Avice Barewell, Ellen Clipston, Avice Fisher, William Dalby, Matilda Nicholl, Ralph Hurleman, Thomas Wenger, Thomas Denton and Agnes his wife, and John Northburgh, and the masters, brethren and sisters of the fraternity and guild of the Glorious Body of our Lord Jesus Christ and the Glorious Virgin Mary his mother who are now in the Church aforesaid or who for the time shall be whilst we shall be in life, and for our souls when from the light of this world we shall have departed, as well as for the souls of all benefactors of the chantry aforesaid, and of all the faithful departed for ever according to the ordinance of the masters of the Guild aforesaid therein to be performed. In witness of which etc. Witness the king at Westminster the 4th day of July.

"By writ of Privy Seal and for 20 shillings paid into the hanaper."

Breder it was ordeyned and stablisshed hereafter that none of the seid Brether' in no wise secretly ne openly in no cause ne mater repreve rebuke ne dishonoure by worde ne dede none of them oder but that eūy of them in absence and in psēnce reporte and sey wele be oder on payne of fforfete vn to the chambur of the Towne of leycestr eūy of them the ffirst tyme knowen with the faute—iij.[s] iiij.[d] the secunde tyme —vj.[s] viij.[d] and thoes paynalties forthwith to be leueued by the maire and the ij. mastres of Corpus Xp̄i gylde for the tyme beyng of the Trespāson and put into the Tresoure of the Towne of leycestr. And yf any of them so forfett and at the disire of the maire and the seid maistres wilnot pay his paynalte then he to be com̄itted by the maires comāundement to warde there to contynue w[t]oute redempcōn till the payne be leueyed. And yf the maire be lacheous in execucōn on that behalf the same peynaltiez then to be leueied upon the maire by the maisters of Corpus Xp̄i gylde for the tyme being. And yf any of the seid Brether be obstynate and wilnott be reconciled and . . . . by the to paynalties affore noted the third tyme he to be deposed and discharged of the Bynke and excluded of the ffeleship of the Breder for eū more.

"And if it so fortune that eny of the seid Breder have any resonable cause or mater to other, eny of them y[t] fyndeth hym greued showe his cause or greff to the maire and masters of Corpus Xp̄i gylde for the tyme being. And the maire and masters in that be half to take a rule be twene the pties and nether for love ffaūoe or aliaunce as ryght and good conciens requireth so det'mine awarde and ende the cause betwene the pties. And that none of the pties Dishobeie the warde of the seid maire and maistres on the peynalties and discharging off the bynke and ffeleship as is affore written. And also that eūy of the seid Breder put them in ther moste vttermoste and effectuall devōrs to saue and increce the hoñoe of the mairalte and contynually reporte in eūy place and company by ther maire the moste hoñoe worship and godenes thei con and may. And to ther heryng or knolech if any . . . psone in worde or dede repreue or dishoñoe their maire that then eūy of the seid breder in siche cause put hym in his moste effectual devōrs to rebuke reconcile and reforme eūy siche symple psone to his pouer on the payne and deposicōn affore written.

Moreov̄ it is ordeyned and acte by the seid Maire and Brether that if any of them disclose open or vtter to any psons any mañ of councell meoved comēncd or detmȳned amonge them or to his power alter or contrary any mañ of agrement among themself concluded as in namyng of ther new maire upon Seynt Mathewe even or for chosing of Burges for the plement or any or' mater consrnyng gode rule or pfite to the Towne the maire or of his Breder he or thei ffurthwith to be deposed and discharged fro the Bynke and excluded of the ffeleship of the said Breder eū more.

Also it is ordeyned and acte that no maire hereaft[r] yn the tyme of his mairalte sett no mañ of man upon the bynke with oute avise councell and agrement of all his Breder or the most part yn payne of hymselfe to be discharged of the bynke and excluded of the ffeleship of the said Breder for eū more aft[r] the tyme of his office of the mairalte.*

It is evident from this Order that the two masters of Corpus Christi Guild were at that time closely connected with the Corporation in the government of the town, and to some extent were invested by the mayor and his brethren with superior authority, inasmuch as they had power to inflict penalties upon the mayor himself in case he neglected his duty, as laid down in the curious regulations just quoted. This close connection is also further shown by the fact that even so early as the fifteenth century "Common Halls" or, as we now term them, meetings of the Council, were occasionally held in the Hall of the Guild, then, as now, standing on the west side of S.

* *Hall Book*, in manuscript, i. pp. 223-5.

Martin's Church. In the *Hall Book* we are told, "In ye tyme of the mayraltie of Mr Hurst yan beyng mayre At a Comon Hall holden in leycestr at Corp. Xpi Halle on fryday nyxt after xij.te day the x. yere of Kyng Henry vij.te" etc. etc.* That was in the year 1495. At that time the Town Hall, in which the mayor and his brethren usually met for the transaction of the public business of the town, and in which they held their assemblies, was situated in Blue Boar Lane. This use of the Guild Hall by the Corporation soon became not only an occasional, but a frequent occurrence, and may, in somewhat later times, be accounted for not only by the circumstance already alluded to—namely, the importance of the Guild—but also by the fact that the Town Hall in Blue Boar Lane was then becoming an old building, and was not so central, and probably not so convenient, for the transaction of public business as the Hall of the Guild.

Fortunately, there are preserved amongst the Records in the Muniment Room, at the Guild Hall, Leicester, several of the original Rent Rolls and Accounts of the officers of the Fraternity which erected that interesting fabric, and within whose walls its members so frequently met prior to their procession to S. Martin's Church, and again assembled after attending their solemn services there to feast together in brotherly love and good fellowship according to the wise and social regulations of their Guild. Some of these documents have been referred to by local antiquaries, but such as are given in the following pages have been copied from the originals by the writer, who was much facilitated in his

* *Hall Book*, i. p. 57.

search by the friendly aid of Mr. William Kelly, whose knowledge and appreciation of our local Records (in conjunction with the labours of Mr. James Thompson, the author of *The History of Leicester*) have been the fortunate causes of their preservation so far as the inadequate means placed at his disposal allowed. Surely the time is not far distant when a proper depository for the mass of Documents belonging to the Corporation will be provided, in which they will be preserved from damp, and when some inducement will be offered to local antiquaries to lend their aid in effecting their proper assortment and classification.

The earliest of these original documents met with in the Muniment Room is a Rent Roll, written, like the others there preserved, relating to the Guild, upon parchment. The heading is imperfect from the effect of damp. It is, however, dated

. . . Ano dio 1476.

and the purport is to tell that what follows is a Rental of the "Chawntre or gilde of Corpus Xp̄i in the chirch of Sent Marten," and that it extends from "the fest of sent Jerome," in the sixteenth year of Edward IV., "vnto the said fest next foloing." This Roll is here copied. The names of Leicester men and Leicester streets at that time are not without their value and interest. The property of the Guild is arranged according to its situation in the different parishes and streets thus :—

" *The parishe of sent marie.*

Of a crofte in the tenor of Thomas . . . . bi
pulcre well* . . . . . xvj.[d]

* "Pulcre well,"—a well near S. Sepulchre's Chapel, on the site of the present Infirmary.

Of a tenement in the tenor of Hew Bore in the sore lane		vj.[d]
Of a tenement of sent mare . . . in the tenor of Thomas Garett		xij.[d]
Of a tenement in the tenor of Mastur . . . . Curtes called the pecoke . . .		xij.[d]
Of the lorde lovell a pece of grownd be gosling crofte	ij.[s]	
Of a tenement in the Hi strete now rafe peches .		vj.[d]

the Newarke.

Of the colleg of the Newarke for a tenement in the parishe of senicolles*		xij.[d]
Of the same for a tenement in the tenor of Rechard Chavnse	ij.[s]	
Of the same for a tenement on the cornar in gallotre gate	ij.[s]	
Of a tenement in the tenor of the wekar of Senecolles	ij.[s]	
Of a tenement of robard Stewynes in the tenor of John Simsn̄ in appillgate		xij.[d]

the parishe of sent Petrus.

Of a tenement in the tenor of Thomas innocent .		xij.[d]
Of a tenement in the tenor of elisabeth Prestin .	iiij.[s]	& iij. hens.
Of a tenement in the tenor of John renolds .		xij.[d]
Of a garthen be the Shire Hall in the tenor of Emot Danke		vj.[d]
Of the Ospitall of sent John for a garthen there .		ix.[d]

the parishe of sent Martens in the Hi strete.

Of Thomas Melkinn̄ for a tenement in the tenor of Richard Wygstn̄	iiij.[s]	vj.[d]

* Saint Nicholas.

Of Thomas Wigstn̄ for a tenement on the toder cornar of p^{t} lane*	iij.^{s}	
Of a tenement of burley of coventre in the tenor of Johñ . . . wyfe		xij.^{d}
Of a tenement of John Wygstn̄'s in the tenor of Rechard Coke in ye cherchyard . .	iiij.^{s}	vj.^{d}
Of a tenement of the gylde of Corpus Xp̄i in the tenor of Wyłłm	xxj.^{s}	
Of roger Wygstn̄ for iij. cotages in the Hote gate†	x.^{s}	
Of the same rog^{r} for a yate howse . . .	iij.^{s}	iiij.^{d}
Of the same rog^{r} for a shop sm̄ time rechard Knightn̄s	ij.^{s}	
Of the same rog^{r} for the en that is callid the george		vj.^{d}
Of a tenement of Wyłłm . . . . . in the Hote gate	v.^{s}	
Of a tenement of the abay in the tenor of lawrans Crewis on the cherch lane cornar . .	ij.^{s}	
Of a tenement in the Kyrke lane‡ in the tenor of John Horn.	v.^{s}	
Of a tenement in the tenor of Margere barear .	iij.^{s}	
Of a tenement in the tenor of Alis Waturman .	iij.^{s}	
Of a tenement in the tenor of Thomas Hall .	ix.^{s}	
Of a tenement in the tenor of Thomas Bold .	viij.^{s}	
Of a tenement in the tenor of . . . . Skyner	ix.^{s}	
Of a tenement in the tenor of robard Stewn̄s .	xij.^{s}	
Of a tenement of gylds in the Hi strete§ nexte Robard Stewn̄s late in the tenor of Wyłłm Makepes	viij.^{s}	

* Parchment Lane, now New Bond Street.

† Now Silver Street.

‡ Probably the same as Church Lane, sometimes called Holy Rood Lane, now Town Hall Lane.

§ Now High Cross Street.

Of a tenement of Wyllm Daltons late in the tenor of Rychard Langtofte in the Hote gate .		xxiij.^{d} ob.
Of a tenement of Wyllm Hoir of the cornar of the Hote gate end	iij.^{s}	
Of a tenement callid the Cardenall Hat in the tenor of Rychard Smyth	vj.^{s}	
Of a tenement of thomas Avin in the tenor of Thomas Burḡs	x.^{s}	
Of ij. cotagis in the tenor of John Danett . .	v.^{s}	& ij. hens.
Of iij. tenements of the gylde of Corpus Xp̄i in the appill gate gyfyng a hows vj.^{s} . .	xviij.^{s}	
Of John Mai Draꝑ for sarten grownds & crofts .	vj.^{s}	

*in the swines market.**

Of a tenement of the gilds at the Hi cros in the tenor of John Leg		xxij.^{d}
Of a tenement of John Cutlers in his own hands .	v.^{s}	
Of ij. tenements of mastur Fildings in the tenor of Wyllm Cowentre & Wyllm Waleing .	x.^{s}	
Of a tenement of nycks̄ tempulls in the tenor of Wyllm Holbecke	iij.^{s}	
Of a tenement of Wkllm blacwens	v.^{s}	
Of a tenement of Thomas Wyllers in the tenor of John Whitwell	x.^{s}	
Of a tenement of thomas Guskes in the tenor of thomas Jacksn̄	iij.^{s}	
Of iij. tenements of John Austens y^{t} wed Wyngars wyfe	vj.^{s}	
Of a tenement of Rog^{r} Wigstn̄s late in the tenor of Clement Smyth		vij.^{d} ob.

* Now High Street.

Of a tenement of mastur langtuns in the tenor of Clement Smyth		x.[d] ob.
Of a tenement of Corpus Xp̄i gild in the tenor of Wyllm Brown	xij.[s]	
Of a tenement in the tenor of Rafe gyles . .	iij.[s]	
Of a tenement of John tomsn̄ in the tenor of Robard flecher		vj.[d]
Of a tenement of Wyllm Dawes in the tenor of Thomas Hurst	v.[s]	
Of iiij. tenements of thomas Coks in the tenor of Thomas Gylls John Weste sadler & thomas Hurst	viij.[s]	
Of a tenement of George Astey of . . . . in the tenor of John Smyth . . .	ix.[s]	vj.[d]
Of a tenement of ye gilds late in the tenor of Xp̄ower Dyc̄nsn̄	xv.[s]	
Of a tenement of ye gilds in the tenor of thomas stone	xiij.[s]	iiij.[d]
Of a tenement of ye gilds in the tenor of John Pakyngtn̄	xl.[s]	
Of a tenement in the tenor of Rychard Burgs .		xij.[d]
Of a tenement of the gilds in the tenor of Jone Cathelere	xiij.[s]	iiij.[d]
Of a tenement of the gilds in the tenor of thomas Lyllyng	xiij.[s]	iiij.[d]
Of a tenement in the tenor of Wyllm Moke .		iij.[d]
Of a barn in parchement lane in the tenor of John robards		vj.[d]
Of a tenement of the gilds in the tenor of ye same John robards	xxj.[s]	
Of the same John for a tenement in the tenor of Hare Hemsworth . .	vj.[s]	

Of the same Joħn for a tenement w^{tt}owt the north yate in Sõ lane	ij.^{s}	

in the Shepys market.

Of a tenement in the tenor of elisabethe yats .	x.^{s}	
Of the same elisabethe for a garden in sooꝑ lane .		vj.^{d}
Of a tenement in the tenor of Joħn Wyllomot .	iij.^{s}	
Of the same Joħn for a tenement next hym .		xij.^{d}
Of the same Joħn for a tenement of George Asley of		vj.^{d}
Of a tenement in the tenor of Joħn Stamvycke walear	vj.^{s}	& two hens.
Of a tenement in the tenor of Rychard Wakefeld	iij.^{s}	
Of a tenement in the tenor of Wyłłm Coke wryght	iiij.^{s}	
Of a tenement in the tenor of thomas jee .	v.^{s}	

Wyth owt the yest yate.

Of a tenement of the gilds in the tenor of Joħn Tesdell Cowꝑ	xxvj.^{s}	viij.^{d}
Of a tenement of the gilds in the roundell* in the tenor of Wyłłm Pakyngtn̄	x.^{s}	
Of a tenement of the gilds in the tenor of Wyłłm Wetherbooke	x.^{s}	viij.^{d}
Of a tenement in the tenor of Wyłłm Whittoy	ij.^{s}	& j. hen.
Of a tenement in the tenor of thomas gifte .		xij.^{d}
Of a tenement in the tenor of Joħn Grene draꝑ .	ij.^{s}	& j. hen.
Of a tenement in Hommrstone gate callid thomas rathris in the tenor of Wyłłm Wynsley .	iij.^{s}	
Of a tenement in Belgrave gate late Marget Gumles noy in the tenor of Rychard Mapurley .	v.^{s}	
Of a ley next ij. leis† of the mastur of sent Jonis in the tenor of Joħn May mercer .	ij.^{s}	

* The Haymarket. † A Ley, pasture-land.

Of a crofte in Normande nexte the beshope grownd of lincolne in the tenor of Wyłłm mysshell feshar	iij.s	iiij.d

in the seterday market & the chirch yard.

Of a tenement of the gild in the tenor of Rogr . . .	xx.s	
Of a tenement in the tenor of Robard Sheringam	ij.s	
Of a tenement in the tenor of Rychard Clarke .	ij.s	& j. hen.
Of a garthen of the gilds be the town wall in the tenor of ye same Rychard . . .		xviij.d
Of a tenement of Corpus Xpi gild in the tenor of John Erele	xiij.s	iiij.d
Of a tenement of Phn Walles in the tenor of John Davis	iiij.s	
Of a tenement in the tenor of thomas Pallett .		xij.d
Of a tenement of Wyłłm Hores in the tenor of John	v.s	& ij. hens.
Of a tenemant in the tenor of John May ñcer .	v.s	
Of a tenement in the tenor of Robard Cat . .	v.s	
Of a tenement in the tenor of Sr Wyłłm Yrland .	iij.s	iiij.d
Of a tenement ondur the same chambur in the tenor of Sr Thomas Glen*	iij.s	iiij.d

The total amount of this Rent Roll, which is not given in the original, amounts to nearly £28. This, however, must not be considered as all clear revenue. There were chief rents to be paid, a large outlay for reparations, and a considerable loss from what are called in the accounts "decays," that is, losses arising from tenements uninhabited, abatement of rents, and from various other causes. The Rent Roll was

* Sir Thomas Glen was one of the Rent-gatherers of the Guild in 1492-3. He was a priest: the title "Sir," as is well known, was at that time accorded to the clergy.

simply a list of the houses, lands, and rents belonging to the Guild placed in the hands of the Rent-gatherers for their guidance in collecting. Those officers then collected all they could, noted the cause of nonpayment in cases where the rent was not forthcoming, ordered (under the sanction of the Stewards) the necessary repairs to be made, and made other payments for carrying out the objects of the Guild, and for a decent observance of its articles and customs. At the close of their year of office they made out their account, which probably first received the sanction of the Stewards, and was then submitted to all the members assembled in the Guild Hall upon one of their days of meeting. It is one of these original accounts which next claims our attention. It, like the Rent Roll just quoted, dates from the Feast of S. Jerome —30th September—and is for the year 1492-3, and from it we learn that Sr Thomas Glen and Thomas Gillot were in that year the rent-gatherers, and Thomas Wyke and Robert Croft Masters or Stewards of the Guild.

The account is headed :—

> This ys the acompt of Sr. Thomas Glen and Thomas Gillot Rentgedārs of the Gylde of Corporis Xpi yn the paryshe of Seynt Martens of Leycester from the feste of Seynt Jerome pste the viii.th yere of the reigne of Kynge . . . . the vij.th unto the same feste . . . . folowynge the ix. yere of oure seid lorde kyng for a yere complete.

The "Charge" (or receipts) is thus given :—

Itm̄ of Rents of Wylle and of Asyse ꝑtenynge to the same Gylde as hit apereth pleynlyer be a Rentall thereof made . . . xxxiij.*li* vij.*s* ob. q.

Then follows the "Discharge" or payments, a portion of which may be quoted as showing the manner in which the accounts were kept, and as giving some curious information respecting the customs of the Guild.

I. Under the special head of "Discharge" are the following selected from a long list :—

It' to the kyng for the talbot . . . . . ij.^{s}
It' to the kyng for v. Cotages yn the Dede lane . . xv.^{d}
It' to the Newe Colegge for a crofte late the seid John psons . . . . xxij.^{d}
It' to the same for the owt shote of the waƚ of the teñ late yn the holdyng of Robt Coup goyng owte throwe the Anteloppe . . . . . iij.^{d}
It' to Seynt M^{r}getts Gilde for the Roundell . . iij.^{d}
It' to the Kyng for layng of swepyngs at the ffrere yate ij.^{d}
It' to the ffrary clerke . . . . . iiij.^{d}

The total of this section is :—

Sm̄ . . xxvj.^{s} iij.^{d} ob̄.

II. Under the head of "Deykeyes" are :—

A grownde called the Pecokke at the Rede Crosse because hit standyth yn varianse bytwyxt Peres Curtes and the Gilde . . . . . . xij.^{d}
Itm̄ xx^{d} abated of a teñ* that Joh̄n Mey dwelles yn.
It' viij.^{d} abated of a close that John Blownt holds.
It' a teñ yn the Swynes market late yn the holdynge of Joh̄n Pyman . . . . xvj.^{s} viij.^{d}

The whole of the decays amount to

Sm^{a} . . iiij.^{li} xvj.^{s}

* Tenement.

III. Then comes a List of miscellaneous payments: the most interesting part of the document, and which is here copied entire:—

Payd to the iiij. Chauntre prestes xxj.[li] vj.[s] viij.[d] for talough Candall for kepyng of the morwe mas* ij.[s] It' for kepyng of the auter† iij.[s] iiij.[d] It' for beryng of the ffertur & for torches on Corp Xpi day ij.[s] vj.[d] It' payd for John psons obet xv.[s] It' for Ryngyng of the belles at Dirige and masse for the brethern and Systers soles xj.[d] It' to the belman ij.[d] It' for washyng of auter clothes and awbys‡ xiiij.[d] It' for mendyng of Awbes v.[d] It' for iiij. tukkyng stryngs iiij.[d] It' for makyng of the Rentall vj.[d] It' for wax brynnyng§ a bowt the auter xiij.[li] & halffe ix.[s] It' the Rentgēydars ffee xl.[s] It' for pchement paup & ynke & for makyng of the cownt ij.[s] vj.[d] It' for writynge of ye brod' & systs̄ yn the tabull‖ ij.[d] It' to Jone Babers xx.[s] the whiche is graunted hyr for tēe (term ?) of lyffe. It' for swepynge of the plar (?) and the Halle ij.[d] It' to Joh̄n Assheby for makynge of a Dede iiij.[d] It' for selyng wax ob̄. It' spent yn ale of maist[r] mayre and his compeny when he went to se the lyvelode ¶ of Corpus Xpi Gild iiij.[d] ob. It' spent of the men that brought the gret tymbre o[d]. It' for halowynge of a auter clothe & a corpas vj.[d] It' for a citation for Joh̄n Goldson vj.[d] to the somner vj.[d] It' for Rebyn for makyng of a corpas case vj.[d]

Sm̄ xxvj.[li] vij.[s] iiij.[d]

IV. The remainder of the Discharge consists of a very long list of "Repacions" or Repairs at the various houses be-

* Morrow Mass. † Altar. ‡ Albs. § Burning. ‖ That is, writing the names of the Brethren and sisters of the Guild on the table or tablet at the altar of the Guild in S. Martin's Church. ¶ Property.

longing to the Guild: a few of these are given to show the scale of wages, etc. etc.

Repacions of John May house ffyrste for beryng oute of mukke ij.[d] It' to Ric. Bradfeld & his man for v. dayez & a halfe v.[s] vj.[d] It' to an other of his men for v. dayez ij.[s] vj.[d] It' for a gruer un to them for v. dayez and a halfe xxij.[d] . . . . . It' paid to ij. dawbers for iiij. dayez & a halffe iii.[s] Repacions of the chauntre ffyrst paid to Ric. Bradfeld & his man for a day & a halffe xviij.[d] It' to his gruer for a day & a halffe vj.[d] . . . It' paid for vj. ston leyd & a halffe iiij.[s] x.[d] ob. It' paid to a plumer for sod[r] & his labur xij.[d] . . . . It' paid to a thakker for iij. dayez xv.[d] . . . It' for iiij. cartfull lyme xiij.[s] j.[d] It' for beryng yn of the same iiij.[d] . . . It' paid for vj crestez vj.[d] . . . .

Sm . viij.[li] x.[s] iiij.[d] ob.

This document is thus endorsed:—

Sm of the whole charge . . xlij.[li] vij.[s] ob. q.
Sm of the Discharge . . xlj.[li] iij.[s] vj.[d] ob.

and remayneth clerely alle thyngs rekened and alowed to the Gilde . . . . . xxiij.[s] vj.[d] q̄.

The other original documents formerly belonging to the Guild of Corpus Christi which I have seen, and which are now preserved in the muniment room at the Guild Hall, are a Rental for the 10th year of the reign of Henry VII. (1494-5), showing a total of £31 : 8 : 9¾; a Rent Roll the date of which is not decipherable, and in which the following entries occur:—

Itm̃ of Wittm Shawe for a close Besyde Seynt James churche . . . . ix.^{s}
Itm̃ for a tent̃ a lyttell north brygge . . . . . vj.^{s}
Itm̃ of the horsleche wyff for a tent̃e . . . . . vj.^{s} viij.^{d}
Itm̃ of Thomas Grene for xxx. ac̃s land gyffen to the gyld by Agnes White . . . . x.^{s}
Itm̃ for a close in the holdyng of M$^{r.}$ Dalton of the gyfte of M$^{r.}$ Thomas Hurst . . . . . . xij.^{s} iiij.^{d}

Among the chief rents is :—

Of John Reed for a tent̃e cald the Cardenall Hatte . xj.^{s}

A Rent Roll, dated the Feast of S. Michael the Archangel, 20 Henry VII. (1504-5), in which this entry occurs :—

Itm̃ of Ric Reynolds for iij. tenem̃ts that almes men dwell in by yẽr . . . . xij.^{d}

The total of this Roll is £36 : 14 : 8¼.

A Rent Roll for the year 1519 (?) in which is found :—

Itm̃ for a tent̃ late M$^{r.}$ Chaundlers called Sent Katerns howse . . . . xj.^{s}

The next document as to date is of more interest, and requires fuller notice. It is the account of the Stewards of the Guild for the year 1525-6, and is here given entire. It is thus headed :—

The Accompts off us Sr Joh̃n Cappe & Thom̃ Cotton Junior Stewards off the Gild off Corpus Xpi in Leycet$^{r.}$ ffrom the feest off sent Michell the archangel in the yere off o$^{r.}$ lord god m^{l}vcxxv^{ti} unto the sayd ffeest off sent Michell in the yere off o^r. lord god a m^l vcxxvj^ti & ffyrst for the ffoott off our last accompts in Bylls & Reydy money sm̄ nyehill. Itm̄ more wee the sayd stewards charg us w^t Rents at Wylle as aperith in the Rentall sm̄ xxiij.^li xviij.^s iiij.^d Itm̄ more wee charg us w^t Rents of Assise aperyng By the Rental sm̄ x.^li xvij.^s vij.^d q̄.

Sm^d to^ll charg } xxxiiij.^li xv.^s xj.^d q̄.

Cheffe Rents paid owt

Imprimis peyd to the Kyng By the hands off Wm Schawe ffor a pece off ground called long Crofts xix.^d ob. It' to the same Wilłm ffor a close of the gefte of M^r. psons xxij.^d It' pd to W^m ffor a close late Thom̄s Burges xij.^d It' to the same ffor iiij. cotags in gallowtregate ij.^s It' to the same ffor a pece off grovnd in Blankney iij.^d It' to the same W^m ffor ij. closses late M^r. Hurst xiiij.^d Itm̄ peyd to Wyłłm Gybson ffor the Kyng off a tenn̄et in the holdyng off Wm Provdluff iiij.^s iiij.^d ob̄. It' to the same W^m ffor a ten̄et late in the holdyng off Raffe Gyllit xij.^d It' to the same W^m for v cotages in Ded lane xv.^d It' to the same W^m ffor a ground in the northgate j.^d It' to the same W^m ffor a pece off ground in the hye stret iij.^d It' to the same W^m ffor a ten̄t in the holdyng off Robr̄t Elliatt iij.^d Itm̄ peyd unto my lord abbott of leycet^r ffor dyvers Ten̄t in the chyrche lane vij.^s Itm̄ more p^d to the Chamburlens off leycet^r ffor a close late Wm Daltons xij.^d It' p^d to John̄ Blyth ffor a closse late Mr Hurst xij.^d Also p^d to sent Margretts gild ffor a ten̄t in the Rondill iij.^d It' to the same gild ffor a closse late M^r. Hurst vj.^d Also p^d to the Newerk of leycet^r ffor a closse late M^r. psons xviij.^d It' to the same ffor a closse late Thom̄s Burgesse xij.^d It' to the same ffor a ten̄t w^t owt the est gate in the holdyng off W^m poloffe iij.^d Itm̄ p^d to Thom̄s Pultney ffor s̄ten land in the Sothfields off the gift off Agnes Whyte iiij.^s Also p^d ffor s̄ten land in Barkbie in the holdyng of Wm Clyston j.*d* It' p[d] for s̄ten land off the Vic̄ ij.*d* Also pd to the Ayres of M[r.] Belgrage vij.*d* ob̄. It' p[d] Henry Clare ffor the kyng ffor s̄ten land in the Sothffild late Hawes xij.*d* It' pd to the sayd Henry ffor a tent̄ late W[m] Beytts xij.*d* It' to M[r] Reynolds ffor ij. tent̄s in the Canke viij.*d* ffor the Newerke.

Sm̄ off the Cheffs . xxxv.*s* j.*d* ob̄.

Dekeys off Rents at Wyll & Rents of Ass̄

i. Impm̄ys In Dekey ij. Cotags late in the holdyng off Thom̄ Butlar & Allyn Bradford in the Ded lane vj.*s* viii.*d* Itm̄ dekey ther a cotage late in the holdyng off the curiar iij.*s* iiij.*d* It' in dekey a tent̄ in the holdyng late off Widow Hatmaker iiij.*s* It' a tent̄ late in the holdyng off W[m] Vynnys vj.*s* vj.*d* It' in dekey a tent̄ at the hye crosse late in the holdyng off John Tomlys̄on vj.*s* It' in dekey a tent̄ in the holdyng of John Sadlar iij.*s* It' a dekey a tent̄ in the holdyng off R . . . Wodde xxiii.*s* iiij.*d* It' in dekey a tent̄ in the holdyng of R . . . Hill & now a gardyn iij.*s* viij.*d* It' a dekey a tent̄ late in the holdyng off W[m] Mavnbe iiij.*s* It' in dekey a tent̄ in the Holdyng of Ryc̄ Stapley v.*s* iiij.*d* It' dekey a tent̄ in the holdyng of Jamys Sadlar vj.*s* viij.*d* It' dekey a tent̄ in the holdyng off W[m] Cockyn xiij.*s* iiij.*d* It' a dekey a tent̄ in pchm̄et Lane in the holdyng off John Smyth iij.*s* iiij.*d* It' in dekey a Barne in the Ded lane callid the store howse iij.*s* iiij.*d* It' in dekey off s̄ten chamburs in sent M'tyns chyrchyard v.*s* It' dekey a tenn̄t in the Canke late in the holdyng of John Sharpe & now in the holdyng off Ann . . . . vj.*s* vj.*d* It' in dekey ij. tent̄s in the aplegate late in the holdyng off Th' Cham̄brs iiij.*s* It' dekey a closse in the holdyng off nycolas Shaw viij.*d* It' in dekey sent Catryns howse xij.*d* It' a dekey acre of medow in the holdyng off Raffe Swyllyngton ij.*s* It' a dekey of a grownd in the Ded Lane sometyme Margrett Innocents xij.*d* It' a deky ij. tent̄s in the hye strete now M[r.] Dannett's v.*s* ij.*d* It' dekey in the Swynys m'kett ij. tent̄s of M[r.] Wynge vj.*s* It' a dekey a tent̄ late in the holdyng off

Clement Smyth x.*d* ob. It' in dekey a grownd upon the towne wall late John Wygstons xviij.*d* It' dekey a tent at the hye crosse now Mr. Raff Peksals vj.*s* It' dekey off a closse besyde the schyre Hall ix.*d* It' dekey a tent in the Hotgate late Mr. Meys iij.*s* iiij.*d* It' dekey a tent late John Androo off Branston vj.*d* It' dekey a tent late in the holdyng off Ch' Beyard ij.*s* It' dekey ffor Mr. Peksals poleyard ij.*s* It' in dekey a tent at sent Sondays Brygge vj.*s* viij.*d* It' a dekey a qrt Rent of the howse off Wm Prodluff v.*s* It' a dekey of the howse off Ryc Schevalis (?) in pment Lane nt. In dekey of a tent in the holdyng of Grene plastorer xij.*d* It' dekey a tent late Wm . . . . galowtregate vj.*s* viij.*d*

Sm off the Dekeys . . viij.*li* ij.*d* ob.

Obitts & ffees peid owt of gilde — Imprimys pd ffor the kepyng off John psons obitt xv.*s* Itm pd ffor the kepyng off the Obitt ffor the Breder & sistrs xiij.*d* Itm ffor the kepyng off Mr. Svyks obitt iiij.*s* x.*d* It' pd ffor the kepyng off Mr. Davers obitt iiij.*s* v.*d* It pd ffor kepyng off Mr. Thoms Hurst obbitt v.*s* ix.*d* It' pd ffor the kepyng of Mr. Beylese obitt viij.*s* ix.*d* It' pd ffor the kepyng off John Whytwele obitt v.*s* Itm ffor the kepyg off Wm Chandlars obitt ij.*s* It' ffor washyng off the awter clothes & othr. the ornyments abowt the awter in our lade chappell ij.*s* j.*d* It' ffor mendyng off corpas case iiij.*d* It' ffor waxe spend at or ladise awter vij.*s* viij.*d* It' ffor tawlowe candill to the morowe mass ij.*s* It' ffor garneshyng off the awter iij.*s* iiij.*d* It' ffor Brownyngs masse evy (?) Wenysday iij.*s* viij.*d* Itm pd the clerke off sent Johns ffrare iiij.*d* It' ffor ffees off the too stewards off the gild xxvj.*s* viij.*d* It' ffor the makyng off the acompts ij.*s* viij.*d*

Sm off the obitts & ffees . iiij.*li* xv.*s* vij.*d*

Repracons — Impmys pd vnto a smyth at West Brygge ffor mendyng of the Chantre Wykkett & iiij. keys vj.*d* It' ffor wedyng of the cort & clensyng off the howse ageynst Corp^s^ Xpi dynar viij.*d* It' s̄ten thyngs done in the stoor (?) Chamb^r^ x.*d* It' ffor mendyn of a wyndow in Sr. Nycolas Chamb^r.^ xij.*d* It' ffor s̄ten Repacions done at Joh̄n Schawards howse at the Crowne be the advise of the stewards ij.*s* iij.*d* It' Repacīons at John Lanys howse iij.*d* It' at the Ieyngmongars shopp off lutt^r^worth v.*d* It' ffor Repacōns done at sent Sondays Brygge as aperes by the ps̄els in S^r.^ Wm. Reeds Booke x.*s* vij.*d* It' ffor s̄ten hooks & hyngs to John Sharard to the howse of Robr̄t Elliatt xij.*d* It' ffor Bords & neyles to the same howse p to Mr Reynold xxj.*d* ob̄. It' p^d^ to Joh̄n tom̄lyson for workmanshypp v.*d* It' p^d^ vnto John Scharard ffor iiij. hooks & ij. hyngs to Ellyn Arthurs howse in the Losbe lane v.*d* It' ffor bords & neyles to the same . . . . to Mr. Reynald n^tt^. It' for the Remevyng of Tymb^r^ & slate & other stonys at Schevals howse in p̧chment lane xvj.*d* It' p^d^ to Wm Abbott for iij. keys to dyvers ten̄ts vj.*d* It' ffor a days work . . . at store howse by Joh̄n tōlynson for makyng of a . . . . . vij.*d* ob̄ It' p^d.^ to Harre Tomson ffor neyles to the same ij.*d* It' ffor a bunch of lath ffor a latic (?) in the chantre v.*d* It' to Wm Abbott ffor a key of a ten̄t in Chyrch lane ij.*d* It' pd to Mr. West ffor Repaciōn done by hym at dyvers tymys in sclatyng & other thyngs as aperes by his byll off the same sm̄ xxxiij.*s* vij.*d* It' pd vnto Thom̄s Grene ffor sand & other Repācion made by hym in Sr Joh̄ns tyme of the last yere & not sett into the Booke v.*s* iiij.*d* It' a skyn of p̧chment to make a new Rentall w^t^ & a Rolle of the gilds detts w^t.^ iij.*d*

Sm̄ off the Repaciōns iij.*li* ij.*s* vj.*d*

Peyments off ye Prests Wags To the Mast^r^s off the gild

It' we the sayd Stewards dysharg as pd & delyverd vnto the mast^r^s of Corpus Xp̄i Gyld ffor & towards the chargs & peyments off the chantre prests off Corpus Xp̄i gild And p^d^ By the hands off Sr. John Cappe sm̄ v.*li* Itm̄ p^d^ & delyv^r^d by the hands off S[r] Wyłłm Reyde syns S[r.] John Cappe deptid hense* sm̄ viij.[li] vj.[s] viij.[d]

Sm̄ off Both ther peymēts } xiij.[li] vj.[s] viij.[d]

Sm̄ w[ee] dysharg } Amont xxxj.[li] j.[d]

And so dew vnto the sayd gild By the stewards off the same sm̄ iij.[li] xv.[s] x.[d] q The wiche we the sayd stewards dysharg us delyv̄d vnto the mast[r]s off the same gild off Corpus Xp̄i Robr̄t Harwar & Roger Gillott mast[r]s ffor the ffoott of this our Acompt the yere & day afforsayd to the vse of the same gild."

The next Manuscript belonging to the Guild is a Rent Roll—much damaged by mice—apparently for the year 1533-4, dating "frome ye feast of Sent Mychell y[e] archangell anno dn̄i a M V. hondereth . . . . Unto the foresayde feast year followyng a M . . . . . ondreth xxxiiij." Then is found a Rent Roll (in very good preservation) for the year 1535, at the head of which is figured the sacred monogram I. H. C. within a shield, the letters I. N. R. I. appearing on a label passing through the upper part of the letter H. The total rents for that year amounted to £29 : 7 : 2¼. And lastly, there is a Rental of the Guild for the year 1542, showing a total of £27 : 2 : 6, at the head of which is (what was undoubtedly) the cognizance or badge of the Guild. This, as is shown by a facsimile of it given on the opposite page, was the Chalice and Paten, symbols of the sacred elements in the Eucharist, which after consecration—according to the teaching of the Roman Catholic Church—became the veritable Body and

* Departed hence.

COGNIZANCE OF CORPUS CHRISTI GUILD.

(From Guild Roll, dated 1542.)

Blood of our Saviour. Upon the Chalice itself is figured a bleeding heart, which, with the two hands and two feet, all pierced, shown upon the shield, exhibit the "five wounds" inflicted upon our Saviour's sacred body, the symbols of the Passion so familiar to all interested in mediæval ecclesiastical antiquities.

Even a cursory examination of the documents here brought before us gives a not uninteresting picture of a Fraternity which filled an important place in Leicester in mediæval times. Its officers took part in the administration of justice; exerted their utmost to uphold the dignity, and to claim public respect for the municipal authorities; its priests sang daily at the altar of the Guild for the spiritual welfare of its members, and so tended to keep alive in the minds of all a sense of the importance and reality of religion—however much that religion was clouded by superstition and vain ceremonies; its annual Festival, with its public processions, would be one of the holidays of the year, whilst its annual Feast would bring rich and poor together clad in one common garment or livery, and their social differences would, for a time at least, be forgotten, and all would be in reality, what they were in name—brethren.

It has been shown that the articles of the Guild required the members to meet at All Saints, Christmas and Easter, for the transaction of business, and for the payment of the Guild dues. But it was upon Corpus Christi day that the grand procession and feast took place. In preparation for that day, the altar in the lady chapel at the east end of the great south aisle of S. Martin's Church, where the priests of the Guild served, was decorated and made as attractive as possible. In the accounts for 1492-3, already quoted, are :—

It' for kepyng of the auter . . . iij.[s] iiij.[d]
It' for washyng of auter clothes . . xiiij.[d]

1525-6.

It' ffor washyng off the awter clothes & oth[r] the ornyments abowt the awter in owr lade Chappell . ij.[s] j.[d]
It' ffor garneshyng off the awter . . . . iij.[s] iiij.[d]

Wax lights were, of course, provided for the altar, upon this and other occasions :—

1492-3 :—

It' for wax brynnyng a bowt the auter xiij.[li] & halfe . ix.[s]

1525-6 :—

It' ffor waxe spend at o[r.] ladise awter . . . vij.[s] viij.[d]

One or two references are made to the fittings of the altar :—

1492-3 :—

It' for halowyng of a auter clothe & a corpas vj.[d]
That would be at the abbey.
It' for Rebyn & for makyng of a Corpas case vj.[d]

1525-6 :—

It' ffor mendyng off Corpas case . . . . iiij.[d]

The vestments of the priests and others are noticed :—

1492-3 :—

It' for washyng of . . . . awbys . . . xiiij.[d]
It' for mendyng of awbes . . . . . . v.[d]

On the eve of Corpus Christi day the members assembled before the Guild-altar to hear Evensong for the dead members of the Fraternity. Early on the following morning the brethren and sisters were summoned by the bellman of the Guild going round the town and ringing a hand bell, and also by the church bells, to assemble and hear *dirige*, or matins for the dead, sung at the Guild-altar :—

1492-3 :—

It' for Ryngyng of the belles at Dirige and Masse for the brethern and systers soles . . . . . . xj.[d]

It' to the belman . . . . ij.[d]

High Mass of Requiem following. In the Accounts are entries probably referring to this :—

1492-3 :—

For talough Candull for kepyng of the morwe mas . ij.[s]

1525-6 :—

It' ffor tawlowe Candill to the morowe mass* . . ij.[s]

During the office of the Mass of Requiem, upon this occasion, the names of all the deceased members of the Guild were read by a priest, standing in a pulpit, from a bead-roll, or from a tablet or table upon which they were painted, and which stood by or upon the altar in order that all individually might upon that occasion at least have the benefit of the prayers of the whole brotherhood. This table is referred to in the account of the Rent-gatherers of the Guild for 1492-3 :—

It' for writynge of y[e] brod' & syst's yn the tabull . . ij.[d]

The reading of the bead-roll usually took place immediately after those present had offered their gifts at the altar—the "mass penny"—and from ancient bead-rolls now existing we

* Morrow Mass (I have been led to think since writing the text) was a term used for the early Matins, sung every morning.—See Dr. Rock's *Church of our Fathers*, ii. 85.

know the priest generally began the roll by saying, Of your devout charity ye shall pray for all the brethren and sisters of the Guild of etc. etc., founded in this Church etc. etc., or some such-like words.*

Occasionally the list was prefaced by a short account of the formation of the Guild, its original objects, its founders, and the alterations in the statutes from time to time, as greater wealth or numbers necessitated.† After the service doles of money, bread, or fuel were given to the poor, and no mass for the dead was considered complete without that work of charity.

But beyond the prayers of the members of the Guild, secured by each of the fraternity at least once a year, and those of the Guild priests offered every day at the Guild altar, sometimes gifts were made to the Guild for special obits or masses for the good of the souls of the donors, to be performed upon the anniversaries of their deaths. Thus, in the account of the Rent-gatherers of Corpus Christi Guild for 1525-6, are found chief rents paid for "a close the gift of Mr. Parsons," and "for two closes late Mr. Hursts," whilst in the discharge are seen, with various other similar payments :—

Imprimis pd ffor the kepyng off John psons obitt .	xv.[s]
It' pd ffor kepyng off M[r.] Thom̄ Hurst obitt . .	v.[s] ix.[d]

By the will of Thomas Eyreke, or Heyrick, dated 25 August 1517, we find that he also secured a yearly service by the priests of Corpus Christi Guild for the good of his soul,

* Dr. Rock's *Church of our Fathers*, ii. 409.

† See an address of this kind in the Chartulary of the Guild of the Holy Trinity, S. Botolphs quoted by Hone, *Ancient Mysteries*, 79.

and that he made many gifts to the local clergy and "religious" for the same purpose. After requesting to be "buried in the parysh Church of Sānt M[r]tens in Lecister," he bequeaths :—

"to the moder church of Lincoln iiij.[d] ; and to the works off the same viij.[d]: also I will that the iij. orduris of freeris of Lecester bring my body to my g[a]ve and eṽy of them to haffe xx.[d]: also I will thatt eṽy prest of Sentte M[r]tyns have vj.[d] and Robert clerk iiij.[d] ; and the other clerk ij.[d] ; and I will that eṽy other preste have iiij.[d] that cūys to my buryall: eṽy child ob: also I will that the warden of the Gray Freers sey v messys at the entering of our Lady in the Frers, and to have xx.[d] for his labo[r]. Also I will thatt y[r] be seid for my solle a trental of messis w[t]in the churche of Saint M'tyne."

After leaving his lands to his children, in default of their having issue he wills :—

"thatt my wyff have the lands to her and to her assines for ever, off thys condicōn, that she do putt in surtye to the gylde of Corpus Xp̄i, to have yerly a dyrige, with mass of reqūire for my sole and my wyeff soule, my father and my mothē solles, and all my frends' sooles, and all Criest'n soulles; and at the same dyrge for to be spende yerly viij.[s] iiij.[d] ; and that to indure as long as the lands be habull to performe the same."*

It was upon this occasion, then, that the members, attired in the livery of the Guild, decorated with its cognisance or badge, and each carrying a torch, marched in procession through the principal streets of the town to and from S. Martin's Church; and although there is little in the documents of the Guild to throw light upon this Procession on Corpus Christi day, still we may be assured that nothing would be wanting to

* Nichols' *Leicestershire*, ii. 615-16.

make it as impressive and jubilant as possible. The "Body of our Lord," represented by the sacred wafer or Host, was the principal object in the Procession. This is referred to in the account of the Rent-gatherers for the year 1492-3 :—

It' for beryng of the ffertur & for torches on Corp. Xpi day . . . . ij.*s* vj.*d*

According to an ancient manuscript in the Town Library, Guild Hall, Leicester, already alluded to (page 135), we find the Latin word "*fertum*" was used for "a nobley" or an obley : now an oble was a term used in mediæval and later times for the consecrated wafer: again, the small shrine in which relics were kept and carried about was sometimes called a *feretrum* or feretory, hence, perhaps, "fertur." It is therefore evident that the word "fertur" in the Rent-gatherers' Account refers either to the Host itself, or to the Shrine, Casket, Pix, or Monstrance, containing it. This fertur borne by a priest * would be carried under a canopy. Machyn, in his *Diary*, describing the Guild processions in London in 1554, says, "Then cam a canepe borne by iiij. of the masters of the clarkes over the Sacrament."† And in an Inventory of articles belonging to Corpus Chisti Guild, Coventry, in 1493, is "a canope of silk brodured w^t gold w^t ij. sidez of the same for y^e ꝑcession on Corpus xpi day." And again, in 1502, the same fraternity possessed, "Itm̃ a canapy to bere ov^r the sac^ament of clothe of

* Machyn, in his *Diary*, under date of 8th December 1554, mentions a procession in which "the prest carehyng the sacrement ryally betwyne ys hands, and on (one) deacon carehyng a senser sensyng anodur the ale-water stoke"—*i.e.* the Holy water stock or stoup.

† Page 63.

tyssew browght in by maist[r] Thomas grove."* At Coventry the canopy over the sacrament was borne by four of the Burgesses, and the same was not improbably the case in Leicester.

The Torches mentioned in the same entry as the "fertur" would be borne aloft upon staffs near to the canopy overshadowing the host.† These were frequently decorated with flowers; indeed, flowers appear to have formed as important, as they would be a beautiful, part of the decorations upon these occasions.‡

In addition to the Guild Priests, the clergy of the various churches, and the ecclesiastics belonging to the religious houses in Leicester, would join the procession attired in their rich copes, and would chant a processional chant as they wended their way slowly and solemnly along the streets. And considering the intimate connection between the masters of the Guild and the Corporation, there is no doubt the mayor and his brethren, attired in their robes, and attended by the Town officials and the waits, would also take their places in the procession.§

* Sharpe's *Coventry Mysteries*, 161.

† Machyn's *Diary*, 63.

‡ In the parochial accounts of S. Margaret's, Westminster, are the following entries referring to these processions on Corpus Christi day:—

Payde for garnyshyng the iiij. torches for Corpus Christye day ij.[s]
flowres to the same torches vj.[d]
Payde for flowres for the torches on Corpus Christie day vij.[d]
for v staf torches x.[s] x.[d]
for the garnyshyng of them xx.[d]
for flowres the same day iiij.[d]

—Dr. Rock's *Church of our Fathers*, ii. 425.

The Churchwardens of S. Martin Outwich, London, charge:—

1524.—Itm̃ for rose garlands on Corpus Xp̄i day . . . . . vj.[d]

—Nichols' *Illus.* p. 272.

§ This was the case at Coventry.—See Sharpe's *Cov. Mys.* 167.

But in addition to these representatives of the Church, the Local Government, and the Guild, the Procession most probably comprised within its length other characters which would attract the gaze and elicit the comments of the townspeople more than any of the others. Those were men and women dressed to personate celebrated characters in Holy Writ, or in the Annals or Legends of the Church. In the Corpus Christi procession at Coventry were persons representing the Virgin Mary * who was specially provided with new gloves for the occasion, S. Katherine, S. Margaret, the angel Gabriel, S. James, S. Thomas of India, "x other apostells," "viij virgins," and Herod who rode on horseback.† There is no reference to these or similar characters in the few documents relating to our Guild at present found in the muniment room: yet knowing the custom in other places it is scarcely probable that Leicester would form an exception. It should be remembered, too, that the procession at Coventry comprised within it another Guild and several city companies, and that the clothing of the persons represented was contributed by them, and not found by Corpus Christi Guild. This would probably be the case here. S. Martin's Church could send clothing for a representative of S. Martin, of S. Nicholas, of Herod with his sword, and probably of the Virgin Mary crowned with a gilt crown.‡ S. Margaret's Guild would contribute its titular saints Margaret and Katherine, St. George's, a representative—always popular—of S. George slaying the dragon; and so the number would

* 1501.—"payd for a Crown of sylv[r.] & gyld for the Mare on Corp[s] Xpi day xliij.[s] ix.[d]"—Sharpe's *Cov. Mys.* 161.

† *Ibid.* 162-4.

‡ See pp. 41, 73, 114.

soon be considerable, whilst all would send a display of Banners and Pensells which formed in mediæval times no insignificant part of the adjuncts of the Processions.

The procession terminated at the Guild Hall, which was made decent for their reception. In the account of the stewards for the year 1525-6 is:—

It' ffor wedyng of the Cort & clensyng off the howse ageynst Corp[s] Xpi dynar . . . . . viij.[d]

The cost of the dinner appears from the Constitutions of the Guild to have been paid by a proportion from each person, and not out of the "common stock," for we are told each person paid for his own "eating."* The only reference I have met with in our local documents at all bearing upon this part of the annual festival are the following entries in the Chamberlains' Accounts for the year 1552-3, relating to the "Vessel of the Guild"—what that vessel was is left for others to determine:—

Itm̃ receuyd for the Chantrey Vessell . . . . xxvj.[s] viij.[d]
Itm̃ pd for the Chauntrye Vessell . . . . xxij.[s] ij.[d]
Itm̃ pd for carryeng the same Vessell to wayeng and to the hall agayn . . . . vj.[d]

After dinner the loving cup or mazor bowl was passed round, of which all, without distinction, partook.†

According to the original articles of the Guild the Wardens would on Corpus Christi day render an account of their receipts

* Page 191. For a list of the articles consumed at the annual dinner of Trinity Guild, Leicester, see Nichols' *Hist.* vol. i. part ii. p. 306, etc. etc.

† Rock's *Church of our Fathers*, ii. 338.

and payments for the past year; new wardens would be chosen; and questions as to the relief of poor members of the Guild, or as to the expenditure of the funds in other acts of charity, would be considered, and the wardens instructed thereupon. There are two such cases in the Guild accounts already referred to:—

1492-3:—

It' to Jone Babers xx.[s] the whiche is graunted hyr for tene (term ?) of lyffe

1525-5:—

It' ffor Repačions done at sent Sondays Brygge,* as aperes by the psels in S[r] W[m] Reeds Booke . x.[s] vij.[d]

The property of the Guild was inspected annually by the Mayor and his brethren. In the payments for 1492-3, is found:—

It' spent yn ale of maist[r] Mayre and his company when he went to se the lyvelode of Corpus Xpi Gild . iiij.[d] ob.

And the Guild appears to have adopted a custom, then prevalent, of placing upon the houses belonging to it the crest or cognisance of the Fraternity:—

1492-3:—

It' paid for vj. crestez . . . . . vj.[d]

The Fees then paid by the Guild to its officers were—

	£	s.	d.
To each of the four priests . .	£5	11	8
To each of the stewards . . .	0	13	4
To each of the rent-gatherers . .	1	0	0

* The making or repairing of Bridges is one of the Acts of Corporeal Mercy.

In establishing a Guild care was usually taken to procure a chamber for the priest, or, in cases where more than one Chaplain was provided, a larger residence. The foundation Articles of S. John's Guild in Leicester provide that the "mayster and his successours shall gyffe to the seide gylde preest mete and drink sufficiently, or allȳd evwry yere for his borde x.[li] of lawfull money. And the seid steward and his successours to pay him the income of his salery as they can agree, and fynde him a chambur w[t]yn the seid seynt John."* And so with regard to our Guild of Corpus Christi, we find that in addition to the Hall in which to hold its meetings and its feasts, the Fraternity possessed its Chantry or residence for the Guild Priests. This is referred to incidentally in the manuscripts of the Guild now existing. In the Rent-gatherers' account for 1492-3 are among the payments :—

Repacions of the Chauntre : ffyrste paid to Ric. Bradfeld
& his man for a day & a halfe . . . . xviij.[d]
It' to his sruer (server) for a day & a halfe . . . vj.[d]

And again in the Stewards' account for 1525-6 are found :—

Imprm̄ys pd vnto a smyth at West Brygge ffor mendyng of
the Chantre Wykkett & iiij. keys. . . . . vj.[d]
It' for wedyng of the Cort & clensyng off the howse ageynst
Corp[s] Xpi dynar . . . . viij.[d]
It' for mendyn of a wyndow in S[r.] Nycolas Chamb[r.] . xij.[d]
It' ffor a bunch off lath ffor a . . . in the Chantre . v.[d]

In accordance with the usual practice we should expect to find the Chantry in close proximity with the Hall, as that

* Throsby, 293.

again was with the Church in which the altar of the Guild stood. That expectation is somewhat strengthened by the entry above, referring to the weeding of the Court or yard, and cleansing of the House in preparation for the annual dinner in the Hall. The inference from that would be, that whilst the Hall occupied one side of the Court, the parlour another, the Chantry, or residence of the priests, occupied the third or south side, where in after-times were the kitchens and culinary offices of the Corporation, and where now stand the modern residence and offices of the Chief Constable. There is, however, so far as can be discovered, no documentary evidence to show the locality of the Chantry, and the inference just drawn is only partially borne out by the statements of our local historians. For whilst Throsby and Nichols both state that the Hall and four houses belonging to the Chantry Priests were situated on the west side of S. Martin's Church,* both also state (but apparently without any authority) that a house in the High Cross Street now occupied by Mr. Wingate, surgeon, was the Chantry house belonging to this Guild. That it did belong to a Religious Body of some kind is evident from the existence there in Throsby's time of a series of paintings in stained glass in a range of lights (which lights are still remaining) on the side of what was formerly a long room, hall, or refectory, but which in Throsby's time was divided into a hall and kitchen, and which has since his time been again altered. The subjects, twenty-eight in number, represented in these

* This statement is strengthened by the entry just quoted showing the purchase of four keys for the "Chantre Wykkett," apparently a key for each of the Chantry priests occupying the four houses referred to in the text.

lights, were events in the life of our Saviour, the seven sacraments of the Romish Church, five Acts of Mercy, the birth and assumption (?) of the Virgin Mary, figures of S. Margaret, S. Christopher, S. Catherine and S. George, and the Town Arms and crest. The ancient front of this house was taken down, and the present one erected, about seventy years ago, thus destroying externally its antique appearance. The stained glass was also removed many years ago by a gentleman—the then owner of the property—and is now in the possession of his descendant, the Rev. Richard Stephens of Belgrave.*

It has before been shown that in the fifteenth century the Mayor and his Company held their business meetings in the Guild Hall, and this they continued to do in the next century. For in 1524-5 the Chamberlains of the Borough charge in their Accounts :—

> Itm̃ pyd ffor Charke colls for M[r] Myer and his brether' at
> Corp' Xpi Hall diũse tymes . . . . . vj.[d]

It was not, however, their business only which was now transacted within its walls, but those presents to officials of the Crown and others, which were then so commonly made by the Mayor, were presented, and not unlikely sometimes consumed there. The Chamberlains in the same year say :—

* Nichols, speaking of the Guild Hall and the four houses states, in error, that they belonged to the Guild of S. George ; and Throsby speaks of the Guild of Corpus Christi and of "a Chantry belonging to this Church"—S. Martin's—as being distinct Foundations, whereas they were identical, as a careful reader of his History will at once discover.

Itm̄ payed for a galon off wyne to spend upon the Comyssion[r] at Corp' Xpi Hall . . . . xvj.[d]

Again when a neighbouring nobleman sent the Mayor a fat buck (which was not unfrequently done) it was in Corpus Christi Hall that he and his brethren assembled to feast upon it. The Chamberlains in 1541-2 charge:—

Itm̄ ffor the denn[r] at Corpus Xpi Hall . . . viij.[s] iiij.[d]
Itm̄ paid at Corp[s] Xpi Hall ffor Allee (ale) aft[r] y[t] Mr. Ma'r had eton veynesson . . . . viij.[d]

The last recorded public act of the Guild of Corpus Christi for the benefit of the town of Leicester was upon the granting by King Henry VIII., in the year 1540, to the Mayor and inhabitants, Letters Patents under the seal of the Duchy of Lancaster for holding two new fairs. The Guild then subscribed ten pounds towards the charges incurred in obtaining that privilege.*

At that time Henry VIII. was laying, or had laid, his hands upon the possessions of the Church. Leicester Abbey had surrendered, and the revenues of the Collegiate Church in the Newarke had passed into his hands. Guilds and similar fraternities were allowed only a short respite, for on the 15th December 1545 Commissions were issued to examine the state and value of the lands belonging to Chantries and Guilds. Injunctions were sent "to the Parson, Vicar, Curat, Chaunter, Priests, Churchwardens, and two of the most honest Persons" in each parish where such Fraternities existed, requiring from them an exact return showing the Titles,

* Nichols' *Leicestershire*, i. 59.

Statutes, Possessions, and Rental of the Guild or Chantry, and the uses, abuses, or misuses connected with the same: also specially enquiring whether any property had been sold or otherwise transferred since the 4th February in the 27th year of the King's reign.'*

The Return made—apparently in accordance with this Injunction—as to the Guild of Corpus Christi is fortunately preserved in the Augmentation Office,† and gives the following account of its origin and of its state at that time. The Return is creditable to the Fraternity, as showing that its priests were useful and ready helpers of the Vicar of the parish, among his (what was then considered) large number of parishioners:—

FOUNDED by Wylliam Humberstone and John Ive the younger under the license of King E. the III. to the intent to fynd iiij. priestes to celebrate dyvyne service within the paryshe church of St. Marten in Leicester, and to pray for the founders soules in which paryshe is D. houselyng people‡ or above, and no mo prestes but only the viker, whose stypende or lyvyng ys so sore decayed that he ys not able to fynde any other preste to serve there, so that withowte the helpe of the seyd chauntrye prest many of the seyd paryshoners in tyme of sicknesse shall be lyke to perishe withowte the rightes of the churche: also the churchwardens wth aleven other honeste men of the seyde parishe hath the presentacon and eleccon of the same; and at thys present tyme there ar but ij. of the seyd iiij. prestes nowe syngyng for that the rentes of the same ar so ferr in decaye and lesse of rent than they have here to fore bene, and there be no lands or possessions

* Burnet's *Refor.* ii. part ii. No. 27.

† No. D. 9, 31.

‡ "D. houselyng people," that is 500 people who were Communicants, from *housele*, an old word for the Eucharist.

solde or alyenated syns the tyme before lymyted* and an Inventory of the same here after doth appere.

The value of the Guild—its income and expenditure—is thus given :†—

The Chantry of Corpus Christi within the town of Leicester	is worth in	Rent and farm of all the tenements and cottages within the town of Leicester to the Chantry aforesaid belonging as in particulars by a rental therein made and renewed appeareth per annum.	18^{li} 17^{s}	xxvij.^{li} xix.^{d} qr.
		The farm of divers other tenements cottages and gardens there demised to divers persons by indenture as in particulars by the rental aforesaid therein made and renewed appeareth per annum.	19^{s} 8^{d}	
		Rent of assise of divers free tenants there as by the Rental aforesaid therein made and renewed in particulars appeareth.	6^{li} 14^{s} $11\frac{1}{4}^{d}$	
		The farm of a dwelling house with garden to the same belonging situated on the western part of the Church of the blessed Mary there valued per annum.	10^{s}	

* That is, since 4th February, 27 Henry VIII.

† Translated from the original.

The Chantry of Corpus Christi within the town of Leicester				
	is worth in	Rent resolute to divers persons following, viz, to our lord the king for divers small rents issuing out of divers tenements aforesaid of his duchy of Lancaster (vij.^{s} x.^{d} ob.) to William Overede gentleman issuing out of certain lands in Southfield (xij.^{d}); to the aforesaid Lord the King as of his duchy of Lancaster aforesaid for divers other small rents allotted to our Lord the King (xij.^{s} ix.^{d} ob.) in the right of the late monastery of Leicester (vij.^{s}); to divers other persons in all as in the particulars in the rental aforesaid more fully appear (xij.^{s} v.^{d}) per annum.	41^{s} 1^{d}	xviij.^{li} vij.^{s}
		Decay or vacation of divers tenements there per annum.	xvij.^{s} viij.^{d}	
	Reprisals viz. in	Stipend of Henry Grymys the chaplain celebrating divine service within the church there per annum.	vj.^{li}	
		Stipend of John Foster the chaplain there per annum.	cvj.^{s} viij.^{d}	
		Obits and alms there annually expended per annum.	xliiij.^{s} ij.^{d}	

The Chantry of Corpus Christi, etc.	Reprisals viz. in	Fees of steward or bailiff there per annum.	xx.^{s}
		Monies paid for wine, wax, and lanterns as well for the two aforesaid chaplains as for one other chaplain celebrating the iiij.^{s} mass called Jesus mass within the church aforesaid annually expended per annum.	ix.^{s} vj.^{d}
		Repairs upon divers tenements there annually done per annum.	viij.^{s} xj.^{d}

And there remains clear per annum viij.^{li} xiiij.^{s} vij.^{d} q^{r}.

The death of Henry VIII. appears to have stayed further proceedings with regard to Guilds and Chantries. The respite was, however, short, for soon after Edward VI. had ascended the throne a Bill for giving their possessions to the king was brought into the House of Lords, and (notwithstanding considerable opposition from the Bishops) passed into law.* Visitors or Commissioners were sent to inquire into the state of the different Fraternities, and to arrange for the sale of their possessions. These visitors were in Leicester in the year 1547-8, when the mayor, as was then usual, regaled them with wine. The Chamberlains for that year say in their accounts :—

Itm̄ payd for ij. gallons of wyne that was gyven to the
Kyng's maiestes vicetors for chauntres . . ij.^{s} iiij.^{d}

* Burnet's *Reform*. ii. 85.

The result of this visit is soon apparent. The lands belonging to the Guild were sold by King Edward VI. to Robert Catelin, Esquire, a native of Leicestershire. He was sergeant-at-law in the reign of Philip and Mary, and in the first year of Elizabeth's reign was made Lord Chief Justice of the Queen's Bench. He was also the purchaser of all the lands once belonging to the dissolved Guild of S. Margaret, Leicester, and of those belonging to the Collegiate Church of the Blessed Virgin Mary in the Newarke, Leicester.*

The Guild Hall was sold to John Pickerill of Norwich, or to his widow Cicely, for by a deed of release made in the year 1563, Cicely Pickerill of Norwich, widow, formerly wife of John Pickerill, gentleman, sells to Robert Braham of Barrow-on-Soar a tenement, with appurtenances, situate near the Cemetery of S. Martin's Church, in the tenure and occupation of the Mayor and Burgesses, and formerly of the Guild of Corpus Christi. The purchase was made by Mr. Braham the Recorder in trust for the Mayor and Burgesses, and the occurrence is thus notified in the Chamberlains' Accounts for the year 1562-3 :—

Itm̃ paid for wyne shewgar and cakes at the possessyon takyng of the Hall . . .	iij.*s* vj.*d*
Itm̃ paid to Mr. Manby that he laid out for the pr.chase of the hall.	x.*li*
Itm̃ paid more to Mr Recorder for the same Hall that he lead out & for his peans. . .	liij.*s* iiij.*d*

* Nichols' *Leicestershire*, i. 562, iii. 169.

S. George's Guild.

Having written somewhat fully upon the origin and purposes of Guilds, and upon the customs connected with them, in the Section devoted to the Guild of Corpus Christi, there is the less reason for saying much upon the other Guild whose altar stood in S. Martin's Church in pre-Reformation times—that under the patronage of S. George. This is a fortunate circumstance, inasmuch as there are but few facts relating to it to be gathered from existing documents, and still less to be deduced from traditionary lore. The dates of its foundation and of its suppression are alike unknown. There is, however, ample proof, as we shall see, of its existence, and of the interest attaching to it, during parts of the fifteenth and sixteenth centuries. And from reference to documents relating to Guilds formerly existing in other places, dedicated to the same titular saint, we shall be able to form a tolerably correct idea as to its customs and peculiarities.

As we do not possess a copy of the original Statutes of the Guild, it cannot be stated from what its income was derived, or in what manner it was directed to be expended—whether the Guild was a purely religious one, like that of Corpus Christi, or whether it combined secular business with religious advantages, as was so frequently the case in these Fraternities. We may, however, infer that it possessed little or no real property; for, under date of the 21st of September, in the fifteenth year of Henry VII. (1499), " In tempe Witti Wigston senior," is found the following entry in the Hall Book of the Corporation of Leicester :—

"Be it Remēbred yt. it is cōdecended agreed & stablyshed at a comōn Hall . . . . that eůy of xlviij. yt hathe ben chambleyns shall pay to the vp holdyng of saynt Georgys Gild by yēr vj.d & the yt hathe not ben chambleyns shall pay at the leyst iiij.d or mor̄ if the pleasse."*

It is evident from the fact of this contribution that the income of the Guild from its own resources was inadequate to its necessities, and the extract from the Hall Book also proves (what will be more fully shown hereafter) that the Mayor and his Brethren upheld the Guild and enforced the observance of its customs with considerable energy and perseverance.

As with the Corpus Christi Guild, so with this, its Annual Festival was a leading feature in its yearly existence. This Festival was called "The Riding of the George." The Mayor and Corporation took their places in the Procession, and to it all the inhabitants were summoned by a constable or other official. Absence incurred a penalty in money which went into the coffers of the Guild. These facts are shown in a long list of Ordinances

"Made by Richarde Gillot Maire of the Towne of leycestr . . . . at a Comon Halle holden at leycestr. the Thursday next afore the ffeste of Symonde day and Jude yn the yere of the reigne of our Soůayen lorde Kyng Edwarde the fourthe after the Conquest of Ynglond the vij.t

"The Mayre comaundeth on the Kyng's behalfe

(*amongst other things*)

* Vol i. in MS. p. 65.

also that all mañ men inhabitauntz w^t^inne this Town that be warned or somened by the constable or any other of the maires officers to come (at an owre) to the Comon Halle or to attend vppon the maire to ryde agenst the Kyng or for (Riding of the Georg or) eny other thing that shalbe to the plesure of the maire and worshyppe for the Towne yff any man so warned absent hym w^t^oute cause resonable or speciall licence of the maire he or they shall forfett that is to sey eñy of the maires Brethren xij.^d^ and eñy comener vj.^d^ that to be leuyed by ye Chamberlayns to the vse and ꝓfete of the Comons . . . . . &c.*

The Festival was held between S. George's day (23d April) and Whitsunday. The following enactment, passed at a Common Hall held in 1523, shows that if default were made by the master of the Guild in "riding the George" within the limit of those dates, he subjected himself to the payment of a heavy fine, to be levied by the Mayor. If the Mayor were negligent, he and his Chamberlains were also ordered to pay heavy penalties for their tardiness :—

"Allso it is enactyd at the same Comon Hall be the seyd meyr & hys brethern the xxiiij.^ti^ and the xlviij.^ti^ electyd of the Comyns that the acte ffoloyng to be of effect and eñ more to theym that shall com̃ here aft^r^ to be ferme and stable that who soñ be the Maist^r^ off Seynt Georges Gylde shall cavse the george to be Rydyn accordyng to the olde auncient costome y^t^ ys to sey be twyx sent Georges day and Wytsondey except a causse reassonnable and he or they that make deffaute in Rydyng of the seyd george of ye seid Maist^r^ or Maisters to fforfet ffrome the day of this acte forthwards, v.^li^ ; and that to be leuied of ye seid maisẗ or maisters to ye behewe & use of the seyd gyld by the Mey' ffor the tyme beyng and the chamburleyns and yf ye seyd Meyr & Chambleyns be necligent or lachius in levyeng of y^e^

* *Hall Book*, i. 236.

seid fforfet that then the Mere to fforfet xxvj.[s] viij.[d] and eyther Chamburleyn to fforfet vj.[s] viij.[d] and to be peyd to the ꝑfet of the same gyld.

"More oũ it is agreyd at the same acte that all forfetts mayd by the masters that have been seyth [*since*] the laste tyme that the George was Ryden shall be browgh in and payd to the behowe and ꝑfet of the same Gyld of eũ mast[r] beyng be hynd xxvj.[s] viij.[d] *

The Procession would doubtless partake of the character of that formed by the Guild of Corpus Christi already described. It would, however, have distinctive features of its own, bearing special reference to the legend of its titular Saint. S. George would be personated by a man representing a knight in armour over which he would wear a surcoat figured with his traditionary bearings—a red cross on a white ground. The horse upon which he rode would also be richly caparisoned, whilst over horse and rider was borne by four men a canopy similar to that carried over the Host in the Corpus Christi procession. S. George would be attended by his standard-bearer (also sometimes in armour) carrying his banner—a red cross on a white ground—and by his henchmen or pages; whilst near to him frequently rode the lady Margaret, that daughter of the King of Egypt who was saved from the fury of the dragon by the valour of the Saint. "The Lady" (as she is sometimes called in old Guild Rolls) would be also attended by her henchman or page. The most conspicuous member of the procession was, however, the conquered dragon, which appeared in all its hideous proportions, its long body being carried, and its wings worked, by a man walking with bended body within it. The only reference in our local manuscripts

* *Hall Book*, i. 160.

(so far as I am aware) to the characters represented in the Procession, is to this emblem of vanquished sin and iniquity. On a fragment of a Roll of expenses incurred by the Chamberlains of the town between the years 1536 and 1541 is :—

Itm̄ paid ffor dryssyng of the dragon . . .	iiij.^{s}

During the time S. George's Guild flourished in Leicester a similar Fraternity existed (amongst many other places) at Norwich, respecting which many particulars are preserved. As the Processions of the two Guilds would be similar in character if not in detail, extracts are here given from an accompt of the latter Guild for the year ended the "Feast of the Annunciation of our Lady, fourteenth Henry VIII." :—

Payd to Master Waade for executyng the state of the George on the daye of the Feste for thys yere past	v.^{s}	iiij.^{d}
Item, for his glovys		iij.^{d}
And payd for iij. payer hoosys, for ij. hensmen and the standerd berer	vj.^{s}	x.^{d}
And for iij. payer showys, for the same hensmen and the standerd berer	ij.^{s}	j.^{d}
And for xij. payer glovys for Angell, hensmen, standerd-berer, foottmen, and ij. pleyers in the Dragon .		xiiij.^{d}
And for the Cross berynge, with other lyts in the tyme of processyon		viij.^{d}
And to them thatt wentt in iij. Angell weeds . .		vj.^{d}
And to iiij. men in Aubys (*albs*) beryng the Canapy over the George, in the tyme of processyon . .		iiij.^{d}
Also payd to the Clerks for syngyng in the tyme of processyon, and att dyner and att sooper . .	ij.^{s}	
And to the iiij. Wayts of the Cyte . .	vj.^{s}	viij.^{d}

Item, to ij. other mynstrells		xvj.[d]
Also to the pleyer in the Dragon and his man for ther labor		xij.[d]
Also to the Banner berer		iiij.[d]
Item for offeryng of the George and hys company (*that was at mass*)		iij.[d]
Also for skorynge of harnes and of ſyne mayle for the George and standered berer		xviij.[d]
Item to . . . . for borowyng of a Sallett . .		ij.[d]
Also to a saddeler for borowyng of a horse harnes for the George, and trymmyng of the same . . .		iiij.[d]
Also for bolyons for the same		ij.[d]
Also for mendyng of an Angell wyngs that was brokyn, and the iryn to the same		xiij.[d]
Also for new poyntyng, hopyng, and new reparyng of the dragon to Braame	vj.[s]	vj.[d]
Also for a reward to hym that browte the George's horse and for ledyng home again		iiij.[d]

S. George in the Norwich Procession was in some years accompanied by "the lady" on horseback: she was sometimes styled "the maid," and "the Margaret," and had her henchmen. Among the payments, 26 Henry VIII. is :—

Paid for half a hundred oranges given for borrowing a gown and kirtle for the Margaret	viij.[d]

The procession sometimes included the Bearer of the Helmet, Coat-Armour, and Target; the Pendant-Bearer; and the Bearer of the Holy-water Stoup.

These extracts, with the following Inventory of Goods belonging to the Fraternity in 1551, in the absence of documents relating to our own Guild of S. George, enable us to form a tolerably correct impression as to the nature of its annual Procession:—

1551.	£	s.	d.
A Vestment of black velvet, with all that belong thereto	0	16	0
A Wast-Coat of white fustian with red sleeves . .	0	4	0
A Jerkin of crimson velvet	0	5	2
A Cap of russet velvet	0	16	4
A Coat-Armour of white damask with a red cross .	0	6	8
2 Coats of Bruges satin, for the Henchmen . .	0	5	6
2 Worsted Coats of S[t] Thomas's for the Henchmen .	0	4	4
A Covering of crimson velvet, for a p[r.] of Brokenders .	0	5	0
A Jacket of fustian with a red cross . . .	0	2	0
A Horse's Harness for the George of black velvet with buckles of copper gilt and bit to the same .	0	5	8
A Horse's Harness for a George, of red velvet with buckles of copper gilt (without a bit) with a feather thereto	0	6	8
A Horse Harness for the Lady, of crimson velvet flowered with gold, without a bit . . .	0	12	6
A Banner-Cloath, stained and garnished, with red damask and knopps of silk, and a banner-staff thereto	2	0	0
An old Banner, and a staff thereto belonging . .	0	16	0
A Standard Cloath of white silk with a red cross, with the Standard and Spear, and a great Bastard sword	0	3	4
A great Mass-Book of parchment	0	2	6
	£7	11	8

The Cognizance of the Guild at Norwich was a red cross.*

On the day of the Procession in Leicester, the members and others taking part in it would assemble at the Hall of the

* *The Norwich Corporation Pageantry*, 5, 6, and 15.

Guild and proceed to S. Martin's Church, where the usual services (already described in speaking of the Fraternity of Corpus Christi) would be performed at the altar of the Guild then standing at the Western end of the great South aisle. This altar, as we have seen (pp. 49, 50), had a "vowte" over it; and hanging behind it, or near, was "a payntyd clothe" upon which was probably depicted the saint slaying the dragon. Upon the altar itself would be all the articles necessary in the celebration of Mass, whilst near stood a life-size figure of S. George fully armed (p. 50).

After the Service in the Church and the Procession through the principal streets, an assemblage would again take place at the Hall of the Guild, where the Annual Feast would be held, and the business of the Guild transacted.

Throsby describes the day as being "the greatest solemnity of the Town;"* and from an entry in the Chamberlains' accounts for the year 1530-1 it appears that occasionally noblemen and others living in the neighbourhood came to Leicester on that day, and were—with the then usual hospitality of the municipal body—presented by the Mayor with wine:—

> Itm̃ gyfud to my lorde Hastyngs ye same daye ye gorge
> was Ryddn̄ ij gallons off wyne . . . . . xx.^d^

The year following this it was agreed by the "wole assentt" of the Corporation that for "dyueres cōsidderasions" . . . "Mast̃ Kryst̃ Clughtt shud nott Ryde ye George" that year, the old act to remain in force notwithstanding.† The master had to pay a fine for "ye redymyng ye Rydyng of ye George" of 26^s.^ 8^d.^

* *Hist. Leic.* 222. † *Hall Book*, 290.

The Mayor had frequently to enforce the fine against the Master of the Guild for not "riding the George" in accordance with the order made at the Common Hall held in 1523 already quoted. Thus in 1533-4 the Chamberlains credit themselves in their account:—

Itm̃ reseuyed of Mr Garsett for not Rydyng of ye Gorge . . . . iiij. marks.

And again, between 1536 and 1541:—

Itm̃ receyvd of Mr Thomas Cressy ffor not Rydyng of the George . . . . xl.^s^

And again, in the *Hall Book* on the 5th October 1543, Mr. Clough being then Mayor, the following entry occurs:—

M^d.^ that at ye same Comõ Hall before Mr. Meyre his brethren and the xlviij.^ti^ Mr. Mey M^r.^ of Sent Georg's gyld pd to Hew Barlo & Wiłłm Alsope becawse the georg was not Rydyn . . . . . . xl.^s^

The Hall belonging to S. George's Guild stood in Town Hall Lane (then called Holy Rood Lane or Churchgate) probably on the East side of S. Martin's Church. In the Chamberlains' accounts are some scanty entries referring to that building after the suppression of Chantries:—

1591-2:—

Itm̃ of Mrs. Darker for a house called St George Hall and Two Gardyns thereunto belonging in the sev̄all Tenures of Wm. Hobbye & Mr Pottell Rent ꝑ ann̄ . . . . vj.^s^ viij.^d^

Itm̃ of Wm. Hobbye for a messuage or Tent^e^ wth thappurtenances called the Meyden headd and a garden thereunto belonging lying on the *East syde* of St M'tyns churche in his occupacoñ Rent ꝑ anñ . . . . xiij.[s] iiij.[d]

This probably joined S. George's Hall.

1594-5 :—

In Holye Roode Lane or churche gate.*

Itm̃ of John fflampson for a house called S[t] George's Hall with thapp. . . . . . . vj.[s] viij.[d]

In the next year's account the Hall is called a "howse or Barne," indicating that it was a large room suitable for a large assembly.

I have not met with any information respecting this Guild later than the year 1543, when the master was fined for not "riding the George," until the overthrow of the altar in the Guild Chapel, and the sale of the Chalice, etc., belonging thereto, together with the figure of the titular saint as recorded on a previous page.†

From the paucity of documents relating to this Guild, and from the absence of any record of its possessions in the Augmentation Office, it is presumed that it possessed, as before indicated, no real property in lands or houses, and that there was nothing, when the change in Religion doomed these Fraternities to destruction, worth the notice or the grasp of a needy, if not an avaricious and unscrupulous government.

* In the Chamberlains' Accounts for 1665-6, this is called "Holye Roode Lane or S[t.] *Martyns* Churchgate."

† P. 98.

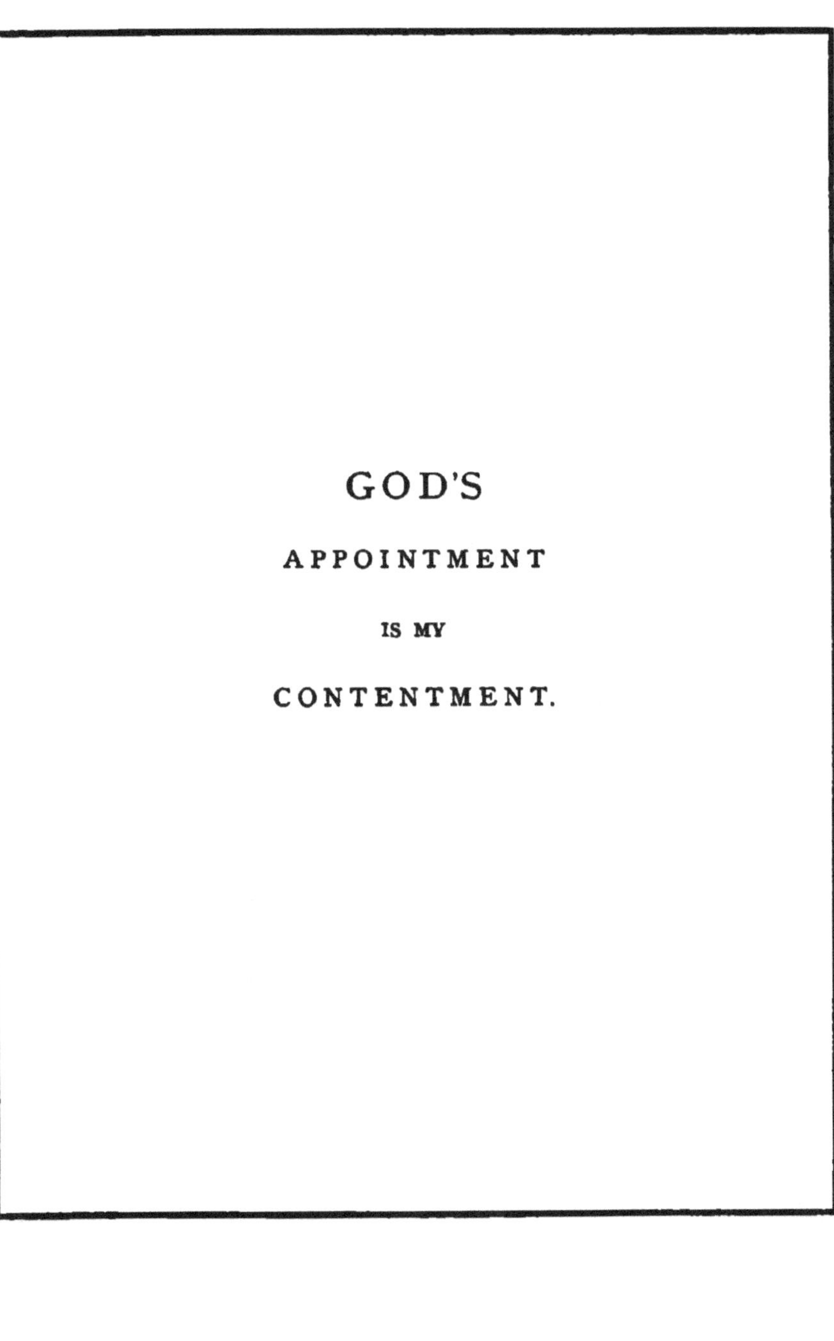

GOD'S APPOINTMENT IS MY CONTENTMENT.

INDEX.

Printed by R. CLARK, *Edinburgh.*

ERRATA.

P. 160, line 18, *for* "provided" *read* "providing."
P. 160, line 24, *for* "Gospelles" *read* "Gospeller."
P. 193, line 16, *for* "numbers" *read* "number."

www.ingramcontent.com/pod-product-compliance
Lightning Source LLC
Chambersburg PA
CBHW021053030726
47496CB00006B/1819

* 9 7 8 3 3 3 7 0 0 2 5 5 8 *